Under the Shadow of Nationalism

Under the Shadow of Nationalism
Politics and Poetics of Rural Japanese Women

Mariko Asano Tamanoi

University of Hawai'i Press
Honolulu

Library of Congress Cataloging-in-Publication Data
Tamanoi, Mariko.
    Under the shadow of nationalism : politics and poetics of
rural Japanese women / Mariko Asano Tamanoi.
        p.   cm.
    Includes bibliographical references and index.
    ISBN 0–8248–1944–6 (cloth : alk. paper). —
ISBN 0–8248–2004–5 (pbk. : alk. paper)
    1. Rural women—Japan—Nagano-ken—History—20th
century.   2. Women in rural development—Japan—
Nagano-ken—History—20th century.   I. Title.
HQ1764.N3T35   1998   97–37899
305.42'0952'163—dc21   CIP

University of Hawai'i Press books are printed on acid-free
paper and meet the guidelines for permanence and durability
of the Council on Library Resources

Designed by Jeanne Calabrese

For Fuyu

Contents

Preface

$t$he cover of this book, Takahashi Hiroaki's *Twilight*, "highlights the ideological emphasis on the virtues of the traditional countryside in opposition to the urban, industrial society" (Dartnall 1996, 80). Yet, this depiction represents only half of the story I will tell here. In this woodblock print, a rural woman is shown as part of a natural and a national landscape (note the Shinto shrine, a symbol of Japanese nationalism in the 1930s, in the background). In my story, she is an exhausted woman trying to survive her days.

Since the time of my first stint of fieldwork in 1984, more than ten years have passed. I have incurred so many debts during these years that I may miss the names of some of those who contributed to the completion of this book in one way or another. I extend my thanks and apologies to them first. While working on this book, I have had fruitful engagements with intellectual communities in Tokyo, Chicago, Iowa City, and Los Angeles. In Tokyo, my former teachers were always there whenever I needed their help and support. In Chicago, Norma Field always listened to me despite her busy schedule, and later she read the entire manuscript for this book. In Iowa City, Margery Wolf was a mentor in the area of women's studies, and Stephen Vlastos gave me precious comments on my research and writing. In Los Angeles, Francesca Bray read the first version of my manuscript and offered many valuable comments. Leslie Pincus, Miriam Silverberg, and Karen Brodkin were my best intellectual companions. The members of the Center for Japanese Studies and the Department of Anthropology at the University of California, Los Angeles, gave me their utmost support. I am also grateful to Robert J. Smith, and Patricia Tsurumi, who kindly shared her unpublished paper with me, and Kendall Brown, who found the woodblock print *Twilight* for the cover of this book. My graduate research assistants, Brenda Jenike Robb, Haeng-ja Chung, Jennifer Reynolds, Mayumi Yamamoto, William Horton, and James Jo helped me at various stages in preparing this manuscript.

Patricia Crosby at the University of Hawai'i Press has earned my unending gratitude for her help and courtesy from the beginning to the completion of the publication of this book. My thanks also go to Susan Stone, who painstakingly edited my manuscript and remarkably improved the quality of my writing. I am also grateful for the help of anonymous reviewers, who shared their insights with me, and of Cheri Dunn and Masako Ikeda, who oversaw the production of this book.

An earlier version of Chapter 3 was published as "Songs as Weapons: Culture and History of *Komori* (Nursemaids) in Modern Japan," in *The Journal of Asian Studies* 1991, 50 (4): 793–817, and a slightly different version of Chapter 5 appeared as "Gender, Nationalism, and Japanese Native Ethnology," in *Positions* 1996, 4 (1): 59–86. A different version of Chapter 6 will appear as "The City and the Countryside: Competing Taishō 'Modernities' on Gender," in a book edited by Sharon A. Minichiello, *Japan's Competing Modernities: Issues in Culture and Democracy, 1900–1930*, to be published by the University of Hawai'i Press in 1998.

Support for the research and writing of this book was made possible by grants from the Joint Committee on Japanese Studies of the American Council of Learned Societies and the Social Science Research Council with funds provided by the Japan-U.S. Friendship Commission, the Ford Foundation, and the National Endowment for the Humanities; the United Nations University in Tokyo; the University of Iowa; the North East Asia Council; and the University of California, Los Angeles. I am grateful also for the help afforded me by Shinano Kyōiku-kai in the city of Nagano, Ueda Rekishi Hakubutsukan and Urazato Sonpō Fukkoku Jikkō Iinkai in Nagano, Ie no Hikari Kyōkai in Tokyo, and Josei Shiryō Bunka Kenkyūjo of the Ochanomizu Women's University in Tokyo. The University of California Presidential Fellowships in Humanities made it possible for me to take adequate leave time from teaching in 1997, when the final revisions for this book were completed. My thanks also go to Kuki Yōko of the East Asian Library of the University of Chicago and the wonderful group of librarians at the East Asia Collection of the University of California, Los Angeles, Research Library.

My Ph.D. dissertation, which I completed in 1982, was about Catalonian nationalism in Spain and France. Since then I have traveled a great distance, both geographically, from Europe to Asia, and intellectually. I believe, however, that what I learned in Europe is present in this book, that people everywhere live both for and against the state. The late George Dalton prepared me well for this journey. My parents, Asano Kazuo and Asano Chizuko, have always sustained me, from long before I began my career as an anthropologist. I am grateful that they never molded me to fit the category of Japanese women. The late Tamanoi Yoshirō and Tamanoi Kimiko have also extended their help to me and my family. My most heartfelt thanks go to my daughter, Yōko, who always accompanied me to Nagano, and my husband, Fuyu. Despite his occasional complaint "anthropologists often disappear," he has given me his firm and most affectionate support throughout these years. Lastly, I thank all the women in Nagano who shared their memories with me (I wish I could thank them individually). Although not all of them appear in this book, I hope that the narratives I have translated here represent the complexity of their lives in a way they would find satisfactory. Without their voices, I could not have written this book.

Following Japanese custom, I have cited Japanese names surname first throughout this text.

Chapter 1	Introduction: Japanese Nationalism and Rural Women

Those who would codify the meanings of words fight a losing battle, for words, like the ideas and things they are meant to signify, have a history. —*(Scott 1988, 28)*

While acknowledging that every word inscribed in the present text has a history of its own, I intend to focus on only a few. I single out for study "Japanese nation/nationalism," "rural," and "women" because I am interested in the way in which the category of "rural women" emerged in the discourse of "Japanese nationalism" at the turn of the century and continues to be used to maintain national boundaries to the present.

However, I do not believe that "rural women" is the product of discourse alone. Nondiscursive practices, such as institutional and pedagogic ones, have played important roles in creating "rural women" and making them useful subjects for the construction of the Japanese nation-state (see Das 1995, 11). For this reason, I shift my focus back and forth between the discursive and sociological categories of rural women. The latter comprises a group of women who have lived in rural Nagano, a mountainous prefecture in central Japan. This sociological category is my own imposition. Although they live in what I perceive to be "rural" areas in Nagano, they do not necessarily identify themselves as rural women. They are individuals who have their own thoughts and emotions, and who joined various women's groups in the 1970s and 1980s to reminisce on their own pasts. They are neither identical nor diametrically opposed to the discursively formulated "rural women." In this book I explore the gap between the two categories.

Historian Joan Scott reminds us that even the word "history" has its own history. Hence, history does not exclusively record changes in the past; history also actively participates in producing knowledge about the past (1988, 2). I would like to produce a different history of rural women in Japan that eschews the way in which they are described, depicted, analyzed, and judged in the discourse of Japanese nationalism. This objective requires that I rely on the "voices" of rural women themselves.[1]

In this chapter, I introduce the rural women in Nagano with their own names and voices. I then introduce the discursive category of "rural women," which eventually comes to stand for "Japanese women" in the early twentieth century. I focus separately on "Japanese nation/nationalism," "women," and "rural" in that order, offering a theoretical overview of each concept.

RURAL WOMEN AS SOCIOLOGICAL CATEGORY

The rural women whom I met and whose voices I heard both in person and in documents come from a particular region, Nagano prefecture in central Japan. My choice of Nagano was based on my own judgment of this region's relevance to the formation of the nation-state: the contribution of the rural women of Nagano in building modern Japan is undeniable. These women were born or have lived in various villages and towns near Okaya in Nagano. Okaya, often described as the "capital of the Japanese silk kingdom," was the center of the silk spinning industry during the industrial revolution in the late nineteenth and early twentieth centuries.[2] Yet their contribution was not restricted to this particular, though perhaps most important, industry and historical period. Rural women in Nagano worked, from a very young age, as nursemaids (*komori*), domestic servants, factory workers, and farming women. In whatever capacity they worked, they became the objects of scrutiny in various genres of nationalist discourse not only because of the importance of their labor to the nation, but also because of their gender and place of residence (that necessarily connoted their class position).

I chose Nagano for both historical and contemporary reasons. Since the early 1970s, a significant number of women's groups have been formed throughout the prefecture. At regular meetings, members made deliberate efforts to record their recollections. They gathered at a cultural center (*kōmin-kan*), a public institution that oversees cultural affairs in each administrative unit, or in their friends' and neighbors' homes to talk about their memories.[3] I did not solicit these women to narrate their memories to me. If I had, I would have been the only one to listen to their narratives. Instead, they voluntarily gathered, formed groups among themselves, and talked, each one listening to the voices of the others. They not only listened to each other but read each other's narratives when they opted for writing rather than speaking about their memories. With state subsidies, some of these women's groups published their narratives in the form of books or booklets. Their books, published in small numbers, do not circulate widely but serve largely as keepsakes for the members. These women's groups still exist, continuing to engage in the same task.

I also read narratives of women who died long ago that were collected and recorded by government officials, education specialists, journalists, folklorists, and local historians. Many of these narratives are contained in and by the very discourse of Japanese nationalism. My "textual strategy" here is to read such a discourse against the grain of its ostensible meaning—that is, to read it not simply in terms of the message that the recorders intended it to convey, but in terms of how it might have been received by the rural women in Nagano who heard it (see Rafael 1992, 71).[4]

This is why my field research is somewhat different from the so-called village study. The latter refers to the study of a single rural community. Instead of focusing on women's lives in one locality, I went to various villages and towns in Nagano to hear the memories of rural women.[5] I listened more intensively to the voices of rural women in the village where I lived, the village of Tabata in southern Nagano.[6] However, I did not restrict myself to one particular community.

Why do these women actively continue to engage in the task of relating and writing their memories of the past? To answer this question, I must briefly discuss the nature of memories and their relationship to narratives. Scholars have pointed out in various ways that the past is not unproblematically known. For example, Benedict Anderson argues that all changes in consciousness, by their very nature, bring with them characteristic amnesias and that such changes cannot be "remembered" but must be "narrated" (1990, chap. 7).[7] Thus, the past (or changes in consciousness in the case of Anderson's argument) constitutes a "political field" for anyone who attempts to remember it: anyone can present his or her own version of the past by remembering it in a certain way or even by forgetting it; but he or she must always "narrate" it (see Benjamin 1969; Adorno 1986; Hartman 1986; Young 1993; Boyarin 1994; Watson 1994b; Yoneyama 1995). Thus, memory travels from one person to another because it must be narrated, and when it does, it changes. Michel de Certeau argues: "The strange aspect of memory is doubtless its mobility, such that details are never identical to themselves" (1980, 42). He calls this aspect of memory the "art" of memory, the memory's "capacity to inhabit the space of the other without possessing it" (1980, 41). Rubie Watson also argues this in a slightly different way: new environments produce new pasts; hence "constructing the new is deeply embedded in reconstructing the old" (1994a, 6).

During my field research, the memories of rural women in Nagano traveled to me. Even though I was born many years after they were and I grew up in the city in Japan, I now "remember" these women's pasts. Watson states:

> Many Americans "remember" the American Civil War and many Jews "remember" the Nazi Holocaust, but not because they personally experienced those events or because they have read master narratives written by professional historians detailing great battles or the sufferings in camps. Rather, they "remember" because they share with others sets of images that have been passed down to them through the media of memory—through paintings, architecture, monuments, ritual, storytelling, poetry, music, photos, and film. (1994a, 8)

The rural women in Nagano did not paint paintings, build monuments, create new rituals, write poems, compose music, or direct films. But they themselves told me their stories, and that is how I "remember" their pasts.

I understand the Nagano rural women's activity of forming groups among themselves and narrating their pasts collectively as a political act. Their narratives are often poetic but contain clear political messages. But what kind of politics? One way to answer this question is to formulate the following hypothesis and explore its possibility: the more powerful an individual or a group is, the more effectively such an individual or group member can exercise the politics of memory. Where, then, have these women stood in relation to other individuals and groups who have also exercised the politics of memory in Japan since the 1970s?

Historian Carol Gluck argues that there are four main agents of public memory or custodians of the past in postwar Japan. First are the progressive intellectuals who, though not forming a single group, are united in their commitment to protest against the revival of prewar nationalism rooted in the imperial ideology. I will say more about prewar Japanese nationalism later. Suffice it to say here that it represents an evil for the progressive intellectuals, along with the postwar governments that, in their eyes, have not radically changed since the prewar period. These progressive intellectuals are thus against the political and economic establishment. Gluck, however, argues that "their place in the sun"—they were virtually everywhere in the print and broadcast media in the 1960s and 1970s—has been "increasingly taken by conservative intellectuals who supported rather than opposed the postwar status quo" (1993, 71). These conservative intellectuals then form the second group. This group has wielded the "greatest institutional power" in postwar Japan. Furthermore, unlike the first group, they refuse to see discontinuity in modern Japanese history, but find in the modernizing achievements during the Meiji period (1868–1912) the key to explaining Japan's remarkable postwar economic recovery (ibid.). Third are the media that sell a commodified history of the popular past (p. 73). Japan since the 1970s is indeed a media-saturated society, and this agent of public memory is perfectly at ease incorporating the histories of the first and the second groups of custodians of the past. Gluck then argues: "The fourth agent of public memory is not public at all: it is the individual memories, the life histories, the personal pasts of people whose lives were ineluctably intertwined with the events of history with a capital H" (p. 76).

What Gluck calls "history with a capital H" could be paraphrased as "national," "official," "monumentalized," or "dominant" history (see Anderson 1990, 248; Herzfeld 1991; Watson 1994a, 1994b; Duara 1995). History and the discourse of nationalism are not identical, and yet they are interdependent. Whatever it is called, History is always presented as linear, progressive, and teleological. It is a history of "homogeneous community within a territorial state that had evolved into the present" (Duara 1995, 49). Restated, it is a history of a nation-state. It also represents an arrow of time that suppresses spatial as well as gender divisions. And History is always presented as written. However, as school textbooks of History have been revised repeatedly by the state since the late nineteenth century when compulsory education was introduced, Japan's History does not have a single version, nor has it remained the same. Gluck thus interprets national history as a hegemonic field in which agents of public memory have sometimes supplemented and reinforced one another, but have worked against one another at other times (1993, 78–79).

How should I describe the History that was hegemonic during my field research in Nagano in the 1980s and early 1990s? According to Gluck, such a History was "increasingly weighed away from the critical to the celebratory" (1993, 79). This celebratory History was a part of the discourse of Japanese nationalism in the 1980s and early 1990s. The buzzword in such a nationalist discourse was "postmodern" (*posto modaan*): Japan surpassed what it had acquired from the West in the form of political modernization and material growth, and what had made this swift transformation possible was a cultural property unique to Japan—a self-conceived superiority, implied in the discourse of postwar Japanese nationalism. In it, Japan represented a space in which its "postmodernity" was "officially" endorsed. For example, in 1980, former prime minister Ōhira Masayoshi proudly announced the establishment of a new age of culture, conquering "the modern": "thirty years after the war, Japan has pursued the goal of economic abundance and pushed on ceaselessly without looking aside"; now is the time to transcend the modern and to stress the "special quality of Japan's culture" (quoted by Harootunian 1989, 79–80; see also Gluck 1993, 72).[8]

The "special quality of Japan's culture" was not the only endorsement in the discourse of nationalism in the 1980s. The special quality of Japan's technology also played an important role. Perhaps the term "information society" (*jōhō shakai*) most succinctly captures the quality of Japanese technology. Although it was first coined by a former professor of engineering at Tokyo University in the late 1960s, it had "gained widespread currency in the media, academia and the world of business" in Japan in the 1970s (Morris-Suzuki 1986, 77). The term referred to a society undergoing "social change accompanying the introduction of new information-related technologies" (p. 76). Yet, as Tessa Morris-Suzuki persuasively argues, it became, ideologically, a heavily loaded term in Japan for several reasons. First, it was one of the first Japanese-made pieces of socioeconomic jargon to spread to the rest of the world; this entitled Japan to claim that it was the first to become an "information society." Second, in an "information society," the principal elements in the creation of wealth are information, knowledge, and technology, not direct labor or material inputs (p. 77); this made Japan into a futuristic society ahead of any other country. With the advent of the "information society," Japan transcended the West.

While Gluck treats the four custodians of the past as more or less equal participants in the making of History, I will privilege the fourth, individual memories, over others for the sake of my argument. In Rubie Watson's words below, I have changed "history" to "History" to be consistent in my argument:

> Memory may be a reservoir of History, but it is not the same as History . . . . People maintain personal memories—memories of events and situations that they themselves experienced. These personal memories may remain private, they may be passed on in conversation or storytelling, they may be lost, or they may be written down in the form of diaries, memoirs, and autobiographies. There are also collective or shared memories that are not dependent on a single individual's direct experience of the past. (1994b, 8; see also Connerton 1989)

Here, Watson is primarily concerned with Communist China. Ideally speaking, "people" are the protagonists of History in a communist country. Since people represent the government, History equals the sum of individuals' memories. However, Watson claims this not to be the case: in communist China, people have produced "personal memories" and "collective or shared memories," which are not exactly the same as History, or even opposed to it.[9] I will call these personal and shared memories "histories" with a small h.

As in China, people have produced histories in postwar Japan. Since people experienced social pasts in different ways, each history should be different from another. There may also be, as Watson describes, collective or shared histories. And some histories may be more incongruous with History than others. In this incongruous category of histories, Gluck includes those of Okinawans, Koreans and other minorities, and women,

> whose accounts of their postwar chronology often began with the constitution and other reforms that changed their lives more than the promise of political democracy did. Women were suddenly "allowed to speak," recalled members of the older generation, and

peace and equality of the sexes were frequently mentioned along
with the ubiquitous washing machines and refrigerators. Such differently experienced social pasts seldom appeared in the main narratives, revealing the sorts of exclusion and homogenization that
operated in public memory exactly as they did in society. (1993, 89)

Rural women is a subcategory of women. Unlike "women," however,
the term "rural women" connotes work. The rural women in Nagano
use the term "hataraki" to describe their work. In the first volume of
his *Capital*, Marx distinguishes "work" from "labor": "Labour which
creates use-values and is qualitatively determined is called 'work' as
opposed to 'labour'; labour which creates value and is only mea-
sured quantitatively is called 'labour,' as opposed to 'work'" (1977,
138, n. 16). But the notion of *hataraki* rejects such a distinction and
renders the task of translation impossible. *Hataraki* includes both a
woman's productive and her reproductive labor. The latter includes
the work of childbearing, child rearing, housekeeping, cooking, bud-
geting, shopping for the household, and caring for the sick and the
old. *Hataraki*, for which I use "work" and "labor" interchangeably,
refers to the way in which a woman's productive and reproductive
labor are intertwined. Because their *hataraki* became useful for the
construction of the nation-state, the discourse of Japanese nationalism privileges "rural women." I also privilege rural women among
women because of their *hataraki*, yet I do so to interrogate the nature
of Japanese nationalism.

I do not, however, simply interpret the narratives of rural women
as their "resistance" to History. That is, I do not intend to produce
another linear, progressive, and teleological history of them or of
rural women's liberation. In doing so, I would oversimplify the
nuanced past of each individual rural woman. As Sherry Ortner persuasively argues, resistance literature is still embedded in "dualistic
theorizing": structure versus agency, domination versus resistance,
and hegemony versus authenticity (1992, 1995).[10] The term "resistance" itself, in the sense that it always presupposes the existence of
power, is already implicated in dichotomous thinking. Michel
Foucault, in his penetrating analysis of power and resistance, has
attempted to break down a series of binary categories and to dis-
mantle our dichotomous way of thinking. His "where there is power,
there is resistance" has by now become a well-known dictum in the
discipline of anthropology (1980, 95). And yet, each microcosm created by a specific relationship between those who exercise power and
those who do not still firmly stands on binary categories. According

to Ortner, "dualistic theorizing" generates a number of issues, the most problematical of which is the neglect on the part of anthropologists of the "embeddedness of 'resistance' in a larger social and historical process full of its own complexities and contradictions" (1992, 8). In other words, resistance does not in any way constitute a box fixed in place into which anthropologists can throw narratives of their choice. Rather, the intentionalities of those who resist "evolve through praxis, and the meanings of the acts change, both for the actor and for the analyst" (p. 7). Hence, resistance is continuously and variously experienced by those who resist and is therefore always ambiguous. This ambiguity, however, makes the culture of those who resist richer and more complex. Because my goal is to convey as well as possible the richness and complexity of the politics of Nagano rural women, I do not abandon the notion of resistance completely.

As an alternative to History, historian Prasenjit Duara proposes a "bifurcated" conception of history, in which the "past is not only *transmitted* forward in a linear fashion," but "its meanings are also *dispersed* in space and time" (1995, 5; emphasis in original). He further argues: "Bifurcation points to the process whereby, in transmitting the past, Historical narratives and language appropriate dispersed histories according to present needs, thus revealing how the present shapes the past. At the same time, by attending to the very process of appropriation, bifurcation allows us to recover a historicity beyond the appropriating discourse" (ibid.). I attend to the "dispersed histories" of the rural women in Nagano, as they speak and write in group meetings. I also attend to the process in which History has appropriated their dispersed histories without allowing rural women to speak. This book, then, represents my own resistance to History in order to recover a historicity of the lives of Nagano rural women beyond the appropriating discourse of Japanese nationalism.

THE JAPANESE NATION AND NATIONALISM

In a lecture delivered at the Sorbonne in 1882, Ernest Renan argued that nations were "something fairly new in history": "Classical antiquity had republics, municipal kingdoms, confederations of local republics and empires, yet it can hardly be said to have had nations in our understanding of the term" (1990, 9).[11] A member of an old community such as a municipal kingdom was not a modern citizen or, in Etienne Balibar's words, "*homo nationalis.*" The latter describes a member of the national community, an individual ushered from cradle to grave through a network of state apparatuses and daily practices (Balibar 1991, 93).[12] In Europe *homo nationalis* emerged only in the eighteenth century. Thus, the rise of a nation-state necessarily corresponds to the emergence of the notion of modernity. This is why a "modern nation-state," while sounding like an oxymoron, makes sense.

The Japanese nation-state is also a modern construct. We see its emergence sometime in the mid–nineteenth century, when Japan opened its doors to the West and began to build its modern state structure. Of course, just as "France" had existed centuries before its "peasants" became "Frenchmen" in the late nineteenth century, "Japan" too had existed long before it opened its doors to the West. But the idea of Japan as a body of *homo nationalis* "united according to their own will and having certain attributes in common (not least history)" did not exist before the mid–nineteenth century (Weber 1976, 485). The rise of a nation-state also constitutes a process in which the idea of a nation and that of a "culture" merge together. Hence, the "articulation of a unified Japanese ethnos with the 'nation' to produce 'Japanese culture' is entirely *modern*" (Ivy 1995, 4, emphasis in original; see also Sakai 1991). The Japanese nation-state with its unique culture called "Japanese culture" is thus a quintessentially modern concept.

Benedict Anderson, perhaps the most influential scholar of nationalism, emphasizes that a nation is a "cultural artifact." He argues that a nation has been "imagined" into existence and is therefore an "imaginary" (1983, 1991). We can then understand nationalism as a sentiment or a movement that produces an "imaginary" nation (see Gellner 1983, 1). However, since "there exists, for the nation, no 'normal' way to be or define itself," we must argue nationalism not in terms of a nationalism (singular) or nationalism in general, but in terms of nationalisms (plural) (Parker et al. 1992, 3; see also Bhabha 1990 and Sedgwick 1992). Thus, political historians classify nationalisms into two groups: the first are Western, good, and liberal; the second are non-Western (or Eastern), bad, and illiberal. The first refer to rational and self-conscious attempts to achieve national independence and liberty, while the second refer to irrational and destructive attempts whose inevitable consequence is the annihilation of freedom (Chatterjee 1993a, chap. 1).[13]

When we look at real-world politics, can we classify nation-alisms into good and bad ones? According to Partha Chatterjee, nationalism was once "one of Europe's most magnificent gifts to the rest of the world" (good nationalism).[14] The two destructive wars of this century, however, were the results of "Europe's failure to manage its own ethnic nationalisms" (bad nationalism) (1993b, 4). In the postwar era, nationalism moved to Asia and Africa, where it became a central feature in victorious anticolonial struggles (good national-ism). Along with the "development" and "modernization" of post-colonial societies, however, nationalism lost its vigor. By the 1970s, "nationalism had become a matter of ethnic politics," offering the news-hungry Western media a reason "why people in the Third World killed each other" (bad nationalism) (p. 3). Today, nationalism is "seen picking its way toward Europe," owing largely to the influx of immigrants in the world of late capitalism (bad nationalism) (p. 4). At the same time, once-contained ethnic nationalisms have again erupted in the post–cold war world (bad nationalism). This is why, Chatterjee argues, "nationalism is now viewed as a dark, elemental, unpredictable force of primordial nature threatening the orderly calm of civilized life" (p. 4). Since his eyes are firmly fixed on post-colonial India, his scheme of world politics mainly traverses Europe and its former colonies. When world politics is viewed from anoth-er geopolitical angle, a rather different picture of the genealogy of nationalisms emerges.

In the mid–nineteenth century, Japan appeared on the scene of world affairs after almost three hundred years of isolation during its feudal period. The new Meiji state immediately set out to build its own modern state structure and civilization, which "summoned pur-pose and goal—self-sacrifice and nationalism" (Harootunian 1974b, 15). Japanese nationalism, which emerged around the state and the figure of the emperor, is what Anderson has called "official nation-alism" (1983, chap. 6).[15] To foster nationalism, the state, with its enormous power, mobilized its own subjects through their village communities and/or patriarchal families, all in the name of the emperor. The state then presented these communities and families as miniature replicas of the nation-state of Japan.[16]

Japanese nationalism is also what H. W. Arndt has called "reac-tive nationalism," for which national survival and an "intense desire to stand on an equal psychological footing with the advanced nations of the West" are the most important themes (1987, 14–15). Postwar

Japanese scholars of nationalism, however, name this "official/reactive nationalism" "mass" or "people's" nationalism (*taishū nashonarizumu*). The consequence of this coinage is that the term makes the power of the state magically disappear. At the same time, the masses are rendered as active (or "fanatic") participants in the making of nationalism. When Japan was defeated in World War II, nationalism temporarily "disappeared" from both Japanese and world political scenes (Umemoto, Sato, and Maruyama 1983, 9). Japan was occupied by the American Occupation Forces which, in their own efforts to "democratize" Japanese polity and society, tried to bury nationalism deep below the consciousness of the Japanese populace. By the 1970s, however, nationalism reemerged in the form of History and in a vast body of literature called *Nihonjinron*, the discourse on the essential characteristics of Japanese culture and society. *Nihonjinron* depicts Japan in its relationship to the West, particularly the United States, with which Japan has had an increasingly troublesome trade relationship. It also depicts Japan in its relationship to the rest of Asia, from which an increasing number of immigrants now arrive at the shores of the Japanese archipelagoes.[17] In the end, paraphrasing Chatterjee's words, nothing, it would seem, was left in the legacy of Japanese nationalism to make people in the West and Asia (save Japan) feel good about it (1993b, 3).

However, in trying to understand nationalism, debates on merit—whether it is good or bad—do not seem particularly useful. Chatterjee points this out, arguing that, in political history, nationalism has been treated as the "problem of the bourgeois-rationalist conception of knowledge, established in the post-Enlightenment period of European intellectual history" (1993a, 11). Constituting a universal knowledge and discourse of scholarly power, nationalism as a problem is independent of *cultures*. Here, let me look more closely at how some of the scholars of nationalisms have treated "Japanese nationalism" in particular.

In modern Japan, they claim, not much effort was required to formulate nationalism because of the ethnic and cultural homogeneity of its population. This exceptional homogeneity made Japanese nationalism a particularly strong one. In prewar world politics, such an interpretation of Japanese nationalism as "xenophobic" or "fanatic" offered the West explanations for Japan's aggressive colonial expansion into the rest of Asia. This prewar Western view of Japanese nationalism has left a clear mark on the postwar Western scholarship of nationalism. For example, Anderson argues that "three half-fortuitous factors" explain Japanese nationalism: "the relatively high degree of Japanese ethnocultural homogeneity"; "the unique antiquity of the imperial house . . . and its indubitable Japanese-ness"; and the abrupt, massive, and menacing penetration of "the barbarians" in the 1860s that led the politically aware population to self-defense and nationalism (1983, 90–91). Eric Hobsbawm also presents Japan as one of the "extremely rare examples of historic states composed of a population that is ethnically almost or entirely homogeneous" and its nationalism as antedating the age of nationalism (1990, 66). Modern Japanese nationalism, the continuation of such protonationalism, is therefore necessarily and naturally "strong" (see also Gellner 1983, 49). While this interpretation of Japanese nationalism has been widely circulated, I would like to raise the following questions. Might Japan's ethnic or cultural homogeneity be a consequence of nationalism, rather than its cause? If so, are these scholars themselves implicated in "constructing" Japanese nationalism rather than analyzing it?

We cannot ask these questions without interrogating at the same time our tendency to rely on the nation-state in any research in which we engage. While ignoring the nation-state as a modern construct, historians often rely on it to construct a national history. This is why, as Duara argues, history as a professional institution is fatefully tied to the ideology of the nation-state (1995, 3). Anthropologists too rely on the "representation of the world as a collection of 'countries,' " ignoring that such countries came into existence fairly recently (Gupta and Ferguson 1992, 6; see also Malkki 1992, 1995). Furthermore, anthropologists tend to see the nation-state as the only agency that is allowed to have its history—or, more correctly speaking, History (Duara 1995, 20, 22). Hence, the "tribes" do not have Histories (or have only ethnohistories) because they are "traditional," not modern (Wolf 1982, 19). A group of people that has not yet transcended the "traditional" is not allowed to have its history. Or, its history begins only from the time it is integrated into a modern nation-state.

Weber argues that History is one of the most important attributes of the nation-state, more so than language, kinship, religion, geography, material interest, and military neccesity (1976, 485). Renan too privileges History. He argues that the most important principle of a nation is the "fact of sharing, in the past, a glorious heritage and regrets, and of having, in the future, [a shared] programme to put into effect or the fact of having suffered, enjoyed, and hoped together" (1990, 19). But Renan did not ask *who* would produce such a History; he assumed that a national community would. Hence Renan, like our generation of historians and anthropologists, seems to have been implicated with the ideology of the nation-state: in the end, he relied on the nation-state to speak of its origin. Why is the nation-state almost always the only acceptable and normal unit of analysis, as the term "history of Japan" or "anthropology of Japan" suggests?[18]

In order to entertain this question, I return to Anderson, who argues: "[The nation] is imagined as a *community*, because, regardless of the actual inequality and exploitation that may prevail in each, the nation is always conceived as a deep, horizontal comradeship. Ultimately it is this fraternity that makes it possible, over the past two centuries, for so many millions of people, not so much to kill, as willingly to die for such limited imaginings" (1983, 16; emphasis in original). In many nations, the "actual inequality and exploitation" occurs along the lines of gender and space. Anderson's reference to "comradeship" or "fraternity" already suggests that the nation is often gendered as male and that the actual inequality between men and women and the exploitation of women by men could be suppressed in order to imagine a nation (see Parker et al. 1992, 6; see also Yuval-Davis and Anthias 1989; McClintock 1991).[19]

Anderson's argument also means that nationalism may idealize one particular group in terms of gender and space, and exploit its image metonymically to represent the whole nation to the nation itself as well as to the outside world. This does not mean that such a chosen group is necessarily exploited to represent the nation; the members of that group may enjoy national recognition and actively participate in constructing the nation-state. This is quite important to remember.

In a nation described as almost perfectly homogeneous, ethnically and culturally, which group of people has served as the national signifier, the base for self-recognition and for recognizing others? If we could recognize such a group and explore the formation of Japanese nationalism and the Japanese nation from its perspective, would we reach a better, more enlightening and democratic, understanding of Japanese nationalism and the Japanese nation?

RURAL *WOMEN* AS JAPANESE WOMEN

In the course of my research on Japanese nationalism, I came across the following passage cited in English in *Jogaku zasshi*, a women's magazine published in 1887: "The destiny of Nations lies far more in the hands of women, than in the possessors of power, or those innovators who for the most part do not understand themselves. We must cultivate women, else the new generation cannot accomplish its task."[20] In this quote, "women" are asked to decide the destiny of a nation. The author, German educationalist Friedrich A. Wilhelm Froebel (1782–1852), is a member of "we," the "possessors of power" or "those innovators," who are men. And it is men who must cultivate women. This quote, then, suggests the need not only for new women, but for new men. Denise Riley argues that the categories of "Woman," "woman," and "women" are historically and discursively (over-) constructed and always relative to other categories that themselves change (1988, 1–2). "Women" in the above quote does not simply refer to a group of human beings of the female gender. "Women" and "men" are not parallel concepts. Rather, "women" is the effect of the ideals of men, the new patriarchy, on the place of women (see Mosse 1985, 1). Thus, Froebel publicly acknowledges the role of "women" for the construction of a nation-state. "Women" appear as "national subjects" in his discourse.

I use "national subject" to refer to an individual who takes up a subject position in a homogeneous national (here, Japanese) space, thereby acquiring a new identity (Liu 1994, 172). A national subject is therefore a participant in national history, or History. Note that a national subject can be an active agent, a passive one, or both. A member of a nation is made into a national subject by a network of state apparatuses and daily practices (among which education is perhaps the most important). In this process, one member may willingly accept the position of a national subject, while another member of the same national community may resist doing so; or a member may accept the position at a certain point of his or her life and yet may reject it at another point. Furthermore, this process is intertwined in a complex way with gender, class, ethnicity, place of residence, occupation, and so forth.

In the early Meiji period, only a certain group of women who were exposed to education became national subjects. Yet, the possessors of power represented them as the "Japanese women" (*Nippon no fujin*). For example, the readers of *Jogaku zasshi* were largely upper class, educated (and able to read English), and urban. Few among rural women became national subjects. Those who did were mostly the daughters of samurai, rich merchants, or rich landowners who lived during the last decades of the Tokugawa feudal period

(1600–1867). Indeed, the physical as well as the intellectual strength of the samurai woman depicted by such writers as Nitobe Inazō (1905) and Etsu Inagaki Sugimoto (1925) helped to formulate the image of a Japanese woman as a subject willing to sacrifice herself for the nation. In *Bushidō*, Nitobe emphasizes the difference between Japan and the West (the Teutonic peoples and the Americans) in terms of a gender relationship. He argues: "The respect man pays to woman has in Western civilization become the chief standard of morality" (1905, 155). In Japan, he argues, a woman (of the former samurai class) was already receiving the highest respect and the deepest affection as wife and mother, although she counted for very little on the battlefield (pp. 152–153). Nitobe's book went through twenty-five printings in English, Sugimoto's book through fifteen printings; both were translated into at least one other Western language (Minear 1980, 515). A woman depicted by Nitobe or Sugimoto was no longer a samurai daughter but the "Japanese woman": intellectual, strong, respected as mother and wife, and believing in the virtue of the division of labor by gender, she is far superior to the Western woman, who would endlessly assert her equality with men. English banker Basil Chamberlain endorsed this view and chose "woman" as one of the "things Japanese" along with the tea ceremony, silk, tattooing, and so forth, in order to introduce Japanese civilization to the West (Chamberlain 1904).

At this stage, then, working-class women, which included the majority of rural women, were not counted as national subjects. "Rural women" did not emerge as national subjects until later, in the late nineteenth century. Thus, the question is why they replaced the upper-class women.

RURAL WOMEN AS JAPANESE WOMEN

Scholars of modernism always identify modernism as an urban phenomenon. For example, geographer David Harvey argues that (Euro-American) modernism (after 1848) was "very much an urban phenomenon" and "existed in a restless but intricate relationship with the experience of explosive urban growth, strong rural-to-urban migration, industrialization, mechanization, massive re-orderings of built environments, and politically based urban movements" (1989, 25). Thus, urban modernity was the opposite of "traditional" rural life. Restated, modernity emerged as the transcendence of the "traditional."

History with a capital H also needs the "traditional," because "History is surely one of the most important signs of modern. We are modern not only because we have achieved this status historically, but because we have developed consciousness of our historic depths and trajectories, as also our historical transcendence of the traditional" (Dirks 1990, 25). Marilyn Ivy argues that "modern" refers to the process by which progressive history could be situated against the background of "tradition" (1995, 5). It is therefore modern to imagine a national community by using the "traditional," which can be conceived of either temporally (the past as traditional) or spatially (the countryside as traditional). I argue that this process of imagining a nation has involved two, mutually opposing, forces in Japan. One is the modernizing force that castigates "tradition" and supplants it with urban-based modernity. The other is the force that incorporates "tradition" to imagine a truly modern national community. Here, ironically, "tradition" becomes more modern than merely modern, for it is "tradition" that makes a nation genuinely modern. I argue, then, it was the countryside that became the source of this "tradition" in the History of Japan. This is why "rural women" emerged as national subjects in a variety of official discourses in the late nineteenth century. Note, however, that rural women are also ambivalent national subjects: they are not only "traditional" and "more modern," but also "nonmodern." But why the countryside as "tradition" (or by the same token, as more modern)? I have two answers. The first is ideological, while the second is material. Only when combined do they seem to give an adequate answer.

First, urban modernity in Japan was "Western." The rapid modernization and industrialization in the early Meiji period were largely the result of the Westernization of the society. However, this rapid modernization and industrialization also brought social ills, such as the "break-down of the agrarian order in the countryside and the emergence of new forms of social conflict in the cities and factories" (Gluck 1985, 177). Reawakening an agrarian vision was not new in Japan in the nineteenth century. Gluck introduces us to an eighteenth-century nativist, Ogyū Sorai, who decried the city as the center of unwelcome changes that then spread to the countryside (p. 178). But the resurrection of this vision for the purpose of constructing the modern nation-state was new. The late-nineteenth-century discourse of nationalism responded to urban modernity by identifying the countryside as the locus of an authentically Japanese culture.

My second answer concerns the development of Japanese capitalism. Upper-class women did not offer abundant and cheap labor for various industries, notably the textile industry, which triggered the industrial revolution. The demand for abundant and cheap labor was fulfilled by rural women. Consequently, the contributions made by rural women had to be identified as important. Thus, "rural women" began to appear as national subjects in the 1880s and 1890s. Still, when I compare the discursive category of "rural women" at the turn of the century and the one that appeared later, for example, in the 1930s, they are not identical. This incongruity seems to reflect the difference between the two historical contexts in which the Japanese state and capital integrated rural women as national subjects.

In 1905, a journal called *Den'en fujin* was first published by the Greater Japan Agricultural Association for Women. "*Den'en*" means "rural," but in an idyllic sense. It implies the soundness of the rural environment and the abundance of food. "*Fujin*" literally translates as "women"; it includes all people of the female sex. Fukuzawa Yukichi, an enlightenment scholar, coined this term in the early Meiji period. Using *fujin* to emphasize the notion of women as respectable human beings, Fukuzawa attempted to reject the Confucian notion of women as legal incompetents and appendages to men (Kanō 1989, 10). During the Tokugawa period, the dominant Confucian ideology recognized women as biologically inferior to men and intellectually ignorant. Referring to *ōraibon* (educational and moral tracts) published in this period, Koyama Shizuko argues that the texts hardly mention women as "mothers," but emphasize the stupidity of women and their inability to educate their own children (1986). *Fujin*, then, is not simply a term but represents an ideology that a new patriarchal figure, Fukuzawa, tried to espouse in Japan. *Fujin* could easily have been found among upper-class women, but perhaps not among the majority of rural women. The term *den'en fujin*, however, implies the possibility of finding *fujin* among them: they are rural women who are like urban *fujin*, and yet, unlike the latter, they participate in the production of goods, thereby contributing to the nation's formation.

In an editorial in the third issue of *Den'en fujin*, published in 1906, we find the following passage. The author emphasizes the need to enrich the nation and uses oil as a metaphor for the Japanese nation-state.

As rape oil can be found in each tiny rape seed, the oil of a nation can be found in each family. The wealth of a nation is the totality of the wealth of households. . . . There are many ways to increase the wealth of a nation: the introduction and improvement of sericulture and poultry farming, the promotion of stock farming, the rearrangement of rice paddies, the improvement of irrigation systems, the improvement of crop cultivations, the eradication of harmful insects and crop diseases, the promotion of side jobs, the establishment of agricultural cooperatives, and the popularization of agrarian education. All these increase the wealth of a household, thereby increasing the amount of oil of a nation. And all of these, especially sericulture, poultry farming, and side jobs, involve women (*fujin*).[21]

In this quote, the job of rural women, to increase the nation's wealth, is publicly acknowledged. They thus clearly appear as national subjects. They do not yet suffer from overwork, poverty, or other hardships, but are asked to be involved in agriculture as independent producers, thereby bringing prestige to the nation.

Scholars of nationalism often ignore the fact that, without its wealth or a material foundation, a nation cannot exist. Anderson's thesis, a nation as imaginary, often makes us blind to the material side of nationalism.[22] As Gellner argues, the emergence of industrial society, to which humankind is irreversibly committed, always precedes an age of nationalism (1983, 39). But Gellner's argument should not cause us to take a nation's wealth for granted. On the contrary, we must ask how it was accumulated. In the history of Japanese capitalism, the crucial roles that rural women played cannot be overemphasized. They produced rice and other agricultural raw materials, notably raw silk. They paid increasing taxes to the state. Recruited from the countryside as factory workers, they offered cheap and abundant labor for textile industries.

However, a general liberation of the peasantry did not take place in Japan at the same time. Instead, far from suppressing the essential relations of feudal property, the new Meiji state "introduced these relations into the new Japanese capitalist society by giving them juridical endorsement" (Halliday 1975, 43).[23] Furthermore, owing to the transfer of common lands to private ownership and a huge increase in the landholdings of both the state and the emperor, "368,000 peasant proprietors were dispossessed for failure to pay taxes" between 1883 and 1890 (p. 44). Thus, by the turn of the century, the majority of rural men and women had already been suffering from poverty, and yet nationalist discourse such as that found in *Den'en fujin* did not mention it.

In 1932, another journal called *Nōson fujin* was published by Fumin Kyōkai, the Association for Enriching Japanese Nationals. "*Nōson*" means "agricultural village" and, by extension, "rural." Unlike "*den'en*," however, it is no longer an idyllic concept; *nōson* could be quite poor. In an issue of *Nōson fujin* published in 1932, Kaneko Heiichi describes a rural woman who "smells of fertilizer, wears torn cotton work garb, covers her head with a towel that looks like it was dyed with soy sauce, and has swollen chapped hands and a face the color of sooty copper." She is indeed quite poor. Kaneko, however, praises her as a "sacred mother of the nation." He further writes: "The scene of this sacred mother nursing her infant child, while resting in the midst of hard labor on a footpath between rice paddies, and of this child's brothers and sisters chasing butterflies . . . even the genius painter Michelangelo or Kano Motonobu would have thrown away his paintbrush in the face of her and heaved a long sigh" (1932, 18).[24] The "sacred mother of the nation" was poor and exhausted from her labor. However, precisely because of that labor, she became a beautiful national subject. Poverty here is mentioned and described and yet completely aestheticized. Thus, rural women became laudable subjects because of labor that never made them rich.

However, poverty or, more specifically, rural poverty has many connotations, including ignorance, crudeness, and vulgarity. If the poor are women, it also connotes sexual promiscuity. Even though "rural women" became unmistakable national subjects by the turn of the century, they also became ambivalent national subjects precisely because they were poor, rural, and women. This is why they had to be constantly described, judged, and if necessary, reformed, to be national subjects whose labor was indispensable for nation formation. In this respect, Homi Bhabha argues: "For the nation, as a form of cultural *elaboration* (in the Gramscian sense), is an agency of *ambivalent* narration that holds culture at its most productive position, as a force for 'subordination, fracturing, diffusing, reproducing, as much as producing, creating, forcing, guiding'" (1990, 3–4; emphasis in original).[25] In the discourse of Japanese nationalism, I see the subordination of "rural women" to national identity. This is why the discourse of Japanese nationalism is often ambivalent. Through the voices of Nagano rural women, I would like to explore this ambivalence in the subsequent chapters of this book.

In Chapter 2, I will introduce the Nagano rural space that was the site of my field research between 1984 and 1991. I will also present History that has incorporated this rural space into a national space. I will focus specifically on how the state created and controlled various women's organizations from the beginning of the Meiji period to the early 1970s. I will also describe how Nagano rural women created their own groups in the early 1970s, which I later joined, in opposition to the state-led women's associations.

I have organized my argument in the rest of this book around a pattern of the life cycles of several generations of Nagano rural women as they grow, marry, have children and grandchildren, age, and die. The rural women in Nagano have interacted with History in different ways during their life cycles. They have engaged in various kinds of *hataraki*. While young, they began their *hataraki* as *komori* (nursemaids) (Chapter 3). When the industrial revolution was well under way, they began working at silk spinning factories built throughout Nagano prefecture (Chapter 4). In these two chapters, I analyze the process through which the rural women in Nagano were made into the nursemaids and factory women useful for the construction of the Japanese nation-state. At the same time, I introduce their own voices.

The silk spinning industry, however, declined in the 1920s and 1930s. Some of these silk factory women returned to their home villages, married, and gave birth to their children, while others moved to the city to work in manufacturing or service industries. In chapters 5 and 6, I introduce two different but related discourses, those of Japanese folklore studies and agrarianism. Both became important components of Japanese nationalist discourse in the early twentieth century, and both treated "rural women" as important national subjects. Folklorists depicted them as *jōmin* women but eventually made *jōmin* into "Japanese" (Chapter 5). The Nagano middling farmers depicted them as "truly modern" or "truly cultural" women, superior to urban women, and expected them to work along with men to produce a new nation with agriculture as its base (Chapter 6). In Chapter 7, I present the memories of the rural women in Nagano in the form of their narratives. I also relate them to the discourses of Japanese folklore studies and agrarianism, which were coopted into the state's war discourse by the 1930s.

The nationalist discourse I have read varies. For Chapter 3, I read primarily pedagogic discourse, including documents issued by the Ministry of Education, teachers' records and diaries, and manuals on how to educate nursemaids circulated widely among education specialists. For Chapter 4, I read documents issued by central and local governments with the purpose of promoting the silk industry in Japan. I also read the records of so-called social reformers, who tried to improve the working conditions of factory women. Employers too tried to make factory women into better national subjects and left us their writings. For Chapter 5, I read texts written by Yanagita Kunio, the recognized founder of Japanese folklore studies and his students; and for Chapter 6, I read a variety of articles in village newspapers published by Nagano farmers. Nagano rural women heard all these discourses in a variety of contexts, such as in classrooms, on the street, and at factories. They also read them at home while reading women's magazines and newspapers. I do not know whether these women read the texts written by folklorists. Yanagita and his students claimed that they produced their texts based on the voices of rural women. I will later demonstrate that their claim cannot be justified.

The women's voices, however, are largely voices of memory that I heard in the 1980s and early 1990s. The rural women in Nagano recounted their memories in a context in which the state, the market, and transnational corporations have entered into a new configuration of arbitration and planning. However, *nashonarizumu*, or nationalism, is by no means a dead language. On the contrary, what Michael Taussig has called "talk about order," the talk about Japan's proper relationships with the outside world and about "Japaneseness," floats in the world of transnational capitalism of which Japan now forms an important part (1992b, 17). Chapter 8 deals with the postwar period from 1945 to the present. Although nationalism seemed to have disappeared in Japan under the U.S. Occupation, the discourse of new Japanese nationalism has been heard increasingly since the early 1970s. In such discourse, "rural women," who no longer fit the image of "Japanese women," which surprisingly has not changed much since the prewar period, create a sense of national crisis.[26] In this chapter, my sources of contemporary nationalist discourse are mainly newspaper articles about a variety of events I observed in Nagano.

Nagano today is a part of Japan's transnational capitalism. Since the 1970s, companies based in the metropolitan centers have moved to this region in search of cheap land and labor. Young rural women today have been working as part-time laborers in a variety of manufacturing industries to support Japanese-based multinational capitalism. Hiroko, one of my neighbors during my field research, was one such woman.[27] In the next chapter, I will introduce her narratives. She and her generation of women, however, are not the protagonists of this book. Hiroko's mother, grandmother, and those generations of women are. But it was Hiroko who led me to "discover" these older rural women.

Chapter 2   # Fieldwork

FIELDWORK I: SPACE

Under the warm sun of early afternoon, nothing seems to move. Only once every two hours, an incoming train breaks the silence. The big sign erected by the railroad reads, "Let Us Not Scrap the Iida Line," a testimony to a decrease in local train use and an increase in car ownership.

In the early spring of 1984, my three-year-old daughter and I moved into a house in the village of Tabata, located in the southern part of Nagano prefecture. We rented this house from a woman who had joined her daughter and her family in Tokyo after her husband's death. Though the house was small, we were quite content with its location. Built on the midpoint of a downward slope of the valley, it commanded a great view of at least half of the entire village, the river called Tenryū, meaning a "dragon descending from the sky," and the opposite side of the valley that belonged to the other village. In the past, the Tenryū River repeatedly flooded, causing havoc for dwellers in the valley, until it was tamed by technology and became an important water route for the transportation of various goods. Today highways and trucks have replaced water routes and river boats. Yet the Tenryū River is still an important part of the valley's ecosystem, and its banks provide a space for the people of Tabata to stroll.[1]

Tabata was once described as a "purely agricultural village" (*junnōson*). A passage from a document published in 1876 reads: "The number of households engaging in agriculture and sericulture as a supplement is 438. Two are the households of hunters. Eight, of craftsmen. And there are fourteen other households." The document does not fail to mention the importance of female labor: "There are 228 women who engage in sewing and sericulture, 581 women engaging in agriculture and sericulture, and two who devote themselves to sewing."[2]

Tabata was still a "purely agricultural village" in the immediate postwar period. While the number of households almost doubled between 1876 and 1945, 81 percent of them were still agricultural households.[3] It was not until the mid-1960s that the percentage of farming households began to decline. Searching for cheap labor and land, metropolitan-based companies moved into this area. By 1980, agricultural households represented only 19 percent, a figure that has remained more or less the same until today. While these households rely on agriculture as a primary income source, the other households combine income from several different sources, of which agriculture is the least important.

Although Tabata today is no longer a "purely agricultural village," the village landscape has not changed radically. As most of the factories were built in the wooded area of the upper valley, I could still see the numerous rice paddies and dry fields from our kitchen window. A stream of children, dressed in the same indigo sweatshirts and sweatpants, journeyed to school every morning. When I saw them, it was time for me to wake up my daughter for her long day at the village day-care center. But until they came home from school around four or five o'clock in the afternoon, I hardly saw anybody outside. Where were the people?

I asked Hiroko this question, which to an anthropologist like me was a pivotal matter. She was a young housewife with three children who was constantly busy doing piecework at home. Her work consisted of soldering tiny fragments of metal that were supposedly parts of, in her own words, "some sort of big machines." To meet the company's demands, she had to repeat the same soldering task over three thousand times a day. With a bewildered look in her eyes, as she apparently found my question odd, she said:

"Everybody here works."

"Well, but, where?" I asked.

"They work at factories and at home. We must work hard to fight the increasing cost of everything. I can't enjoy taking a walk with my children in the middle of the day, because that's a sign that I am not working. I don't want anyone to think I'm not working, you see? Do you know what the name of this village means? "Ta-bata," rice paddies and dry fields. Our ancestors worked hard in rice paddies and dry fields. All of us are supposed to work hard in this hamlet."

Indeed, I had moved into this village because I was interested in the changing nature of rural women's work. By investigating this transformation, I believed, the history of the development of Japanese capitalism could be better understood. The discourse of modern Japanese nationalism would have overlooked rural women as important national subjects had they not contributed their labor for the construction of the nation-state of Japan. Tabata is located very close to Okaya. I therefore thought that the women in Tabata would have worked very hard not only in rice paddies and dry fields, but also in factories and homes, spinning silk thread and tending silkworms. Stephen Vlastos describes the enormously intensive work of raising silkworms in the eighteenth century, which must have been repeated in many households in Tabata until just several decades ago.

> Of all the tasks involved in rearing silkworms, feeding is the most demanding. Silkworms sleep only four times, each time for about twenty-four hours, before spinning cocoons, and if not sleeping they will eat voraciously day and night. As the larva grows from a newly hatched "ant" to full size, it consumes 30,000 times its body weight in mulberry leaves, which must be picked, chopped, and distributed fresh at every feeding. (1986, 97)

Additionally, many rural women in Nagano in the late nineteenth and early twentieth centuries went to silk mills, first to small-scale hand-reeling filatures and later to modern spinning factories. At the same time, I thought, they would have worked very hard tending to the needs of their children, husbands, and parents-in-law. Historian Patricia Tsurumi, describing the life of rural women in the pre-Meiji period, writes:

> Women made sandals, bags, baskets, and many other household and farming implements from straw. They were in charge of pickling vegetables, grinding grain, making salt, and all of the laborious processing of food for future use and day-to-day meal preparation—tedious and time-consuming tasks demanding skill and patience. In addition to their many labor-intensive household chores, women bore major responsibility for looking after the very young and the very old and nursing the ill or injured. (1990, 12)

I had cherished this image of industrious and self-sacrificial rural women before coming to Nagano, and I expected to find the contemporary rural women working in a similar fashion, making their appearance on the street, in the rice paddies, and in dry fields. I knew I harbored a somewhat nostalgic image of rural women. I also knew that today's farmer in Japan was not a "farmer" in the strict sense of the term, but someone who worked other jobs to make ends meet. Yet, as a fieldworker and anthropologist, I had at least expected to hear the sounds of rural women and men as they worked, if not in the rice paddies and dry fields, then surely at home, in the village common areas, and in factories. I had not expected this silence.

While listening to my neighbor as she poured cups of tea and served, I began to feel that my concept of "work" was perhaps nothing but a reflection of my own nostalgia for the rural past.

> "But what do you mean by 'work'? You said your ancestors worked hard in paddy fields and dry fields. But people are not working hard in those places any more, are they?"

> "Ah, that 'work,'" she said. "Well, you'll see, when the weather gets a bit warmer, residents of this village will begin to work in the paddy fields and dry fields. But they work there after they come home from their 'real work,' you see?"

As I munched on pickles and digested what she had just said, she continued:

> "'Work' nowadays means working for cash, working a full-time or part-time job in a factory or doing piecework at home—like what I am doing right here. Thanks to the cash I earn, we can go on vacation and buy presents for our children. I can also buy my own clothes and cosmetics, so that I can occasionally surprise Tō-chan ["father," referring to her husband]."

We laughed. Our conversation drifted away from the notion of work to the latest fashions among young village women. But I kept wondering about the meaning of work. Why and how had it been so radically transformed into a nexus with cash, the fetish of capitalism.

Since my daughter and Hiroko's youngest daughter were of almost equal age and attended the same *hoiku-en*, a village day-care center for preschoolers, we gradually became close friends. A *hoiku-en* is a public institution run by the village government and the Japanese Ministry of Health, but it has its own, often "peculiar," rules and guidelines that I, as a parent, must follow. As I did not have a telephone in our rented cottage, I often had to run to Hiroko's house to ask her questions about esoteric rules of the day-care center. For example, the day-care center required that children bring "aluminum," not "plastic," lunch boxes. However, it was hard to find a lunch box made of aluminum in the 1980s. Even when I found one at the store, it was considerably more expensive than the plastic one. One morning, when my daughter resisted taking her plastic lunch box, I had to run to Hiroko's house to borrow an aluminum lunch box. Another rule stated that mothers should occasionally mix rice with some other grain for the sake of their children's health. Other grain? What kind? Where could I find it? I again found myself running to Hiroko's to ask these questions.

As time passed, I found Hiroko constantly complaining about her health: her faltering eyesight, stiff shoulders, shaking fingers, and general fatigue. "Working" was an understatement: for about eight hours a day every day except Sundays, she sat at one of her children's small study desks and soldered tiny chips of metal. Unlike the work described by Vlastos or Tsurumi, in her work Hiroko hardly moved her body while sitting at the desk. The work required only the dexterity of her hands. Furthermore, unlike the work described by Vlastos and Tsurumi, Hiroko's work provided her with cash. But I gradually realized that soldering tiny metal chips was as laborious and tiring as the work of the rural women in the eighteenth and nineteenth centuries. The hours were long and the work exhausting. In this sense, I wondered how much the nature of work had really changed for the rural women in Nagano since the feudal period.

Anthropologist Dorinne Kondo, who worked among female part-time workers at a small confectionary factory in downtown Tokyo, expatiates on the notion of "work" in contemporary Japan. Among such women, she argues, "lack of physical activity would mean a breach of commitment to the family, a blemish on one's moral character" (1990, 278). Ultimately, cash is the tangible sign of their commitment. However, what is important is not the cash itself but the incessant physical labor that earns them the cash. It is their labor that offers these women the ultimate moral conviction that they are doing something important for their families. Kondo, then, compares them with urban middle-class women. The latter willingly stay at home to show their commitment to their families, because, for them, leaving home (to work) is a "blemish on one's moral character." Their job is to instill the value of academic achievement in their children (see also Allison 1996). Thus, I see a commonality among the eighteenth-century farm women, Hiroko, and the part-time workers at the confectionary factory.

But even though I listened intently to Hiroko's dilemma, I, as an anthropologist and fieldworker, could not help wondering about the voices of other women yet to be heard. Like my neighbor, these contemporary rural women in Nagano work tirelessly, and yet they are almost always invisible to an outsider like myself. Should I visit each individual woman at home, even if she is probably not there or busy doing piecework? Should I apply for a part-time job—which is not really part-time at all, but rather a nine-to-five job without fringe benefits—at one of the local factories? I even felt reluctant to visit Hiroko, for I imposed on her work time. If Hiroko was right, no one would be out walking in the middle of the day in Tabata. How could I talk to the people if they had vanished from the streets, rice paddies, and dry fields? Should I wait until the weather gets warmer and people begin to work in the fields, even though Hiroko told me that "just a handful of men do everything with big machines"? If she was right, where would I find rural women who would tell me about their work?

Every morning, at precisely twenty minutes past eight o'clock, Hiroko brought her youngest daughter to the village day-care center on the back of her bicycle.[4] Her other two children had left for school by then. Not all the village parents were entitled to send their preschoolers to *hoiku-en:* mothers (it was assumed that fathers were full-time workers) must be full-time workers or full-time farmers. If they were part-time workers or doing piecework at home, evidence had to be provided by their employers to show that they worked more than four hours a day, twenty days a month. I could send my daughter to this village day-care center only after the village government officer invented rhetoric to the effect that I, self-employed with a research grant, would work more than four hours a day, twenty days a month. When he suggested this rhetoric to me in the village government office, I nodded eagerly and said, "Of course. I will work much more than four hours a day." Around ten o'clock every morning during the week, a man from a company involved with "some sort of big machines" came to Hiroko's house with the day's load of metal chips. I felt as if I was the only one who was not working, not even four hours a day. I remembered what James Scott has called "the elementary fact" for all anthropologists, that is, "an anthropologist is at work from the moment he opens his eyes in the morning until he closes them at night" (1985, xviii). It was indeed depressing to think that I was not doing anything or seeing anyone. I desperately needed to have the sense that I too was working and to demonstrate my "work" to the people of Tabata.

Feeling I was wasting my precious time, I decided to visit the local library in the afternoons. The library was a simple two-story wooden building and unheated. In the dark room where I read and studied, I shivered although I worked in my coat and with a *kairo* (a kind of heat pad) on my back in between my two sweaters. Despite these hardships, I was comforted by the knowledge that I too was working. I biked the distance, rain or shine, because the train came only once every two hours. After a couple of days, I saw a woman slowly pushing a stroller in the middle of the day, and I saw several more such women later on! On some occasions, when a few of them met on the street, they squatted and chatted, while the babies in the strollers were sound asleep. I began to ask myself why these women were not "working." But these women taking a walk during the day were much older than Hiroko: they were in their sixties, seventies, or even eighties; they were "grandmas" (*obā-chan*) taking care of their grandchildren or great-grandchildren. "My daughter is at work today" or "my daughter-in-law (*yome*) is at the factory now," they said, shyly smiling. Their smiles, however, sent me a very mixed message. While they seemed content to be "mothers" again without carrying the greater responsibility of mothers, they also seemed to be mortified by their newly found freedom. They had worked hard in the past. Their work had not been for cash alone. It had been for their survival. And, as I discuss throughout this book, Japan today owes much to the labor of these women. While their work has already been absorbed in the foundation of Japanese capitalism, younger generations of women, such as Hiroko, now contribute their labor for the further expansion of Japanese or Japanese-based multinational capitalism.

Then one day, on my way home from the library, I stopped by the local government office to check its bulletin board. There I noticed various advertisements about women's groups. I also found similar advertisements in the periodicals published by local governments and the local newspapers.

> Study group for women: what kinds of lives should we seek? We solicit participation from any woman.

> The Association to Represent One's Own Pastness (*jibun-shi o kaku kai*): Anyone who is interested can sign up for membership at the village cultural center.

I called up all the places where such groups met, not only in Tabata, but in neighboring towns and villages. After I asked for further information and expressed my intention to participate in their activities, I discovered that these groups shared some common characteristics. They were similar in terms of gender, age, and organization. A detailed description of a meeting of a particular group may help the reader to understand how the members gather, talk, and write. First, however, I will focus on the term *jibun-shi*, "one's own pastness."[5]

I came up with this translation while reading Elizabeth Tonkin's *Narrating Our Pasts: The Social Construction of Oral History*. In it, she argues: "When we consider that representations of pastness—a cumbersome phrase, but more exact here than 'history'—are made by persons in interaction, situated in real time and space, we can see that however modest the speaker's aim, they are purposeful social actions" (1992, 3). "Representation of pastness" is different not only from history but from autobiography. To understand the difference between autobiography and "representation of one's own pastness," we must pay close attention to the process in which each group member constructs oral and written narratives.[6] Each meeting is dedicated to a certain historical theme that is randomly chosen. Such a theme may be an event of short duration or a historical phenomenon of long duration. Hence, the Association to Represent One's Own Pastness is primarily a place where members talk about a past they believe they share. By talking, they hope to elicit their "common" or "collective" memories. These memories could then serve as a historical context for writing one's own pastness. However, in talking about a certain theme, it is often the case that each member remembers the past differently. When this happens (and it often did at the regular meetings I attended), the gap among the members' personal memories or the sum of their "collected" memories challenges History. What I have just described applies not only to the Association to Represent One's Own Pastness but to all the other group meetings.

Let me now turn to one such group that started its activities in the town adjacent to Tabata. The group's name was "A Classroom for Women" (Josei Kyōshitsu) and had been advertised in the town government's publication as the "place to think about how we women have lived and how we should live in the future." On a rainy and unseasonably cold afternoon in the spring of 1984, I hurried to a room on the second floor of the cultural center to participate in the group's first meeting of the year. But I soon realized that I was out of place. All the women who attended the meeting belonged to my mother's generation or were still older. My mother was in her sixties, but some of them were apparently in their seventies or even eighties. They were the generation of women who were pushing the strollers in the middle of the day! I felt as if a woman of my age (I was then in my early thirties) should be working at a part-time job. While wondering whether or not I should leave, the meeting began. I felt every participant's gaze upon me.

First, a female employee of the cultural center told us, about eighty women, to stand up and sing a song, which luckily I remembered from my high school music class in Japan. The felicitous song called "Hana," "Flowers," depicts the spring scenery of the bank of the Sumida River in Tokyo. Ironically, that day had brought a particularly cold drizzle. Then, the director of the cultural center, a man probably in his sixties, gave a short speech. As I never saw him again in subsequent meetings, I think he spoke simply to give a certain formality to the day's event. He said that the group was entering its third year of activities and that their goal was to inspire each participant to pursue the life of a "new woman" (*atarashii onna*). Then, making the excuse that he had to attend another meeting going on simultaneously on the first floor of the same building, he quickly left. Nobody applauded his speech, but as he left the room, everyone politely bowed.

With his departure, the whole room became rather chaotic. The leader told us to form ten groups among ourselves. She also advised us to discuss what we would want to do at subsequent meetings and to choose a group leader. About eight of us who were sitting near one another formed a group. I felt as if all the women, who were now divided into ten groups, suddenly began to talk simultaneously: to counteract this cacophony and to communicate with one another, our group sat close together. To my great relief, everyone seemed to have forgotten my presence. But, with what ease they got to know each other! To be sure, many of these women had been members of the group for one or two years. However, Chikako, whom I befriended at this meeting, later told me that the size of the group grew each year. I was pleasantly surprised that the group incorporated new members so easily.

After having talked for twenty minutes or so, members of our group reached some conclusions about what they (I use "they," since I had not participated in the discussions thus far) would want to do in subsequent meetings: first, to "see ourselves, our experiences, and our lives"; second, to invite a few outside speakers to talk about past and present model women born in Nagano—but not "famous" speakers, as they would ask an exorbitant honorarium; and, most important, to remember to add some recreational elements to future meetings, such as trips or cooking classes. In twenty minutes, however, the discussion went far beyond the three "agenda items" I have just summarized. The discussion often departed from the main theme. "I have seen you somewhere. Ah, you are the one who lives in the corner house, aren't you? How's your husband? I haven't seen him now for quite some time," said one woman sitting next to me to a woman sitting across the circle. The others then smiled and nodded in agreement, and then somehow the discussion resumed.

Among these "agenda items," I clearly understood "inviting outside speakers" and "adding recreational elements," but I did not understand "seeing ourselves, our experiences, and our lives." I decided to intervene in their discussion before they moved on to the next item, choosing a group leader.

> "But what do you mean by 'seeing ourselves, our experiences, and our lives'?"
>
> "Well, that means we will just talk. We will talk about, for example, our hardships during the wartime period. We will talk about what we ate when we were small. Or we will talk about our relationships with our mothers-in-law and daughters-in-law. The cultural center may publish a book about our voices (*watashi-tachi no koe*). Isn't that exciting?"
>
> "A book?"
>
> "Yes, a book. By the way, who are you?"

I jumped at this opportunity to introduce myself: I live in Tabata but study in the United States; I left Japan for the United States as a graduate student a long time ago. I study anthropology and history, and I came to study the history and culture of rural women in Nagano. I somehow sensed what my new acquaintance was going to say. "Oh, my, that is wonderful! Could you please become our group leader?" All the women had been complaining about the lack of time. One woman said she often had to take care of her grandchildren. Another said she was taking care of her sickly husband at home. And another sighed and said that she was too busy taking care of the business of another women's group to which she belonged. I agreed to become the group leader and later became the leader of many more women's groups. I was no longer a lazy anthropologist, but a very busy one indeed.

The number of groups I belonged to as a regular member increased each year. A Classroom for Women was by far the largest group, while other groups had smaller memberships, ranging between ten and fifty. By the time of my second long-term visit to Nagano in 1988 and 1989, I had become extremely busy attending meetings. Some of the meetings were held far away from Tabata. Since local train service had further decreased by then, I had to study my itinerary carefully on the night before each meeting, so that I could make bike, bus, and train connections most effectively. The timetables for trains and buses became my most important fieldwork manuals. Hiroko, who was soldering 3,500 chips a day in 1988 (which indicated not only the development of her dexterity but also the growth of her children), tried to persuade me to buy a second-hand car, but I did not feel confident enough to drive on the narrow "agricultural paths" (*nōdō*) that led to the wide highways.

In Table 1, I list the names, publications (if any), and approximate numbers of members of each of these groups. In each group, there were "active" members, who almost always attended regular group meetings, as well as members who only occasionally attended meetings. The "active" members took a leadership role in reserving meeting rooms in the village or town cultural center, preparing tea and snacks, inviting outside speakers, and so forth. There were also women who rarely attended but, for example, contributed their writings to the group's publications. While these women's groups were not so much "action" as "study" oriented, some groups combined "study" and "action." For example, the members of the "Association to Recount the Stories of Women Living in the Highlands" regularly cooked and delivered meals to the bedridden elderly in their community. On those occasions, the group members casually interviewed the sick and old to explore the past history of their community. Hence, the narratives of those who could not possibly attend the meetings could also be recorded, printed, and published along with the narratives of other, more active, members. The narratives I present in this book are mostly the oral narratives I heard and recorded in my field notes at various group meetings. When I cite written narratives from the groups' publications, many of which are unattributed or women's narratives recorded by someone else, I indicate the source.

The ages of the members of the groups varied, although I have already mentioned that most of them were of my mother's generation or older. I must confess that, when I began field research, I was

TABLE 1

WOMEN'S GROUPS IN THE NAGANO COUNTRYSIDE

Group Name	*Members*	*Publications*
Josei Kyōshitsu (A Classroom for Women)	About eighty active members; each sub-group consists of about eight	None yet
Kōgen no Onna o Kataru Kai (Association to Recount the Stories of Women Living in the Highlands)	About twenty active members; however, the group is theoretically open to all the house-wives living in the village of Fujimi	*Kōgen ni ikiru onna* (Women who live in the highlands; 1984); *Fujimino ni ikite* (Having lived in Fujimino; 1995)
Katari-tsugu Ina no Onna-tachi (Women a in the Ina Valley Who Impart Their Memories to Subsequent Generations)	About thirty-four active members; 207 contribu-tors of articles to the group's book from seventeen villages and towns in Shimo Ina county	*Katari-tsugu Ina no onna-tachi* (1984); working on new publication
Sensō Keiken o Tsutaeru Haha no Kai (Association of Mothers Who Impart Their Wartime Experiences to Subsequent Generations)	About twenty active members; however, the group is theoretically open to all the house-wives living in the village of Kawaji	*Ishoku ni matsuwaru haha-tachi no sensō taiken* (The wartime experiences of our mothers: concerning clothes and food; 1977); no publications since

unable to distinguish between women in, say, their early sixties and women in their late seventies. I always lumped them together in a single category of "the old." After reading the publication of the "Association of Mothers Who Impart Their Wartime Experiences to Subsequent Generations," I realized that the members were either "children" in their early teens during the war and remembered what their mothers did for them, or they were "young mothers" and remembered what they did for their infant children. There was indeed a significant generational difference between these two groups

Group Name	*Members*	*Publications*
Karatachi no Hana (Acacia Flowers)	About seven active members; about 115 contributors to the group's book from the town of Usuta	*Karatachi no hana* (1978); no publications since then
Onna no Rekishi o Kataru Kai (Association to Narrate Women's Histories)	About fifty-two active members; however, the group is theoretically open to all the house-wives living in the village of Kanae	*Hitamuki ni ikinuite* (Having tried to survive; 1984); working on a new publication
Jibun-shi o Kaku Kai (Association to Write/ Represent One's Own Pastness)	About thirty active members; this is the only group with about five male members	Two reports in 1988 and 1996
Rekishi o Hiraku Hajime no Ie (House to Open Up History)	Not so much a group as a place where a variety of grass-roots women's groups from all over Japan gather once a year at the end of August	Annual reports

in terms of how they remembered and narrated the past. But to make generational categories is an almost impossible task; I will let the narratives relate such, often quite subtle, generational differences themselves.

   The activities of these women's groups do not end with the publication of their narratives (although some groups have not yet published their narratives). For example, the members of the Association to Recount the Stories of Women Living in the Highlands published their book in 1984, which they titled *Kōgen ni ikiru onna* (Women who live in the highlands) after the name of their group. In 1988, their leader, Miyoko, incorporating other more "action" oriented groups into hers, renamed the association Wa, meaning "circle."[7] I revisited her village in 1990 and, most recently, in 1996. In that year, Miyoko gave me another book titled *Fujimino ni ikite* (Having lived in Fujimino; 1995). Many women whom I met in 1988 came to meet me. Each of them brought a local dish for a potluck party. It is not that they gathered at my request. They have been meeting regularly to this day, talking, listening, and writing.

Let me place these women's groups in the national context. In 1988, Avon Josei Bunka Sentā (Avon Cultural Center for Women) in Tokyo carried out a survey among what the center called "grassroots women's groups." The center sent out questionnaires to 242 such groups throughout Japan with the goal of understanding the nature of these organizations.[8] The results of this survey were published in the center's report *Kusanone gurūpu katsudō no jittai to riidā no ishiki chōsa* (Survey of the activities of the grass-roots groups for women and the goals of their leaders; 1988). The report shows, for example, that women deciding to participate in such groups had several different motives: 50.8 percent of women "wanted to use their power (*chikara*) to provide for the needs of the others"; 48.1 percent "wanted to contribute something to their own communities"; 28.4 percent "wanted to use their knowledge and skills"; 26.2 percent "wanted to use their free time in the most meaningful way"; and 20.2 percent "wanted to gain new knowledge" (p. 7). Diagram 1, published in this report, shows the kinds of activities in which these women's groups engaged. These activities are broken down by members' ages. The groups that I joined in Nagano fall into the categories I have shaded, that is, groups of the middle-aged and older women studying women's history and women's problems.

How can I relate these older women's group activities to the activities of young women in the Nagano countryside, who are now contributing their labor to Japan-based multinational capitalism? In 1988, Miyoko complained to me that young women were not interested in her group's activities. The oldest active member of the group was seventy-eight years old. The youngest was sixty-three. Hiroko, for example, did not attend any of these meetings in Tabata and its vicinity. Young housewives of my generation were busy working, as part-time workers or doing piecework at home, in addition to attending to the needs of the young and the old. The group Hiroko and I joined together was a jazz dancing group called Danshingu Famirii

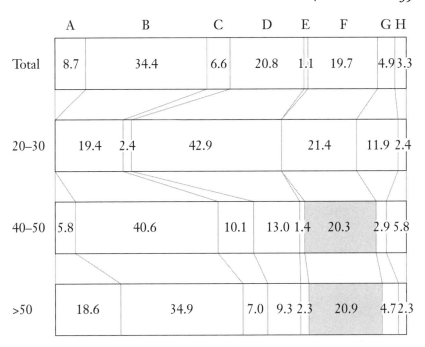

	A	B	C	D	E	F	G	H
Total	8.7	34.4	6.6	20.8	1.1	19.7	4.9	3.3
20–30	19.4	2.4	42.9			21.4	11.9	2.4
40–50	5.8	40.6	10.1	13.0	1.4	20.3	2.9	5.8
>50	18.6	34.9	7.0	9.3	2.3	20.9	4.7	2.3

A: Welfare for the aged
B: Welfare for the handicapped
C: International exchange programs
D: Education programs
E: Environmental problems
F: Study of women's histories
G: Cultural programs

DIAGRAM ONE. **Activities of women's groups in Japan by age (percent).** Based on two diagrams published in *Kusanone gurūpu Katsudō no jittai to riidā no ishiki chōsa* (1988, 12). (Reproduced here with permission of Avon Josei Bunaka Sentā)

(Dancing Family). The group gathered every Thursday night from eight to ten o'clock when our children were either fast asleep or watching television (I had to take my daughter with me, though). According to Hiroko, dancing was the best way to alleviate her stiff shoulders and back pain. Furthermore, she confided to me, the group offered her a place where she could forget about the needs of her family. Although I always wore a comfortable sweatshirt and sweatpants, Hiroko and others showed off their bodies in purple leotards. Were the young housewives of Hiroko's generation not interested in their mothers' or grandmothers' activities? Hiroko teased me more than once, saying that I looked like an "old auntie from the countryside" (*inaka no obasan*) participating in the activities of "more serious kinds" of women's groups. But one night, on our way home from a two-hour jazz dancing class, she told me: "I am not necessarily happy soldering these chips. I am happy only when I get the money. My back hurts a lot these days. I suppose these are things I could talk about if I joined their groups, right?" I will not predict the future of the young rural women in Nagano, but I am greatly interested in which women's groups Hiroko will belong to and what she will talk and write about twenty years or so from now. Since I have placed the women's groups in Nagano in a national framework, I will next discuss them in the framework of the master narrative of modern Japanese history, that is, History. I find it necessary to do so because, according to Miyoko, the groups I joined came into existence in opposition to the "official" (*kansei no*) women's associations that had been established by "the state" (*kuni*) from the late nineteenth century.

FIELDWORK II: HISTORY

For anyone who studies Japanese nationalism, the term *"kuni,"* "the state," represents a particularly troublesome notion. When Nagano rural women use it, they almost always add an honorific prefix to make it *"o-kuni."* The term refers to the prewar Japanese state and implies deference to the state.

A Japanese-language dictionary gives a variety of meanings for the term *"kuni"*: "the earth" (*dai-chi*), "national land" (*koku-do*), "the state" (*kokka*), "the feudal domain" (*ninkoku*), "the imperial throne" (*tei-i*), "region" (*chihō*), "countryside" (*inaka*), "hometown" (*kokyō*), and so forth (Niimura 1976, 636). What the rural women in Nagano mean by *kuni* is very close to the dictionary term *"kokka,"* which I translate here as "the state." But *"kokka"* means not only "the government" but "the nation," "the nation-state," or "the country." And "the state" in English is a concept that is far from clear.

This may be because the Western social sciences lack major theoretical paradigms to study "the state" as either an actor or a society-shaping institutional structure: rather, their paradigms have been "riveted on understanding modernization, its causes and direction" (Skocpol 1985, 6). To Theda Skocpol, scholars of the Western social sciences have been more interested in society than in "the state."

However, she observes a paradigm shift, which is more favorable for studying "the state," in the mid-1970s. One factor that caused this shift, according to Skocpol, is the entry into the social sciences of neo-Marxist scholars who are interested in the role of the capitalist state. Even with this shift, however, "the state" remains an elusive concept. Thus, Philip Abrams argues: "We are variously urged to respect the state, or smash the state or study the state; but for want of clarity about the nature of the state such projects remain beset with difficulties" (1988, 59).[9]

English-language terms such as the "state (State)," "political organization," or "government" are not easy to define. Anthropology is perhaps more deficient than any other discipline of the social sciences in discussing and defining "the state." Indeed, many of the earlier generation of anthropologists simply ignored its very existence. For example, in the preface to *African Political Systems*, A. R. Radcliffe-Brown argues that "the State," in the sense of an entity over and above the human individuals who make up a society, does not exist in a phenomenal world, but is a fiction of the philosophers (1940, xxiii).[10] What does exist is an "organization, i.e. a collection of individual human beings connected by a complex system of relations" (ibid.). When Radcliffe-Brown asserted the absence of "the State" in a phenomenal world, he had in mind various African kingdoms under the British colonial regime in the early twentieth century. Was he aware of the existence of the colonial state, which exerted its enormous power on those African kingdoms? Was he aware that he was part of it? If so, how could he argue for the absence of "the State"?[11]

Abrams concurs with Radcliffe-Brown to a certain extent. Abrams also refuses to see the state as an entity but, then, terms the "non-existence of the state" the "real official secret":

> The state is, then, in every sense of the term a triumph of concealment. It conceals the real history and relations of subjection behind an a-historical mask of legitimating illusion; contrives to deny the existence of connections and conflicts which would if recognized be incompatible with the claimed autonomy and integration of the state. The real official secret, however, is the secret of the non-existence of the state. (1988, 77)

Abrams' argument brings me back to the debate between Marx and Hegel on the nature of the state.[12] In his "Critique of Hegel's Doctrine of the State," Marx argues: "What is crucial in the true state is not the fact that every citizen has the chance to devote himself to the universal interest in the shape of a particular class, but the capacity of the universal class to be really universal, i.e. to be the class of every citizen" (1975, 112). The first step toward this end, according to Marx, is the "extension and the greatest possible *universalization* of the *vote*, i.e. of both *active* and *passive* suffrage" (p. 191; emphasis in original). For Marx, then, the state disappears only when all humanity plays an active part in political society. To achieve this end, all humanity must belong to the truly universal class. But the rural women in Nagano had neither active nor passive suffrage until after 1945. They could not play an active role in political society. Even so, they refer to *"kuni"* as if the state represented the interests of all the citizens, men and women. The *kuni* denied them political roles, and yet they claim to work for the *kuni* (*o-kuni no tame ni*). Restated, *kuni* could conceal its power, representing a "triumph of concealment," for these rural women.

In this connection, I must contrast the women's groups I joined with those that had existed before. The latter were formed not by women themselves, but by the *kuni*. These associations were thus forced to change their nature according to, in the rural women's own words, "the mood of each epoch" (*jidai no sūsei*). And "the mood of each epoch" necessarily reflected the changing nature of the dominant state ideologies. In 1945, the members of various women's associations created by the prewar state were given both active and passive suffrage. But many women whom I met in Nagano described this political power as of the "passive" variety: they were given power, but it was not theirs yet. It was not until the early 1970s that they felt they truly had acquired their own power. This is why various women's associations I joined were formed in the 1970s and 1980s in opposition to the "official" ones. Although some of these were developed from the "official" organizations, I see a clear rupture in terms of how the group meetings and activities are organized. Since the 1970s, it is women who have organized them.

The periodization of more than one hundred years from the onset of the Meiji period to the early 1970s is by no means easy. I can, however, discern the following periods. The first is the early Meiji period (1860s and 1870s), which reflected the mood of "civilization and enlightenment" (*bunmei kaika*). The second is roughly from the 1880s to the 1910s, when the Japanese populace experienced the first two modern wars, the Sino-Japanese (1894–1895) and the Russo-Japanese (1904–1905) wars. Both wars demanded the service and sacrifice of the many rural men who became foot soldiers. This is also the period in which, according to Gotō Sōichirō, "national consciousness" began to grow in Japan (1976, 73). The third period is the brief interlude of the so-called Taishō democracy between the two world wars. This was a time when (male) citizens, energized by the post–World War I economic boom, were allowed to express their political views to a certain extent. Historian John Dower, however, describes Taishō democracy as a period in which "deviance was tested against the polestars of respect for the emperor and for private property" (1979, 306). Fourth is the long and dark period of economic depression and military expansion. This period largely corresponds to the period between the Manchurian Incident in 1931 and the Japan's defeat in World War II in 1945. This is also the period in which *kokutai*, the theory of the Japanese nation as a single extended family with the emperor as its supreme head, prevailed. And finally, we must examine the immediate postwar period, when Japan was occupied by the U.S. Occupation forces, and the subsequent but still called postwar (*sengo*) years until the late 1970s, when Japan's economy fully recovered. Let me briefly examine each of these periods in its relation to the "official" women's associations in the Nagano countryside.

The mood of "civilization and enlightenment" did not last long. I say this because Japanese women's almost dramatic initiation into new social roles was immediately followed by the state's ban on women's political activities. Sharon Nolte points out that "women were permitted to take national qualifying examinations in medicine as early as 1884 but not in law until 1933" (1983, 1). The Regulations on Public Meetings (Shūkai Jōrei) of 1880 barred "public servants"— military men, policemen, and public and private school teachers and students—from joining political organizations. "Women, minors, and those deprived of civil rights" were added to this list in 1890, and only "women and minors" were barred from even attending political meetings (Nolte 1983, 2). Public servants were barred from joining political organizations because their occupations were thought to give them special influence on education and public opinion. Women were barred without any official explanation (ibid.). Even though women won the right to "attend" political meetings in 1922, their exclusion from politics lasted until 1945.

However, the brevity of this first period does not reduce its importance in modern Japanese History. On the contrary, this period offered upper-class women the status of national subjects for the first time. For example, an editorial in a women's magazine published in 1895, *Jokan* (The mirror for women), has the following message for its supposedly female readers:

> Do not forget, for your own sake, that you are first and foremost a happy citizen (*seimin*) and a faithful subject (*shinmin*) in Japan, which has this beautiful scenery, this congratulatory state (*kokka*), and this honorable emperor. . . . Unless you cherish these statuses, you are incomplete and crippled as a Japanese woman (*Nippon joshi*), however much knowledge, ability, and beauty you may have. (quoted in Fukaya 1990, 139)

Such an early nationalist discourse tied upper-class Japanese women—here, the readers of *Jokan*—to the state and the emperor and swiftly made them into national subjects. Furthermore, early Meiji educator Hosokawa Junjirō argued in the same year that the "nation's military power" was increasing only in such countries as England, France, Germany, and the United States, where "women's education" (*joshi kyōiku*) was institutionalized and showing signs of improvement. He thus urged the Japanese state to institutionalize "women's education" immediately, thereby teaching women the importance of the state and their civic duty.[13] In this period of "civilization and enlightenment," we can also observe an increasing number of women's magazines that had *Nippon* (Japan or Japanese) in their titles: *Nippon shin-fujin* (Japanese new women), *Dai-Nippon fujin kyōiku-kai zasshi* (The journal of the Greater Japan Association for Women's Education), *Nippon no katei* (Japanese homes), and *Nippon fujin* (Japanese women).

Do we find such women as national subjects in the Nagano countryside in the early Meiji period? A variety of documents suggest that indeed we do and that they were organized into various women's associations, but these documents do not clearly suggest who they were. These women's associations were not regarded as "political." Rather, they were associations in which women were supposed to exercise their new public/civic duties. For example, a local Nagano newspaper article in 1887 reported the inaugural meeting of Ueda Fujin Danwa Kai (Ueda Women's Conversation Club) in the town of Ueda; the club set goals to reform the "evil customs of the past" and to raise the position and consciousness of women by teaching them "home economics," "hygienic practices," and "proper manners" for "respectable ladies."[14] The mandates of the Ueda Women's Conversation Club parallel the fourth and fifth articles of the "Charter Oath of Five Articles" (Gokajō no Goseimon), which was set forth by the Meiji Government in 1868: "The evil customs of the past shall be abandoned and everything based on the just laws of Heaven and Earth" and "Knowledge shall be sought throughout the world so as to invigorate the foundations of imperial rule" (Hane 1986, 86). "The world" in the charter means the West, in which Japan should seek "civilization and enlightenment" (Harootunian and Najita 1988).[15]

Associations such as the Ueda Women's Conversation Club were also community-based. Hence the membership of each association was theoretically open to any woman over a certain age, usually fifteen years old, who was a resident of a given community, if she paid a membership fee. However, it is unclear who first founded these associations, organized their meetings, and participated in them. The prospectus of the Ueda Women's Conversation Club contained an article that stipulated that "men" (*danshi*) were not allowed to attend the club's meetings "except for honorary and invited members."[16] The prospectus of another women's association suggests that "honorary" members were "aristocrats (*kikan*), gentlemen (*shinshi*), rich merchants (*gō-shō*), and rich farmers (*gō-nō*)," all of whom were men.[17] The lecturers and guests invited to the inaugural meetings of these women's associations were, for example, a prefectural governor, mayors, judges, heads of local tax offices, and school principals. All were, again, men (Nagano-ken-shi Kankō-kai 1987, 941–972). In addition, men working as low-ranking local government officials seem to have taken care of the administrative and financial matters of these women's associations. It is thus difficult to imagine women, even of the upper class, as active agents who formed and ran these associations. It is more likely that the "aristocrats," "gentlemen," "rich merchants," or "rich farmers" first organized the associations for women. They might first have approached women of their own class, their wives and daughters and perhaps female school teachers, who constituted a minority among school teachers. In brief, these early women's associations were *for* upper-class women in Nagano but not *of* them, and they were neither created nor run *by* them.

A local newspaper article from 1899 indicates that the majority of rural women in Nagano were excluded from these early women's associations. The article praised five employers from the silk industry who brought their female employees to a meeting of a local women's association.[18] It commended these employers' actions, for making factory women attend such a meeting was considered to be effective in bringing them closer to "civilization and enlightenment." However, the article also suggests that factory women were not regular members of this women's association. They probably did not have time to attend such meetings, could not afford the membership fees, and attended only when forced to do so by their employers. Many of these factory women were likely transient residents of the community; they were to return to their home villages once their contracted terms were over. But it is unclear whether they became active members of women's associations in their home villages when they returned.

It is well known that early Meiji enlightenment scholars contributed, albeit only discursively, to the policies that led Japanese women to "civilization and enlightenment." They published numerous articles on Japanese women in their journal *Meiroku zasshi* and, in doing so, created novel terminologies. I have already introduced one such term, *"fujin."* Another, *"danjo dōtō,"* is a term these scholars gave to the equality between men and women in terms of "customs and manners" (*fūzoku kanshū*). If such a notion would prevail in Japan, they thought, Japanese women could contribute to the construction of the Japanese nation and the expansion of Japanese capitalism equally with men. Note, however, that *danjo dōtō* is different from another term they created, *"danjo dōken,"* the equality of men and women in terms of their political rights. The enlightenment scholars endorsed *danjo dōtō* but not *danjo dōken*.[19]

Fukaya Masashi discusses this ambivalent position of enlightenment scholars toward women's rights in terms of nationalism (1990). He argues that the introduction of nationalism into public discourse (as in *Meiroku zasshi*) created the "problem": too much nationalism inevitably leads to equality in legal rights between men and women. The state, however, cannot accept such an outcome of nationalism; this is partly because the state must rely on the cheap and abundant labor force provided largely by rural women to enrich the Japanese nation. It was rural women who produced much of the profit that made the nation's industrialization possible.[20] Thus *danjo dōtō* paved the way for the state and the business community to use women's labor, which was substantially cheaper than men's labor precisely because of the absence of *danjo dōken*.

That women constituted a cheap labor force in the nation's industrialization is also a historical truism in the West. But Sievers argues that "the participation of women in Japan's industrial labor force from 1870 to 1930 is unparalleled; in no society has the proportion of women workers reached the 60 per cent that Japan averaged in this critical period" (1983, 84; see also Bernstein 1988; Tsurumi 1984, 1990). Often forgotten, however, is that most of these women workers were recruited from the rural area: "women" in the industrial labor force is emphasized; where they were from is often not questioned.[21] Historian Donald Roden, referring to Japan of the Meiji era, describes it as a "civilization of character, a civilization dedicated to the accomplishment of deeds, the fulfillment of duty, and the exemplification of bourgeois honor and respectability" (1990, 39). He further argues that such a character is synonymous with the "values of masculine domination: asceticism, achievement, and public service" (ibid.). What supported such values, according to Roden, were the "duties of womanhood" to devote themselves to the home as *ryōsai kenbo*, "good wives and wise mothers," another dominant gender ideology similar to that of *fujin* (p. 41).[22] In the countryside, where both sexes were supposed to produce as much rice and silk thread as possible to "enrich and strengthen the nation" (*fukoku kyōhei*), one needs to give serious second thought to the "duties of womanhood" in Meiji Japan. The rural women in Nagano did not stay at home as "good wives and wise mothers," but went out and contributed their labor to strengthen Japan. I have argued that upper-class Japanese women became national subjects in the early Meiji period. By the late nineteenth century (the second period), we observe the separation of classes among Japanese women in terms of how they were expected to behave as national subjects. The working-class women living in the countryside became the source of a cheap labor force, while the upper-class women became the so-called good wives and wise mothers. Put another way, while the upper-class women engaged only in reproductive activities, the working-class women engaged not only in reproductive but in productive activities.

The appearance of working-class women as national subjects dramatically changed the nature of the "official" women's associations. For example, in 1989, the proprietor of Shunmei-sha, a silk spinning factory, established his company's own women's association for his 1,800 women employees in collaboration with a local Buddhist monk. This was a women's association established exclusively for factory women. In 1903, another silk spinning factory, Rokkō-sha in Nagano, established its own women's association for its employees.[23] Factory women, who were excluded from the women's associations in the first period, now became official members. Yet the associations were created for them by their employers. The members of Shunmei-sha's women's association might have been forced to listen to a lecture by a Buddhist monk when they were too tired to keep their eyes open. Thus, we see a parallel in organization between the upper-class women's associations founded in the early Meiji period and the lower-class women's associations founded in the late Meiji period (Nagano-ken-shi Kankō-kai 1987, 951). Both were organized and run by men. I should not overemphasize this, however, for, by the second period, rural women were increasingly willing to attend the associations' activities.

With the advent of the Sino-Japanese War in 1894, the members of Shunmei-sha's women's association made one thousand pairs of socks for soldiers.[24] In a similar act of patriotism, the members of another local women's association, for the female graduates of Aonuma Elementary School in Nagano, raised money to buy as many "winter hats" as possible for sick and wounded soldiers (Nagano-ken-shi Kankō-kai 1987, 963–964). By the time of the Russo-Japanese War, raising money for soldiers, consoling and helping families whose household heads and sons were conscripted, and attaining every possible means of self-sufficiency for such households without their major labor force became the most important functions of the women's associations in Nagano. By the second period, all the women's associations began to be called *fujin-kai*. That working women came to be called *fujin* suggests that they too became national subjects along with upper-class women.

Indeed, Gotō Sōichirō argues that the Russo-Japanese War and the subsequent Hibiya Riots, which occurred on September 5, 1905, mark the beginning of "mass nationalism" (*taishū nashonarizumu*) in Japan. "Even rickshaw men, grooms, craftsmen, and small-scale shop keepers" in the metropolitan center of Tokyo actively participated in the riots, protesting against the terms of the Portsmouth Agreement between Japan and Russia (1976, 124). They demanded more from Japan's victory over Russia, and hence protested against the state that did not satisfy their expectations. John Halliday comments: "The Hibiya Riots of 1905 had shown two things: that there was a large, inflammable anti-regime potential among the working masses and that officially sponsored 'nationalism' and chauvinism had sunk deep roots among the people" (1975, 73). This seemingly inconsistent argument suggests two things: nationalism had begun to take root among the people and yet, in the early twentieth century, the masses still perceived the existence of the state or regime. Michael Lewis asserts that a series of city riots triggered by the Hibiya incident represents an "expression of *democratic nationalism* that demanded respect for the person and the rights of the individual and pledged loyalty to the emperor but not to unpopular policies or policy makers" (1990, 113; emphasis added). However, when the "mass" of "mass nationalism" becomes synonymous with "Japanese," it carries the potential to incorporate even "unpopular policy makers" into the "mass" and to make them disappear. I think this is what eventually happened in the fourth period of Japan's imperial expansion. In this respect, Hannah Arendt once wrote: "Totalitarian movements use and abuse democratic freedoms in order to abolish them" (1973, 312). I will reconsider the implication of Arendt's argument when I discuss the fourth period.

"Mass nationalism" steadily grew in the city as well as in the countryside. Perhaps it grew more rapidly and strongly in rural than urban areas for the following reasons. First, both the Sino-Japanese and Russo-Japanese Wars demanded the sacrifice of a great number of soldiers, most of whom had been recruited from the countryside. In the single county of Kita Saku in Nagano, for example, twenty-three local young men were killed in the Sino-Japanese War and 144 in the Russo-Japanese War. The majority of these victims were below the rank of corporal, the sons of tenant or small-scale tenant-owner farmers (Morosawa 1969b, 7). Second, both wars also demanded the sacrifice of many rural women as a cheap labor source; they were often described as "soldiers of peace" (see Chapter 4). And finally, these wars marked the first instances in Japanese history in which rural women and men were given officially recognized, and therefore visible, opportunities to serve Japan. Both rural women and men were injected with a sense of national pride in this period of Japanese history, a sentiment that the state expected them to nurture from then on.

Around the turn of the century, women's associations started to mobilize for national goals in Japan's external relationships. The first nationwide women's patriotic organization, Nippon Aikoku Fujin-kai (Japan Women's Patriotic Association), was established in 1901 with Princess Chieko, a member of the imperial family, as its president and the wife of Count Iwakura as its director (Aoki 1987, 252; see also Smethurst 1974, 43–49). The Nagano chapter of the Japan Women's Patriotic Association increased its membership during the Russo-Japanese War by making use of the already existing network of local women's associations.[25] In her numerous speeches in towns and villages throughout Japan, the association's founder, Okumura Ioko, dramatized the "hardships of Japanese soldiers" in the Sino-Japanese and Russo-Japanese wars.[26] In this way, she could recruit an increasing number of women into her association (Nagano-ken-shi Kankō-kai 1987, 957).[27] One of her speeches given in an unknown locality contained the following passage: "To whom do we owe this pleasure that we are not looked down upon or despised [by foreigners]? Of course, to His Majesty the emperor. But we also owe it to these dying soldiers."[28] As the ranks of infantrymen were largely recruited from rural areas, her speeches must have moved the rural women who were worrying about the safety of their sons, husbands, fathers, and lovers. However, because the association's higher echelon included the wives of high-ranking politicians and bureaucrats at the local and national levels, the majority of the women in the Nagano countryside could not and would not become a part of it.[29]

Did the so-called Taishō democracy between the two world wars affect women's associations in Nagano in any noticeable way? Despite the post–World War I economic boom, which was after all largely a city phenomenon, the 1920s in the Japanese countryside were a period of mounting economic recession (I will discuss this more in detail in Chapter 6). Nevertheless, Taishō democracy advanced to the Nagano countryside. The introduction of so-called free thought (*jiyū shisō*)—socialism, communism, and anarchism—created a space for the mostly male rural youth. They then engaged in public debates on a variety of topics such as capitalism, labor unionism, and the erosion of agriculture. In the cities enjoying the post–World War I economic boom, Taishō democracy created a confusion in gender relationships: women began to act more like men; they were more outgoing, more independent, and more "political." The disruption in Meiji gender relationships, however, remained largely an urban phenomenon. Rural men remained patriarchal in their relationship to women (see Chapter 6). As I will argue in Chapters 5 and 6, important nationalist discourses of this period relied on the dichotomy between the city and the countryside; the countryside was depicted as a sacred and authentically Japanese space in its relation to the city. And rural women were depicted as the "sacred mother of the nation," thus "superior" to urban women. Rural women were not supposed to be affected by urban turmoil. Hence the "official" women's associations in Nagano underwent little change during the period of the Taishō democracy: they remained "official" women's associations.

The mobilization of rural women for national goals reached its peak during the fourth period. By the early 1930s, national goals referred less to the construction of the nation-state and more to the expansion of the Japanese empire.[30] The young unmarried women in each village and town were mobilized through the "association for virgins" (*shojo-kai*). This association was later renamed by the state the "association for female youth" (*joshi seinen-dan*). It eventually merged with its counterpart for men and became the "association for youth" (*seinen-dan*). The progression of terms, from "virgins" to "female youth" and finally to "youth" suggests the state's desperate efforts to make young rural women into national subjects: *seinen* (youth), a gender-neutral term, connotes "equality" between men's and women's potential contribution to the expansion of the Japanese empire. But the state used this "equality" to mobilize everyone, irrespective of gender, class, and even race for Japan's imperial expansion (see Chapter 7). Rural women did not achieve "democratic freedoms." Rather, the state gave such freedoms to rural women precisely in order to "abolish them" (Arendt 1973, 312).

Married women were also mobilized for the same goal. The Japan Women's Patriotic Association found it hard to increase its membership in the countryside. Instead, Dai-Nippon Kokubō Fujin-kai (Great Japan National Defense Women's Association), founded in 1934, swiftly increased its membership. A 1934 prospectus of this association's local branch in the village of Hirano contains the following passage:

> The economic depression that has hit the silk spinning industry has led to closures of many factories and has resulted in an increasing number of unemployed men and women. The poverty among village residents has mounted, but the government has so far not issued any effective policy that might give us a ray of hope. Instead, dangerous thought [socialism, communism, or anarchism] seems to be emerging in our village. Japan must now meet this crisis with all its might. . . . All of us in this village must create humble but strong families, raise once again our national spirits, and break through this most difficult period as one body of people. . . . We have so far had only the Japan Women's Patriotic Association. We now establish the Hirano branch of the Great Japan National Defense

Women's Association, which can meet the needs of the masses more effectively (*mottomo taishū-teki*). (Nagano-ken-shi Kankō-kai 1987, 875)

Instead of protesting against a state that "has so far not issued any effective policy," the members of the Great Japan National Defense Women's Association promised to work for it "as one body of people." They were not only mobilized by the state; they also mobilized themselves.

For some rural women in Nagano, the class and ideological differences between the two national patriotic organizations did not matter: they became members of both associations. The central and local governments commended these women publicly for their "patriotism" because of their double commitment to the two patriotic associations. The Home Ministry closely controlled the activities of the Japan Women's Patriotic Association, while the military maintained a close relationship with the Great Japan National Defense Women's Association. The tension between the Home Ministry and the military became the tension between these two women's patriotic organizations. The two patriotic associations eventually merged and formed the single body of the Dai-Nippon Fujin-kai (Greater Japan Women's Association) in 1942. The members did not make this decision to merge but were told to do so by government officials. As the international situation made it increasingly difficult for Japan to win the war, the state could not afford to let the "differences" between the two organizations prevail.[31]

Ella Wiswell, who conducted field research in Kumamoto prefecture in the mid-1930s, comments on the women's association in the village of Suye:

On entertaining soldiers on the day of the coming muster, the mayor told them [the members of the Great Japan National Defense Women's Association in Suye] that it will not be necessary to prepare *sekihan* [glutinous rice with red beans, a congratulatory and auspicious dish served on ritual occasions] this time. Ice water would be enough, for it will be hot. What is more important, he has heard, is that all the members of the Women's Association should join in the review rather than just entertaining the soldiers. He believes that the men will be made more attentive and serious if they are being observed by their mothers and acquaintances. (Smith and Wiswell 1982, 27–28)

The women of the village of Suye quietly accepted what they were told to do by the mayor "in view of the present grave international situation" (p. 27). Wiswell's fieldnotes suggest the absence of women's definitions of their own political roles. And yet, they also suggest the women's active participation in the patriotic organization.

On August 15, 1945, Japan offered the unconditional surrender demanded by the Allied Forces. "Japan had risked all and lost all" (Reischauer 1978, 102). From 1945 to 1952, under the American military occupation, the women's associations in Nagano were dissolved but then reorganized. Interestingly, the Occupation used prewar organizations to disseminate the idea of American-style democracy to rural Japanese. But the radical shift from militarism and fascism to democracy seems to have confused (male) local government officials, who continued to use their patriarchal power to control the affairs of the postwar women's associations. For example, an officer of the Nagano prefectural government wrote: "We must educate our women so that they will cultivate their female virtue (*futoku*) inherent in our tradition, develop their morality and knowledge, work for the reconstruction of our nation (*kokka*), and contribute to world peace.[32] Except for "world peace," his narrative could easily pass for prewar discourse. The notion of "female virtue" is clearly the legacy of Meiji gender politics.

Such a lack of understanding of democracy is also reflected, for example, in the letter sent by the female leader of the renewed (by the Occupation) Nagano Prefectural Women's Association to the representatives of its branch associations in 1945: "Utilizing the traditional organizational network of our women's associations, we now have every intention to work harder for His Majesty the emperor, his imperial nation (*kun-koku*), and the development of our race" (quoted in Tsujimura 1966, 77). The emperor had declared himself a human being, not a living god as he had professed to be before Japan was defeated; the nation had lost its imperial glory; and the Japanese race had barely survived. The author of this letter, still clinging to the old values, is incapable of understanding the new ones and is at a loss about what to do next.

Ironically, it was out of this confusion that these women began to search for their own independence. It is not that they suddenly broke their ties to the state and its ideologies. The "new" women's groups I joined are still loosely connected to the state, as we have already seen: most depend on the state subsidies for their existence. And yet,

I also see a clear rupture between the "old" and "new" women's groups, for the latter were created exclusively by local women. Furthermore, these "new" groups, which are still community based, are open to any woman. The voices I heard are the voices of the women who are the members of these new groups. The following chapter marks the beginning of my endeavor to listen to the voices of Nagano rural women remembering the days when they were very young and yet already working for the nation.

Chapter 3   *Komori*

"*k̲omori*" is a generic term that consists of a noun, *"ko"* (child), and a verb, *"moru"* (to protect or to take care of); Japanese use it to refer to any person, male or female, old or young, who takes care of children. In this chapter, however, I focus on the young girls, hired by families in need of child care in the Nagano countryside in the late nineteenth and early twentieth centuries, who were called *komori*.

In his *Centuries of Childhood* (1962), Philippe Ariès explains that "the idea of childhood," that is, an awareness of the particular nature of childhood, did not exist in Europe until the seventeenth century, when the "coddling" of children was criticized by moralists and pedagogues; and childhood, which had thus been isolated, was further "prolonged," primarily through the school system. But Ariès notes that, for the working class and for girls, "brief childhood" remained the norm until much later than for the upper and middle classes and for boys. The children of the working class, and particularly girls, were supposed to work just like their parents instead of enjoying their "childhood." This was indeed the case in the Nagano countryside in the late nineteenth and early twentieth centuries; the children of farmers, particularly girls, were expected to behave like adults in terms of their *hataraki* (see also Miyamoto 1969, 39).

At a group meeting in the village of Kanae, Chieko, looking back on her childhood in the 1930s, said:

> Even though I was then perhaps ten or eleven years old, I worked just like my mother. Silkworms needed our attention for twenty-four hours, so that I too was involved [in the task of taking care of silkworms]. I always ran to school, because I had to work until the last moment before school began. But my parents told me I should be thankful for being able at least to attend school. Many *komori* in my village could not go to school.

Indeed, *komori* was the work available for the rural women in Nagano when they themselves could be described as "children."

Wiswell, describing the everyday life of *komori* in the village of Suye in the 1930s, writes:

> [In the summer] children are very active in the *dō* [village shrine compound]. The nursemaids devise all sorts of means to keep their charges out of the way of their games. They tie them to the posts in a sitting or standing positions, like horses, persuading them that it will be fun to be tied up. They play blind-man's bluff or will get a sash and try to catch someone and tie her up, provoking much laughter. The smaller babies carried on the back merely ran the chance of being knocked down, but the older ones in the *dō* are often left to their own devices. If all else fails they put them on their backs and go on with their own games. (Smith and Wiswell 1982, 234)

Like their European counterparts, nursemaids and nannies, *komori* began to appear in the discourse of nationalism in the late nineteenth century.[1] Their appearance corresponded to the emergence of a subculture among *komori* that is the focus of my analysis in this chapter.

In contrast to the practice of hiring *uba* (wet nurses), which was seen mostly among the elite families in urban areas,[2] *komori* were confined largely to villages and small towns.[3] Unlike European nursemaids and nannies, *komori* were not status symbols but, rather, an economic necessity for the employers, whose own labors left them no time to devote to child rearing. Furthermore, *komori* were not sheltered in the homes of their employers; forming small groups, they spent most of their days with their charges in "public" places such as shrine compounds, playgrounds, river banks, or simply the streets. They had to stay in such places so their employers, who were busy working, would not be bothered. Even when it rained, they often could not stay at home (Miyamoto 1984, 185). Although the majority of *komori* were indentured to their employers for a certain number of years, girls who took care of their own siblings or their neighbors' children at the request of their parents were also called *komori*. All *komori* shared one essential characteristic: they were daughters of poor families (see Figure 1).

In postwar Japan, *komori* have disappeared from the countryside, which is itself rapidly disappearing.[4] But *komori* are still remembered in songs and pictures with a keen sense of nostalgia, and many who grew up in Japan in the 1950s or 1960s recall seeing little wooden figurines (*kokeshi*) of *komori* or drawings of *komori* in school textbooks; she almost always carries her charge on her back, wears a

FIGURE ONE. Photograph of a group of *komori* by French journalist Felicien Challaye, published in his *Le Japon illustré* (1915, 55).

colorful jacket that covers them both, and holds in her hand a balloon or a pinwheel to soothe the baby. Furthermore, those still remembering their days on the back of *komori*, who are somehow almost always men, tend to idolize *komori* and see in them an idealized version of maternal love. For example, the internationally known Japanese writer Dazai Osamu, who was born into an affluent landowning family in Tsugaru (Aomori prefecture) as the sixth son and tenth child, had a *komori* named Také. He writes the following about her when he visits his birthplace: "Také was someone whom I particularly wanted to meet during this trip to Tsugaru. I think of her as my own mother. It was close to thirty years since I last saw her, but I had not forgotten her face. I might even say that it is because of her that my life has any direction at all" (1987, 152–153; translated by Westerhoven). Dazai was brought up by his aunt Kie, as his own mother was "sickly and worn out with child-bearing." Také went into service as Kie's personal servant and stayed with Dazai for five years beginning when he was three. For her part, Také said that she "had always assumed that Shūji [Dazai] was her mistress' child and thus had taken such special care of him" (Westerhoven 1987, xvi). Although she was only thirteen, Dazai writes, "yet the Také I remember is not a young girl at all, but a mature person in no way different from the Také I now see before me" (1987, 168; translated by Westerhoven).

Také was given an opportunity to speak in Westerhoven's introduction to Dazai's *Tsugaru* because of her relation to an internationally known writer.[5] But Také was a very rare exception. *Komori* are almost always rendered "voiceless" in their representations, the quintessential example of a group without a history who never represented their own pasts, emotions, and presence (cf. Said 1979, 6). I will show, through ethnographic reconstruction of the everyday life of the *komori* in Nagano, that *komori* represented their culture and history in terms very different from the representations of them in postwar nostalgia.

The everyday lives of *komori*, however, were powerfully shaped by the historical development of the nation-state of Japan, especially the state's broad effort to incorporate the masses into a newly articulated "civilized" and "enlightened" Japanese citizenship. *Komori* became one of the objects to be, first described, then examined, and finally reformed to make Japan a respectable nation in the international community. *Komori* were by no means the only group of individuals to become the object of such description, examination, and reformation. Almost every commoner, male or female, was expected to be civilized and enlightened as a new Japanese citizen. However, the state was particularly concerned with the "evil customs of the past" among farmers, who still comprised more than 70 percent of the nation's population in the late nineteenth century. For example, the habits of rural young men who, in the words of official decrees, "acted in groups, made merry, argued with each other, and drank and ate in public," thus "damaging local customs and mores," became the state's target for reformation.[6] Furthermore, local people were expected to get rid of publicly displayed phallic images, abandon the custom of mixed bathing, and wear shoes instead of walking on bare feet (see R. Smith 1983, 77). But as *komori* were one of the most marginalized groups because of their class, gender, location of work, and age, the discourse of nationalism relied on the most radical rhetoric to incorporate them as Japanese citizens.

As I will show later, *komori* did hear and manage to read what was spoken and written about them; they were frustrated by how others represented their lives and often attempted to resist these descriptions. Such resistance, however, did not lead to widespread protest, nor did it bring about any profound change in their situation. Rather, the *komori*'s resistance should be understood as part of everyday practices in which they tried to communicate their conscious rejection of the representation of their culture in the state's discourse on elementary education. Such practices may have served not only "to give shape to resistance" but also "to consolidate existing hegemonies" (Comaroff 1985, 6; see also Willis 1977). Thus, *komori* were further despised by society as marginalized subjects. What were these practices? They were to create songs, to express their thoughts and emotions in the verses of those songs, and to sing them in public.

Folklorist Akamatsu Keisuke argues that there are two distinct kinds of *komori* songs: the first is a lullaby or a cradle song, and the second expresses the emotions as well as the living and working environments of *komori* themselves (1993, 99).[7] Like Akamatsu, I am interested in this second group of *komori* songs. Akamatsu introduces us to the following song, which he heard in the Ise region of western Japan in the early twentieth century:

> *The job of komori is to sing.*
> *We walk from the west to the east*
> *(carrying our charges),*
> *always singing.*
>
> *You think we are noisy,*
> *but unless we sing,*
> *the day never ends. (1993, 105)*

Scholars have widely reported on songs as weapons of resistance among the illiterate and the powerless, such as antebellum slaves, low castes, peasants, racial and ethnic minority groups, and women. But until social historians began to pay attention to them, songs were treated as historical sources secondary to written documents. This is because songs are oral and, "in 'the West,' . . . literacy has enormous prestige even when people are not skilled in its uses, and oral skills can be devalued" (Tonkin 1992, 14). Furthermore, singing is performing; each act of singing is a unique performance. An irony here is that oral performances such as singing songs must be written down if they are to be analyzed and preserved (ibid.). Hence, orality and literacy are often hard to discern.

I was interested in the meaning of the verses of ballads sung by *komori*. I therefore tried to collect *komori*'s songs myself. Often, however, those who had once worked as *komori* no longer remembered them or could recall only a portion of each song. Furthermore, the *komori* of the 1930s, unlike the *komori* of the late nineteenth century, were exposed to various other songs through mass media. Thus, I read the verses of the songs collected, written, and analyzed by scholars, the orality of which has been completely removed. As for the contexts of the singing as performance, I can only rely on the memories of former *komori* or on ethnographies about them: they sang in public places so that passersby could hear them. They also sang in company with other *komori*. Songs thus provide me with a weapon to explore the thoughts and emotions of *komori* in rural Nagano. (Note that the state and powerful individuals could also create songs and use them as weapons to disseminate their own dominant ideologies among the illiterate and the powerless; see Chapter 4, page 94.)

Until I began my field research in Nagano, I was unaware that *komori* as "work" had existed in the history of modern Japan. My understanding of the term was purely at the level of its etymology, that is, "to take care of children." When the women of various groups presented it as a kind of work, I understood that the work of *komori* marked the beginning of their consciousness as "working" women (see also Akamatsu 1993, 87, 119). Takayama Sumiko (hereafter Sumiko) told me of her mistress who "kicked her feet every morning at four o'clock to wake her up." She then had to carry her charge on her back and hold the hand of a three-year-old toddler all day long except when she was at school. Her "mistress was always waiting for her impatiently outside her house with her two kids" when she came home from school.[8] Her mistress had to work "until midnight everyday," but so did Sumiko, even though she was then a fourth grader at the elementary school.

WHO WERE THE *KOMORI*?

It is unclear when widespread employment of *komori* started and when *komori* began to appear in public places. Matsunaga Goichi says that *komori* first appeared on the public scene in the mid–nineteenth century. There is evidence of *komori* in the Tokugawa period (Matsunaga 1964, 111; Uno 1987; Akamatsu 1993, chap. 3; Note-helfer, personal communication; Walthall, personal communication), but the identification of full-time child care with young female employees seems to be a later development. Kathleen Uno argues that, in the Tokugawa period, elite families depended on a variety of hired child-care givers such as wet nurses, domestic servants, and *komori*, whereas ordinary families could not afford them and instead had "any" family member of either sex take care of infants and toddlers in turn (1987, 1991). If allowed to speculate boldly, I would say that the custom of hiring caregivers spread from the elite to ordinary families during the Meiji period, while elite families gradually absorbed the idea of the mother as the sole caregiver. The fact that, in the very beginning of the Meiji period, boys also worked as indentured *komori* and that their numbers dropped off sharply in the same period could be understood as a legacy of the pre-Meiji custom.[9] But as the disappearance of boy *komori* seems to have much to do with the emerging notion of "manliness" in Meiji Japan,[10] the appearance of a greater number of girl *komori* would be related to the emerging notion of "womanliness." In this sense, *komori* is sui generis a Meiji phenomenon, a phenomenon that emerged along with the emerging nation-state of Japan.

Tables 2 and 3 are lists of *komori* who attended special educational programs, which I will discuss shortly, in the town of Nagano in 1907 and 1941. Data for both years indicate that the employers and parents of *komori* were engaged in a variety of small family enterprises or combined several different income sources. Table 4 is a list of *komori* who worked in several villages in the southern part of Nagano and were enrolled in similar educational programs in the early twentieth century. The employers and parents of these *komori* were engaged not only in farming, the production of rice and other cash crops, but also in sericulture and various kinds of household employment. Together, these tables suggest that, in the families that depended on the labor of *komori*, everybody, except for the babies and toddlers who had to be taken care of by *komori*, worked.

TABLE 2

EXAMPLES OF *KOMORI* WORKING IN THE TOWN OF NAGANO, 1907

Komori's Identification Number	Year of Birth	Year Entered Education Program[a]	Status[b]	Father's Occupation and His Spouse's Occupation, if Different
1	1897	1906	Employed	Owner of canning business
2	1893	1907	Employed	Owner of restaurant
3	1895	1907	Employed	Merchant
4	1895	1907	Not employed	Rickshaw man; cart-pusher (spouse)[c]
5	1895	1907	Not employed	Manual laborer; dressmaker (spouse)
6	1897	1907	Not employed	Bricklayer (summer job); rickshaw man (winter job)

Source: Katei hōmon roku: Komori Ji-ai no kumi (Records of a teacher's visits to the families of *komori* and their employers: The Ji-ai class for *komori*; 1907). My special thanks go to Mr. Takeshima Yoshishige, the principal of Gochō Primary School, Nagano, at the time of my fieldwork in 1988, who kindly let me copy the records used in tables 2 and 3.

[a] The year a *komori* entered the special education program roughly indicates when she began to work as a nursemaid. Special classes were established for *komori* at the Gochō Primary School in the town of Nagano.

[b] "Employed" means the *komori* had a master; "Not employed" means she took care of her own siblings and/or her neighbors' children.

[c] Cart-pusher (*kuruma-oshi* or *tachinbō*) refers to men and women who waited for a client's cart to arrive at the bottom of the hill, pushed the cart from behind, and were given a little money by the cart driver for their help (see also Yokoyama 1949, 39).

This explains why *komori* spent most of their days in public places. The presence of the *komori* and her charge at home was not welcomed by family members who worked hard in the fields or at home. The *komori*'s job was to let the adult members of the family work to make their living. McBride (1978) has argued that the employment of a nursemaid in Victorian and Edwardian England signified two contradictory feelings of the mother of the house: her callousness toward her children as well as her devotion to child rearing. This contradiction, experienced by many middle-class English

TABLE 3

EXAMPLES OF *KOMORI* WORKING IN THE TOWN OF NAGANO, 1941

Komori's Identification Number	Year of Birth	Year Entered Education Program	Status	Father's Occupation
1	1926	1939	Employed	Innkeeper
2	1928	1941	Employed	Wholesaler of fish
3	1923	1934	Employed	Manufacturer of roof tile
4	1927	1939	Employed	Owner of confectionery store
5	1925	1936	Not employed	Secondhand clothes merchant
6	1924	1935	Not employed	(Unknown)

Source: Gakuseki-bo: Ji-ai no Kumi (School records: The Ji-ai class) (Gochō Primary School, Nagano, 1941).

TABLE 4

EXAMPLES OF *KOMORI* WORKING IN THE VILLAGES IN THE SOUTHERN PART OF NAGANO

Komori's Identification Number	Year of Birth	Entered Education Program	Status	Father's Occupation
1	1895	1907	Not employed	Agriculture, sericulture, fruit vendor
2	1896	1907	Not employed	Agriculture, sericulture, charcoal vendor
3	1896	1907	Not employed	Agriculture, sericulture
4	1924	1934	Employed	Agriculture, papermaking
5	1925	1931	Employed	Agriculture, sericulture

Sources: Katari-tsugu Ina no Onna Henshu Iinkai, *Katari-tsugu Ina no onna* (The Women in the Ina Valley who impart their memories to subsequent generations; 1983); Masuda Sayo, "Geisha," in Y. Usui, ed., *Gendai kyōyō zenshū (1957);* and Takayama Sumiko, *Nono-san ni narundayo* (You will become a little buddha; 1987).

The juxtaposition of this table and tables 2 and 3 may give the reader the impression that there were more *komori* working in towns than in villages, but this was not the case. Although an almost equal number of special classes for *komori* were established in the towns and villages in Nagano, the school records seem to have been better preserved in the towns.

women, seems not to have been a problem in rural Nagano, because the housewives who depended on the help of *komori* had very little time to devote to child rearing. This also means that, upon entering service, *komori* hardly found "their personal horizons widened," as their English counterparts did, by an exposure to the very different lifestyle of the middle class (McBride 1978, 55).

Indentured *komori* worked for three, five, or even ten years. A *komori* either moved from one house to another, as she was successively hired by several families, or took care of the younger siblings of her first charge.[11] It is unclear for how long a *komori* carried her charge on her back. I was often told in Nagano that *komori* carried "very grown-up" (*zuibun ōkina*) toddlers on their backs. Oki Kiyoshige, a teacher in the town of Ueda, wrote that some *komori* attended school carrying even four- or five-year-old charges on their backs. These charges naturally "did not want to be on their *komori*'s back but wanted to play by themselves" (1893, quoted in Kōzu 1974, 128).[12] In the mid-Meiji period, kindergartens were mostly for the children of upper-class families, however (Uno 1987). They were usually attached to women's normal schools. Oki further wrote: "I therefore asked a teacher to gather them [those older toddlers] in one room and take care of them. I must say this is a kindergarten created out of the necessity [to educate *komori*] and not a luxurious institution" (1893, quoted in Kōzu 1974, 128). In this quote, Oki tries to justify the creation of a kindergarten that is not for upper-class children. As Wiswell has described, *komori* with older charges must have invented ways to free their hands so that they could study and play.

The contracts for *komori*'s services were usually oral agreements through the employers' relatives or friends, and the employers paid the parents of *komori* in either money or rice at the beginning of the contract period. The families who sent their daughters out to work as *komori* found in this practice a way to lessen the number of mouths to feed (*kuchi berashi*), but hardly opportunities for the girls. While employed, *komori* received room and board, and occasionally small gifts such as a kimono, an apron, or wooden clogs, but usually no wages. Only when *komori* were considered to be old enough were they expected to receive wages, in exchange for cleaning the house, cooking, and doing other housework. Older *komori* who received wages could thus be considered domestic servants.

Sumiko began to work as a *komori* in 1933 at age ten for the family of her father's cousin. According to *kimegoto* (oral agreement) between him and her parents, Sumiko could have free room and board, attend the elementary school for three years, and receive two *tan* of silk after she completed her service.[13] However, she had to quit in the middle of her service owing to illness, which she now believes was caused by "lack of sleep." She received only one *tan* of silk instead of two.

Komori began child-care work at a relatively young age, much younger than their counterparts in England (McBride 1978, 49). Tables 2 through 4 suggest that a *komori* could begin service as early as the age of nine. But it is quite possible that these *komori* began child-care work long before they entered special education programs. Masuda Sayo (hereafter Sayo), who worked as a *komori* in the town of Shiojiri in the 1920s, wrote in her autobiography that she began her work as a *komori* at five years of age (1959, 138). Since she was born out of wedlock, Sayo was raised by her uncle and sent out to work as a *komori* for the family of a large landowner. Until she was sold as a *geisha* at the age of twelve, she worked from five in the morning until very late in the evening. Since she was not even given a pair of socks during the cold winter, she had to stand on one leg (with her charge on her back) "in order to warm the other leg." The children in her neighborhood thus began to call her Tsuru (meaning "crane"). Since Sayo did not even know her name, she became convinced that it was Tsuru (p. 139).

Where did the *komori* come from? We must consider two different kinds of movements between socioeconomic classes and between geographical areas. Tables 2 through 4 suggest that the *komori* who worked for their own parents were born into the lower-class families of rickshaw men, cart-pushers, manual laborers, dressmakers, bricklayers, secondhand clothes merchants, and, most probably, landless or small-scale owner-tenant farmers. The indentured *komori* working for masters also came from this specific stratum of society, and some of them had endured a miserable childhood before becoming a *komori*. For example, the housewife employing *komori* number 3 in Table 2 is reported to have told her teacher: "My friend asked me to hire this girl as our *komori*. According to my friend, her parents had already died and she has only one brother, whom her father had with his mistress. When she was brought in here, she indeed looked like a beggar's daughter, so I gave her my children's old clothes that I had washed."[14]

Regions that were economically depressed tended to send out a large number of *komori* to more prosperous regions. Many girls were sent to Nagano from the neighboring regions of Niigata, Gifu, and

Toyama. But the majority of *komori* seem to have worked in their own or neighboring communities, or oscillated between their home villages and small towns within Nagano according to changes in economic cycles. Such a cyclic flow of *komori* is difficult to document, but historian Kōzu Zenzaburō reports that the number of *komori* coming into the town of Nagano from neighboring villages increased substantially when the market price of silk thread fell (1974, 177; see also Aoki 1987, 85–86). In this sense, *komori* were the products of economic hardship.

The increasing number of new middle-class families of bureaucrats, journalists, educators, managers, technicians, and other white-collar workers did not depend on the labor of *komori*: to the contrary, they despised the practice of employing them. *Jogaku zasshi*, the women's magazine that increasingly attracted the readership of the women in this emerging middle class, said the following in an 1887 editorial:

> The majority of indentured *komori* were born into poor families and are totally illiterate. We often cannot tell whether they are boys or girls, as they often resort to violence. When they are sent into the street carrying their charges, they do not care a bit about the babies. When they cry, *komori* shake them ruthlessly. If they do not stop crying, *komori* pinch them on their buttocks or put sweets stolen from the store in their mouths.[15]

This editorial is the third in a series of essays published in the same year about the responsibility of the "mother" and the "wet nurse." In his first and second essays, the author links the tasks of the mother and the wet nurse to the formation of the nation-state. The mother must be an educated and scientifically minded woman to raise children of and for Japan. Because of new economic conditions that permitted upper- and middle-class women to devote greater time to child rearing, they gradually accepted a mother-centered approach to child care. Uno argues: "The new conception of motherhood diffused slowly, gaining acceptance mainly among upper- and middle-class circles, in which conditions of life permitted women to devote greater time and energy to child-rearing" (1987, 183). In order to carry on a social life, upper-class women found the wet nurse to be a necessary evil. The author, however, discourages readers from hiring wet nurses, for some of them behave like *komori*. *Komori*, then, are deemed completely inappropriate to raise children of and for Japan. The author believes that they have no redeeming value, for they do not know how to raise children properly. People cannot even tell the gender of a *komori* because of her crude language and violent behavior; the author, in the third essay of the series, thus "sincerely hopes that *komori* will cease to exist in our society" (p. 123). Clearly, the author judges the *komori* not as an adolescent girl who needs to be educated, but as a surrogate mother.

Middle-class families of older types, merchants, craftsmen, and large-scale farmers, seem to have favored continued reliance on hired child-care givers. But they seem gradually to have shifted their preference to somewhat older women who could take care of children as well as tend to other domestic chores. If they had to rely on *komori*, they felt they had to justify the practice by trying to reform her language and behavior. The master of *komori* number 1 in Table 2 had a fairly large canning business, and his wife "seemed to have a certain education."[16] She was reported to have said the following to her *komori*'s teacher: "I hired this *komori* last September, but I really could not put up with her bad manners and language, and thought I should not let her take care of my children. This is why I sent her to school in October, and her manners and language have improved greatly since then."[17] The special education program for *komori* must be understood in this context. The old middle-class and working-class families in the Japanese countryside still needed the help of *komori*. But a *komori* now had to approximate the figure of the upper- and middle-class educated mother.

THE NATIONALIST DISCOURSE ON *KOMORI*

A variety of documents concerning the elementary education issued by the central and local governments in the early Meiji period do not single out *komori*, but include them among the "children of impoverished families." The term for "children" (*shitei* or *shijo*) is a gender-neutral category that included both boys and girls. For example, the Nagano prefectural government issued a document in 1877 titled "How to Persuade the Children of Impoverished Families to Attend School," that included in the category "children of impoverished families" those who worked "as apprentices in merchants' houses and craftsmen's shops, day laborers, and indentured servants such as *komori* " (quoted in Kōzu 1974, 16). One of the most important goals of the Meiji state was to make these children into "Japanese" citizens and into sources of productive labor and military power.

As Foucault has suggested in regard to Europe, the quantitative and qualitative control of the human population were essential to the construction of the modern nation-state of Japan (1980). Quantitatively, the goal was to increase the population. The state prohibited all forms of abortion: medicinal, self-induced, and through the aid of an unlicensed midwife (Mitsuda 1985, 103). The Meiji state also introduced a new set of hygienic practices and public health measures at the local level to improve both maternal and children's health. Qualitatively, the state was determined to educate its population and to establish the institution of compulsory education.[18] Thus the Fundamental Code of Education issued in 1872 urged that "every person (*ippan no hitobito*) should pursue learning" and stated specifically that "there should be no gender difference (*danjo no betsu naku*) in receiving education" (Monbushō Kyōiku-shi Hensan-kai 1938, 277).

In order to support the state's new goal to establish compulsory education, the Nagano local newspapers published numerous "fine episodes" (*bidan*)" of "poor" peasant women who nevertheless understood the importance of education. For example, *Gekkei shinshi* published the following story in 1879: "A clever woman as is rarely found in this world: Iwabuchi Jitsu in the village of Nakagawa in Chikuma County became a widow eight years ago at the age of thirty-two. Living in poverty, she took great care of her three children and sent all of them to school. The eldest particularly was absent from school only one day last year."[19] In another story published in *Shinpi shinbun*, a woman surnamed Takahashi, upon attending a local school lecture, realized, "for the first time in her life," the importance of learning and bought books for her children.[20]

Jitsu and Takahashi represented "new" women. In order to demonstrate this, I will cite another "fine episode," about a woman named Katsu from a certain village in Nagano in the eighteenth century.

> Katsu's family was very poor. She often found no rice to cook at home. Her mother-in-law had been sick for the past twelve years. Whenever Katsu obtained something good to eat, she offered it to her mother-in-law, while the rest of her family ate "wretched stuff" (*asamashiki mono*) to kill their hunger. In the hot summer, Katsu changed the bedding of her mother-in-law everyday. In the cold winter, she warmed her mother-in-law's bed with her own body, leaving her little children by themselves. In the year of a famine in 1786, she pawned one of the only two kimono she had to buy rice

and rice cakes, which she offered to her mother-in-law. The region-al lord, upon hearing Katsu's story, gave her rice and money in 1790.[21] (quoted in Morosawa 1969a, 167)

Katsu conformed to the dominant Confucian ideology of her time, in which a woman's chief duty is to honor her parents-in-law (see Kaibara 1906, 37). To the contrary, Jitsu and Takahashi dedicated their lives to their own children; and, to that end, they tried to educate themselves. Their stories represent a radical transformation of the Confucian discourse on women.

However, despite the massive efforts of the central and local governments to enforce compulsory education among farmers, craftsmen, and merchants and particularly among the poor, school attendance rates remained low overall, and substantially lower among girls, until the turn of the century. For example, in the school district composed of three villages in southern Nagano, an 1883 report stated that 111 children were unable to attend school because of poverty. Among the ninety-six girls, fifty-six worked as *komori* (Kōzu 1974, 41). In view of such a gender discrepancy, the official explanations for the poor record of school attendance became increasingly "genderized," and among the children of impoverished families, girls gradually became the marked category. An editor for a local newspaper commented in 1883: "Because many parents do not believe in the necessity of education for girls, they must work as *komori* or at silk filatures. These are the primary reasons for the poor school attendance record for girls."[22] In this passage, three conditions that had hitherto been only loosely associated were conjoined: being female, being poor, and working as *komori*.

By the late 1880s, the idea that *komori* were daughters of impoverished families who were unable to attend school and therefore ignorant seems to have been firmly established among the new middle-class people. In order to more clearly define themselves as a separate class, the emerging middle class in Nagano scorned both *komori* and their employers. They thus shared the opinion expressed by the editor of *Jogaku zasshi*, who sincerely hoped that *komori* would cease to exist in Japan. Typical of these attitudes are sentiments expressed by a local journalist in 1898: "Whenever I see a group of *komori* wandering about the streets and making noises, I feel sick and nauseous. . . . We must be ashamed of our town because there are *komori*."[23] Schoolteacher Maki Yoshitarō in the town of Yashiro wrote: "*Komori* have nothing to do except to soothe the charges on their backs so that they will not cry. They sing vulgar songs, damage carts and horses, and make fun of people passing by them. One cannot even mention their behavior, which is too crude, nor their language, which is too rude" (1893, 30). Perhaps, as Challaye's photograph shows (see Figure 1), small groups of *komori* who sang "vulgar songs," engaged in "rowdy behavior," and shouted crude words to each other and to passersby roamed the streets and gathered in open public spaces. For the middle class, the speech and behavior of *komori*, particularly when they were in groups, became intolerable.

Another journalist for a local newspaper concocted the idea that the sexuality of *komori* was outside the control of their parents, masters, and mistresses and that *komori* were therefore by nature promiscuous. Thus, in explaining the causes of venereal diseases among military conscripts in Nagano, he commented: "Entertainers and prostitutes, female servants and *komori*, female factory workers, and widows are all responsible for these diseases."[24] Another newspaper article reported the illegal abortion of a seventeen-year-old *komori*: she worked for a certain master and had had an affair with him for the past five years.[25] Another article reported that an eighteen-year-old *komori* had an illegitimate affair with a young man in the village.[26]

Except for the older *komori* mentioned in the last two newspaper articles (who were exceptions to the general rule in terms of age), the majority of *komori* were elementary-school-age girls. Despite their young age, however, their mature sexuality is cited as a threat to society. In Dazai's description of his *komori*, he recalls that Také was only thirteen and yet the Také he remembered was not a young girl but a mature woman. We must take into account the time gap between "then," when Dazai was taken care of by Také, and "now," when Dazai was remembering the past. References by the middle class to *komori*'s sexuality, then, are less actual descriptions of *komori* than projections of the future for *komori*. They believed *komori* would become sexually promiscuous entertainers, factory workers, domestic servants, or even prostitutes. What made them believe so, I think, are the words of *komori*'s songs, which I will describe later in detail.

A variety of government documents published toward the end of the nineteenth century began to single out *komori* not so much as subjects of education, but as objects to be scrutinized and reformed, emphasizing the rudeness of their behavior and the crudeness of their language. A notable result was the establishment of special classes at a number of local schools in Nagano so that *komori* could attend school at the same time they tended their charges. The Meiji educational authorities used the carrot and the stick to enforce compulsory education when it was not yet tuition-free (Nagai 1976; see also Tsurumi 1984a, 276–277). The creation of such special classes was the result of a compromise among several institutions and groups of people: the state, which saw the need for increasing school attendance rates; the local government, which saw the same need and yet was aware of local conditions; and the parents and employers of *komori*, some of whom increasingly wanted the language and behavior of *komori* reformed. Kōzu (1974) reports that the officials of several other prefectural governments traveled to Nagano to learn about special educational programs for *komori* with the intent to establish similar programs in their own prefectures. There was, however, yet another group of people who endorsed the idea of special education for *komori*: the school teachers who began to worry about the possible effects of the behavior and language of *komori* on regular school children and sought to separate the *komori* from the latter (Maki 1893, 34).[27]

But how "rowdy" was their behavior and how "vulgar" was their language? To answer this question, we can listen to the discourse produced by *komori*'s teachers, which not only emphasizes the need to reform their language and behavior but also reveals some facets of *komori*'s everyday lives. For example, Oki wrote in his personal diary in 1893: "*Kono ama, kono yarō, gaki, chikushō yarō, temei, una-a*, all these are second-person references. *Komori* do not consider them obscene words." *Komori* used such second-person references to express disdain for and possibly abuse others. Oki wrote that "*komori* belong to the lowest rank of society and their language is indeed unmentionable" and that "it is horrible to think that their language would eventually become their charges' language." Many other school teachers and local journalists also characterized the songs of *komori* as crude, as they were riddled with what these intellectuals thought to be immoral criticisms of *komori*'s masters and neighbors, as well as allusive references to body parts and sexual intercourse. Thus, by the 1890s, the primary goal of education for *komori* became, as one local journalist put it, to "sanitize (*issen suru*)" their rude behavior and obscene language.[28]

I must introduce here the term *kagaku-teki ikuji-hō*, the "scientific method of child rearing," as this became the key notion used to incorporate *komori* as new citizens of Japan (Sawayama 1980). The "scientific method of child rearing" refers to a body of ostensibly "scientific" knowledge that a "good wife and wise mother" should have in order to raise children appropriate for the modern nation-state. In other words, it refers to the knowledge of public health and hygienic practices. By the end of the nineteenth century, this "scientific method of child rearing" was incorporated into the discourse concerning the education of *komori:* as any "good wife and wise mother" should know the "scientific method of child rearing," *komori* should know it as well. For example, the prospectus for a special class for *komori* established in the town of Yashiro in 1893 uses a horticultural metaphor to explain the role of *komori: "Komori* are gardeners who protect the buds of plants and help them to grow. If the gardeners do not master the art of gardening, they inhibit the budding of plants and suppress their growth. This is why we educate *komori* to reform their child-rearing practices." This passage clearly downplays the right of *komori* to receive education. Instead, it emphasizes the right of their charges to be raised in the scientific manner. At the same time, this passage points out the role of *komori* in the construction of the Japanese nation. Trying to approximate the role of *komori* to that of *fujin* or mother, who should know the civilized and enlightened way to raise children, the state incorporated the "scientific method of child rearing" into the discourse of *komori*'s education. Thus, efforts to reform *komori*'s language and behavior through general education were increasingly subordinated to efforts at making them *fujin. Komori* came to be seen not as children, much less as school-age children, but as surrogate mothers.

Teaching manuals for the educators of *komori*, initially published at the turn of the century, emphasize the need to reform the child-rearing practices of *komori*. One manual published by a local teacher in 1898 advises *komori* not to give toys with small pieces or sticky food to their charges (Maki 1898, 16). Another manual, published by the Nagano prefectural educational committee in 1900, advises *komori* to wear white cotton hair bands so that their charges will not play with their "dirty" hair while on *komori*'s backs (Shinano Kyōiku-kai 1900). This same manual spells out everything *komori* should be careful not to do so as not to inhibit the proper physical and intellectual growth of the infants. Another teaching manual advises *komori* to learn the different kinds of infant cries to better interpret their charges' needs and includes a long list of different cries for *komori* to remember (Nakamura 1900, 20–21). A manual published in 1903 explains the proper tying of the sash to counter the *komori*'s tendency to move around freely while carrying their charges on their backs (Nakamura 1903, 10; see Figure 2).

FIGURE TWO. Representation of *komori* in a
hanging scroll used by teachers in Nagano
to teach *komori* how to use a sash properly. Note
that, in comparison to the *komori* in Figure 1, they
are depictd as more motherlike figures and their
class backgrounds are suppressed. (Circa 1900,
original in color, courtesy of Shinano Kyōiku-kai,
Kyōiku Hakubutsu-kan).

In these manuals, the desirability of educating *komori* is mentioned solely because of their potential to negatively influence their
charges. *Komori* thus came to be seen, in the words of a local teacher,
as "girls who, if not properly educated, may become 'ignorant wives
and unvirtuous mothers' (*akusai mōbo*)" (Nakamura 1906, 21; emphasis added). In this phrase, the discourses of *komori* and *fujin* converge.

Fujin, as agents of morality, should be "good wives and wise mothers," but *komori* could also be made into "good wives and wise mothers" through proper education. The proper education of *komori* was not a general education but rather instruction in the scientific method of child rearing. *Fujin* and *komori*, who were in reality quite different in terms of age, physical maturity, and socioeconomic status, were thus grouped together into "good wives and wise mothers."

The last manual for teachers of *komori*, published in 1920, contains the following twelve chapters (Nagano-shi Jinjō Kōtō Shōgakkō 1920).

1. The role of *komori*
2. How to carry an infant on your back
3. How to feed your charge
4. How to assess your charge's health by examining excretions and discharges
5. How to handle your charge's clothes and diapers
6. How to interpret your charge's cries
7. How to hold your charge
8. How to put down and play with your charge
9. How to get your charge to play with other toddlers
10. How to teach your charge to walk
11. How to clean the body of your charge
12. How to choose appropriate toys for your charge

From the perspective of the state, *komori* had become "mothers," or more specifically, "Japanese mothers." But was this merely the stated ideology of the Japanese nation-state? Did *komori* themselves share this vision of all Japanese women as "good wives and wise mothers"?

THE VOICES OF *KOMORI*

The women who once worked as *komori* in Nagano ranged in age from their fifties to their nineties in the 1980s. They were the most active members of the women's groups. But because these women were *komori* "a long time ago," in their own words, their memories of everyday life during that time tended to be vague. One woman commented: "I began to work as a *komori* when, I think, I was thirteen. I worked for two years and learned the ABCs of child rearing."

Although her narrative helped me to reconstruct the lives of *komori*, it merely exemplified personally decontextualized trends and generalized processes in these women's life courses.

The critical moment for my research on *komori* came at one of the group meetings when I mentioned the verses of a "counting song" (*kazoe uta*) I had found in a book published by a local historian.[29] The author writes that this song was created by one of the teachers for *komori* in the town of Matsumoto around the turn of the century (Kōzu 1974, 276–277). Indeed, teaching "proper and graceful songs" was an important part of the curriculum of special education for *komori* (Nakamura 1906, 28), since "vulgar and obscene songs" sung by *komori* seem to have greatly bothered the middle class, including the school teachers themselves (Maki 1899, 25). The following is one of those supposedly "proper and graceful" songs (Kōzu 1974, 276–277).

> *One, childhood is the foundation of personhood; the*
>   *role of komori is important.*
> *Two, play carefully, don't choose dangerous play.*
> *Three, you can play, but don't forget your charge on*
>   *your back.*
> *Four, copy good deeds, use polite language.*
> *Five, always be cheerful; if you smile, your charge*
>   *will smile.*
> *Six, don't force your charge to wake up or to sleep.*
> *Seven, whatever you do, do it for your charge; don't*
>   *do anything your charge may not like.*
> *Eight, a child will soon grow into an adult, treat your*
>   *charge as an adult.*
> *Nine, the role of komori is important; the komori acts*
>   *in place of the mother to protect the child.*
> *Ten, don't give any poisonous food or dangerous toys*
>   *to your charge.*

This counting song indeed reflects the moral spirit of the manuals published for the educators of *komori*. Kōzu recorded this ballad in an interview with a former teacher of *komori*. She told Kōzu that she "could not sing this song without tears" of pity for the miserable childhoods of *komori*. Akamatsu, however, argues that songs of *komori* (*komori uta*) are always easy to sing, as *komori* themselves were children (1993, 73).[30] Did they really sing this lengthy and moralistic song?

The participants at one group meeting said they had never heard these verses. They also said, laughing, that it would have been impossible for *komori* to sing such a song. Their version, which they tried hard to recall, is as follows:

> *One, we are all bullied.*
> *Two, we are all hated.*
> *Three, we are all forced to talk.*
> *Four, we are all scolded.*
> *Five, we are all forced to carry babies who cry a lot.*
> *Six, we are all fed terrible food.*
> *Seven, we are all forced to wash diapers in the cold*
>   *water of the river.*
> *Eight, we are all impregnated and shed tears.*
> *Nine, we are all persuaded to leave, and finally,*
> *Ten, we all must leave.*[31]

While the teacher's version instructs *komori* how best to care for their charges, the women's version protests the cruel realities of their lives. None of the women I met in Nagano attended classes held specifically for *komori*. Some, like Sumiko, attended school, leaving their charges in the hands of mothers or other caregivers, while others went to school carrying their charges. Unlike those *komori* whose language and behavior were bitterly resented by the members of the new middle class, the women I met were already "reformed" *komori*. Even so, what had separated them from other children when they were *komori* was not only that they worked as caretakers of their charges, but that they always sang. In this particular meeting and in others that followed, songs, or more specifically, songs of *komori*, became a topic of lively discussion among the members of a variety of groups. The striking difference between the songs the former *komori* remembered and the one the former teacher remembered provided me with a starting point to begin my inquiry into *komori*'s daily lives.

The following ballad recorded by Matsunaga Goichi reveals the harsh realities of *komori*'s work.

> *Komori's work is indeed cruel.*
> *I came to this town of Chaya,*
> *when I was seven or eight,*
> *to work as a komori.*
> *I find my mistress so mean.*

She tells me to do this and that,
all day long.
I wish New Year would come sooner.
When New Year comes,
with my belongings and sandals in my hands,
I will say,
"Thank you my mistress for your kindness."
she will say,
"Do come back again,"
but I will never ever return.—(1964, 119–120)

It is unclear who composed the music and who created the verses of *komori*'s songs, although some songs seem to have originated in pre-Meiji peasant songs. In this sense, *komori*'s songs are "changing songs" (*kae-uta*), as *komori* attached words from their own lives to the melodies of existing folk songs.[32] Because there are usually several "changing songs" for the same melody, it appears that successive generations of *komori* transformed the lyrics to express their own thoughts and emotions. This is why the boundary between the songs of *komori* and other genres of song is often ambiguous. Akamatsu thus argues that there are numerous songs presented to him as *komori*'s songs whose ballads have nothing to do with the work of *komori* (1993, 98). It is interesting that when *komori* quit their jobs and began to work at silk spinning factories, they further changed the verses of their songs to reflect the thoughts and emotions of their entirely new situations at factories and dormitories (see Chapter 4, page 85; see also Akamatsu 1993, 74). Some of the songs apparently express the thoughts and emotions of indentured *komori*, though most of the former *komori* who attended the meetings in Nagano were not indentured. Note that those who were not indentured also expressed the sentiments of the indentured *komori*. Below I discuss songs collectively recalled by the women, along with songs recorded by local historians and folklorists.

First, there are many songs about food. Some describe the kinds of food *komori* were forbidden to eat, thereby expressing their desire for a better material life. There are also songs in which *komori* complain about the meals given to them by their masters.

You call me komori, komori.
You always give me pickled radish and rice
  with water.
Why don't you sometimes give me fish?

Second, there are songs describing the relationships of *komori* to their charges.

> *This baby cries a lot.*
> *I want to exchange it for someone else's.*
>
> *What can we do with a naughty child?*
> *Let's put him on the drum*
> *and hit him with green bamboo sticks.*
> *—(Matsunaga 1964, 129)*
>
> *Sleep, sleep, oh, please go to sleep.*
> *If you go to sleep,*
> *you are happy, and*
> *I am happy too.—(Akamatsu 1993, 81)*
>
> *Sleep!*
> *Are you not sleeping, stupid baby?*
>
> *I do not want to be working as komori*
> *for this crying baby.*
> *Master, could you please give me some time off?*
> *I want to go home.—(Akamatsu 1993, 103)*

In the discourse of special education for *komori*, *komori* were expected to play the role of nurturing and patient mothers. But these songs suggest that *komori* were much less tolerant of crying babies and naughty children than the ideal mother promoted by the "good wife and wise mother" ideology.

Other songs describe the relationships between indentured *komori* and their masters and mistresses:

> *I fear my mistress,*
> *much more than my master.*
> *She always watches me*
> *with her white and black eyes.*
> *—(Akamatsu 1993, 106)*
>
> *Listen my master and mistress.*
> *If you treat me badly,*
> *I may have an evil influence on your kid.*[33]

Among employed *komori*, the quality of their relationships to their masters and mistresses was an important dimension of their everyday lives. In the above song, a *komori* confronts her abusive master and mistress.

Mocking the behavior and language of one's master and mistress was another common theme of *komori*'s songs, as is shown in the following:

> *My mistress is so ill-mannered.*
> *She steps on the boiled-rice container to*
> *   reach the shelf.*

It is uncertain whether *komori* could eat white boiled rice. Perhaps they could not and it was therefore precious food for them. In this song, a *komori* depicts a mistress who disregards such a valuable food. Sayo, whose autobiography I have introduced, records in detail her relationship with her master and mistress. She was tied to a tree when scolded; she was confined to a storage house when two *sen* of money disappeared from the house; and she was thrown into a barn when it discovered that she had eaten fruit from her master's orchard (Masuda 1959, 138–141).

The vast majority of songs, however, express the emotional pain of the *komori*, who were often far away from their own homes.

> *I want to go home.*
> *I want to see my house.*
> *I want to see my mother's face.*
> *Even if I cannot see her, I want to talk to somebody*
> *   about my wretched life.*

This is a song about a *komori*'s homesickness. In this genre of songs, the desire to be loved and to love someone is an important theme. The *komori* wanted mutual affection from her parents (usually her mother). The *komori* also wanted to love and to be loved by someone else, usually a young village man. Such songs also express *komori*'s growing curiosity over their own sexuality.

> *I stand under the eaves of someone's house*
> *   when it rains,*
> *not because I find this baby precious,*
> *but because someone I love lives there.*
>
> *I am the daughter of a cotton-felt maker.*
> *If you think I am lying, sleep with me.*

The latter contains a typical example of a double entendre: in this case, "cotton felt" signifies "softness," that is, the "softness of my body."

Thus, the language of *komori* differs from the language of the state's elementary education in significant ways. First, the language of *komori* is oral. When the verses of *komori* songs are written down, a key feature has been unintentionally overshadowed: its oral tradition. Furthermore, the "changing song" is possible only because of the orality of *komori*'s songs. Thus, Akamatsu criticizes those scholars who have recorded only one version of each song and named it an "authentic version" (*seichō*). They are content with it simply because *they* recorded it.

Second, the language of *komori* is also in the local dialect. The fact that several different dialects are used in various versions of a single song suggests a significant movement of *komori* over a wide geographical area. I was told that certain words I could not recognize in the ballads were Echigo (now Niigata prefecture) dialect. Many *komori* were recruited from there to work in Nagano.

Third, although my translation of the songs may not convince the reader, the language of *komori*'s songs is quite crude, despite the efforts of teachers to reform their language. In the songs, *komori* rarely express "maternal" love for their charges and treat them as objects that often annoy them. They rarely express respect for their masters and mistresses, speaking ill of and caricaturing them. Furthermore, allusive and metaphorical references to body parts and sexual intercourse abound in the *komori*'s songs.

Fourth, and most important, the language of *komori* describes what the discourse of the state's elementary education totally ignores: the painful, mundane life of *komori* that is repeated every day from dawn to sunset and that, in its very repetition, generally hides but also occasionally reveals the *komori*'s physical and intellectual growth. *Komori*'s songs tell us when they wake up, what they do and where they go during the day, and when they go to sleep. They reveal *komori* engaged in a variety of activities, not only soothing their charges on their backs, but also walking, running, playing, speaking, eating, crying, and sleeping. They also reveal the moments of surprise, wonder, joy, and anxiety experienced by *komori* in the context of repeating all these activities day after day. In the *komori*'s vernacular, we see their physical, intellectual, and emotional growth. *Komori* thus gain their subjectivity or, using an anthropological term, become agents in their songs.

In the 1940s, folklorist Miyamoto Tsuneichi recorded the following narrative of an old man who as a boy played with *komori*, because he could not attend school owing to his family's poverty:

On rainy days, a small group of *komori* gathered together in a barn somewhere in the village. After the babies fell asleep, they put down their charges on a straw mat and played by themselves. Since there was nothing particular to play with, they jumped into the stack of straw, shouting and laughing, or opened the front of their kimonos to compare the size of their vulvas. (1984, 135)

In comparing the teacher's and the women's versions of the counting song above, we see that *komori* do not have their own subjectivities in the teacher's version. Instead, *komori's* everyday lives are described entirely in terms of the ideology of the *fujin*, or "good wife and wise mother." In the *komori's* version, however, *komori* appear with their own voices; the song describes *komori* as they submit their bodies to toil, eating very little. Or, middle-class journalists describe *komori* as promiscuous and emphasize the need to reform their morality. *Komori*, however, sing about their bodies, impregnated by their masters against their wishes.

Furthermore, the language of *komori* demonstrates sentiments of solidarity. Unlike European nursemaids, *komori* were almost always in company with other *komori* and not confined to their master's home. This fostered a sense of solidarity, through which *komori* could acknowledge among themselves their freedom to pursue their material and sexual desires. Of course, *komori* understood that they could pursue this freedom only in the language of songs and that such a freedom would not change the reality of their own lives. The verses of the following song recorded by Matsunaga seem to describe the *komori's* sense of hopelessness toward changing their fates (1964, 186):

> *I like singing songs,*
> *but I hate reciting sutras.*
> *When I die,*
> *let my body become a part of the fields and*
> *   mountains.*

We can interpret the songs of *komori* in the manner in which James Scott interpreted the songs of poor peasants in the post–Green Revolution village of Sedaka in Malaysia. We might then argue that *komori's* songs represent their "inward" or "ideological" resistance. Like Malaysian peasants, *komori* could not change their own fates "outwardly"; instead, they resisted the power of the rich "ideologically" even though they complied with it "symbolically." This is why, according to Scott, the poor did not resort to rebellions or revolutions but to what he calls "everyday forms of resistance," such as "foot

dragging, dissimulation, false compliance, pilfering, figured ignorance, slander, arson, sabotage, and so forth" (1985, 27). Here, Scott
conceptualizes power as something that coerces the body and the
mind separately: power may coerce the body without coercing the
mind. Consequently, Scott understands resistance in terms of the
same separation of the body from the mind; people may bodily
comply with what powerful individuals tell them to do, but they
may be resisting in their own minds. Scott's conceptualization of
power and resistance marked a watershed in our anthropological
understanding of those notions. In this respect, the language of
komori's songs may signify their "ideological" alienation from the
values dictated in the nationalist discourse. In the verses of their
songs, *komori* could express their feelings of bitterness and sorrow
toward their own lives, mock the language and attitudes of their
masters and mistresses, caricature the moral teachings they received
in the name of special education for *komori*, protest the scornful eyes
of their neighbors, and reject the norms of "good wives and wise
mothers," all while affirming their identity as human beings with
their own wills. Regarding songs of the oppressed, Scott also argues
that the more bitter the song and the darker the humor, the more
alienated are the singers from elite values. If that is the case, "we can
no longer take outward deference at face value" (Scott 1976, 235).

However, the conceptualization of power as well as resistance in
terms of the separation of the mind from the body neglects a very
important aspect of the mechanism of power: power may work
"through actually constructing a seemingly dualistic world" (Mitchell
1990, 547). In other words, Scott's conceptualization of power and
resistance carries the risk of endlessly reproducing the dichotomies
of body versus mind, actions versus values, consequences versus
intentions, and outward conformity versus inward resistance.[34]
Komori sang in the streets, on river banks, in playgrounds, and in
shrine compounds. Many years later, they are attempting to recall in
their group meetings what they used to sing. Do they distinguish
actions from values or consequences from intentions? When we hear
them sing about their own bodies, do we see cleavages between their
bodies and their minds?

In this chapter, we have seen how *komori* were forced to become
fujin or "good wives and wise mothers" in the discourse of the state's
elementary education. The illustration of *komori* trying to learn the
proper use of a sash indeed represents their motherlike, not childlike,
bodies. And yet, when *komori* sang about their everyday lives, they

retrieved their subjectivities from the middle-class discourse on their language and behavior. Power, inherent in such discourse, created the separation and therefore the dichotomy of body versus mind. Such a dichotomy is the consequence of power rather than the nature inherent in power. The songs of *komori* have taught me that the dichotomies of body versus mind and actions versus values are our creations as anthropologists. Without the effort on the part of these elderly women to participate in group meetings and to speak about their experiences with their own voices, the *komori*'s songs would have sunken into oblivion and the modern history of Japan would be without the voices of *komori*. If so, we would have had access only to the discourse produced by bureaucrats, journalists, education specialists, and intellectuals who, because of their power, have misrepresented without remorse the culture and history of the *komori*. I admit that the language of the *komori* heard in contemporary group meetings is decontexualized; these women singing their songs are no longer with their charges, oppressed by their masters and mistresses, or scorned by their middle-class neighbors. However, their efforts to speak in their own language cannot be understood without asking at the same time whose history History is.

Chapter 4   Factory Women

*Y*es, *komori* grew, physically and intellectually, protesting in their songs against upper- and middle-class commentaries and observations of them. And in the next phase of their life cycle, most of them engaged in silk spinning at modern "factories," the symbol of the industrial revolution. The transition in their work from *komori* to silk spinners working at modern factories can be discerned in at least three different domains.

First is the narratives of the rural women themselves. "In those days, we could work only as *komori* or factory women. I went to the silk spinning factory after I had worked as a *komori*," said Matsu in a group discussion in the town of Kanae in 1984. The official discourse on the plight of poor rural children endorses her narrative. Recall here the late-nineteenth-century editorial from a local newspaper: "Because many parents do not believe in the necessity of education for girls, they must work as *komori* or at silk spinning factories" (*Shinano Mainichi Shinbun*, March 17, 1883).

Second is the domain of songs. For example, the verse of a song sung by *komori*, "Bye-bye, my master and mistress, I do not want to see your faces any more," was changed to "Bye-bye, chimneys, I do not want to see the face of my foreman any more." These are typical examples of the "changing songs" discussed in the previous chapter. Although the latter of the two was presented to me as a song of factory women (*jokō uta*), the continuity between these two songs is obvious. For this reason, Akamatsu describes *jokō*, factory women, as "nursemaids of machines" (*kikai no komori*) (1993, 74).

Third is the domain of official statistics for public schools. For example, among 113 graduates of a class for *komori* in the town of Matsumoto in 1915, twenty-five continued to work as *komori* and domestic servants, thirty became factory workers in the silk industry, while forty-two returned to their home villages (Kōzu 1974, 351). Some of these forty-two girls may also have worked as factory workers. A significant number of factory women sought employment once again as *komori* and domestic servants when the silk industry declined in the early twentieth century.

The change in occupation from *komori* to silk spinners did not mean an improvement in economic situation: these women continued to be poor. In the very beginning of the Meiji period, however, silk spinners were the daughters of rich families, proud of their contribution to the modern nation-state. Employment of daughters of high-status families represented only a brief, transitionary phase in industrial relations, when modern factory production was subsidized by the state. Yokota Ei, for example, received her training at the Tomioka Silk Mill, founded by the new Meiji state. In her diary, she describes the day the empress and the empress dowager visited the mill, which clearly suggests the importance of the silk industry in the national chauvinism. Led by French technicians, the empress and empress dowager observed women, including Yokota Ei, spinning silk with modern machines. Each of them then received a fan from the imperial household (Yokota 1988, 52–56).[1] The silk industry was indeed the centerpiece of Japanese nationalism from the day it was founded.[2]

In 1874, Yokota Ei moved to one of the private silk mills in Nagano, a more profit-driven capitalist enterprise, to teach modern techniques of silk spinning to its employees. By the 1880s, glamor and prestige attached to working in the modern plants quickly dissipated (Hane 1982, 174). As the size of each factory expanded in accordance with the increasing production, the need for factory women ballooned. Thus, Tsurumi argues: "During the 1880s and 1890s the proud, confident reeler from an ex-samurai or well-to-do commoner family was replaced by a silk worker with a different background, the daughter of marginally independent cultivators or tenant farmers" (1990, 47).

In this chapter, I would like to ask the following questions. Were the silk factory women since the 1880s—the daughters and wives of poor peasants—continuously perceived as national subjects in the discourse of Japanese nationalism? If they were, what rhetoric did the discourse of nationalism depend on? Finally, how did factory women perceive themselves and assert their subjectivities? But let me first describe the nature of the silk spinning industry, which I will eventually characterize as a "rural" industry.

THE NATURE OF THE SILK SPINNING INDUSTRY

There are certain similarities between the histories of the industrial revolution in Western Europe and in Japan. The industrial revolution in Europe removed, although not entirely, labor from the family workshop and relocated it in the factory; the first branch of industry transformed was a "feminine" one: spinning and, later, weaving (McDougall 1977; McBride 1977).[3] In Japan, the first such branch of industry was silk spinning, owing largely to the availability of domestic raw silk. It was not only a "feminine" industry but a "rural" industry.

I characterize the silk industry as a rural one for several reasons. First, the silk spinning factories were built in rural areas, proximate to the regions producing its raw materials. In Nagano, sericulture, or the production of raw silk, became the major industry by the turn of the century, largely because of the industry's ability to attract capital from outside the producing regions (Wigen 1995, 146). Kären Wigen reports that early land expansion for the silk mulberry occurred in the densely populated villages of the Ina basin where Tabata is located (p. 147). Successful sericulture also required constant attention to the silkworms from the adult members of the farming household. This task almost always fell upon the female members of the family, who also engaged in other agricultural and domestic activities.

Second, silk workers' contracts were of relatively short duration (in comparison with those in the cotton industry) (Molony 1991, 219, n. 9; Nakamura 1976, 81). The women's involvement in the silk spinning industry was seasonal: the summer shift (*natsu-biki*) was from the beginning of July to the end of December; the spring shift (*haru-biki*) was from the beginning of February to the end of April. In between these two shifts, factory women went home, but there was no respite. "From the end of April 'til the summer shift started, I worked from dawn to sunset, tending silkworms, planting rice seedlings, and picking tea leaves," said eighty-two-year-old Chiyo in 1988. This means that rural women participated in the entire production process of silk thread, from picking mulberry leaves in the field and tending silkworms at home day and night, to producing silk thread at factories. They also moved between these different places and phases of the production process depending on which part of the life cycle they were in. The silk industry was thus a rural and a feminine industry.

I must caution the reader about the widely used English term "factory girls" for female factory workers in the silk industry in Japan. The silk industry was not mechanized to the same extent as other textile industries, notably cotton. The skill and dexterity required for silk spinning were often viewed as an "extension of the kind of work farm women had traditionally done" (Molony 1991, 219, n. 9). Consequently, silk reeling has often been "erroneously viewed—by both contemporaries and later scholars—as unskilled work suitable for young farm girls" (ibid.; see also Bernstein 1988; Tsurumi 1984b, 1990). This conventional view of the history of the Japanese industrial revolution, I believe, generated the term "factory girls." In reality, a significant number of married women in Nagano worked at numerous silk mills. They simply moved from larger and more mechanized silk spinning factories to smaller neighborhood silk filatures. The latter depended on *zaguri* reeling (which involved hand reeling). According to historian Machida Shōzō, there were still 4,042 *zaguri* factories in comparison with the 836 modern silk spinning factories in Nagano even in 1931 (Machida 1953). I will thus use "factory women" for the Japanese term *kōjo* or *jokō*.

The decision of the rural women in Nagano to work at silk spinning factories explains not only the growth of Japanese capitalism but also these women's physical and intellectual growth. Here, I must be careful in balancing two opposite views of factory women in the textile industry. Historian Barbara Molony argues:

> In the case of Japan, most scholars have promoted the view that female factory workers of rural origin, their major contributions to Japan's development not withstanding, passively accepted their role in the textile industry. . . . It has generally been thought that young girls right out of elementary school were lured to work in the mills by unscrupulous recruiters who offered their parents or guarantors a prepayment of at least several months' wages in return for a contract that effectively made the girls indentured laborers. (1991, 223)

Restated, most scholars have viewed factory women as women whose consciousness as workers was hardly developed and have created an image of them as being dutiful daughters even after returning home.

Molony then argues that factory women in Japan became more and more independent over several decades. Therefore, we should leave the image of factory women as pitied passive victims behind and imagine more or less independent women who decided by themselves to work in industry either to serve their families' interests or even against their parents' wishes.[4] To argue so, Molony discusses socioeconomic changes that would have influenced the way in which women viewed their factory work. First, the working conditions at textile mills generally improved. The Factory Law of 1929, which I will discuss shortly, prohibited child labor and eliminated late-night work for women. Second, the educational levels of factory women rose in the 1920s, and older factory women generally meant a healthier labor force. Labor strikes became more frequent in the 1920s, and activism became "compatible with women's notions of gender identity" (p. 219). According to Molony, the type of textile industry is also important. In comparison with the factory women in the cotton industry, located in large cities, factory women in the silk industry might have been less independent and more submissive to their employers; but, after the decline of the silk industry in the 1920s and 1930s, many of its factory women may have moved to the city and become more independent from their rural parents. Although I largely agree with Molony, I believe that there were always independent-minded as well as much less independent-minded rural women who became factory workers. It seems to me that the earlier view of factory women as victims was constructed by the "Victorian social conscience," which, I believe, is still with us (McBride 1977, 282).[5] The late-nineteenth- and early-twentieth-century middle-class commentators of factory women in Japan, whom I shall call "social reformers," played a vital role in creating such a passive view of factory women. Molony, to the contrary, was influenced by the recent rise in feminist scholarship.

NATIONALIST DISCOURSE AND FACTORY WOMEN

Miwada Masako is one of the early advocates of the "good wife and wise mother" ideology.[6] Commenting on factory women, she argues:

> Recently, along with the development of manufacturing industries (*shokusan kōgyō*), a group of women called *jokō*, who work at a variety of factories, emerged. As *jokō* depend upon their own physical labor to make their living, they are more respectable than those [prostitutes, geisha, barmaids-cum-prostitutes] who waste

time sucking the wealth of others. I also accept favorably the fact that *jokō* usually engage in work suitable for women. Such [textile] industries constitute the source for enriching the nation (*fukoku no moto*). Thus, *jokō* are not necessarily shameful women. (1898, 6)

Miwada uses the term *jokō* for factory women. *Jokō* is the reverse of *kōjo*, which Yokota Ei was. She was never called a *jokō*. A *kōjo* was always a daughter of a rich family, proud of her contribution to the modern nation-state. It is unclear whether Miwada inverted the order of the two Chinese characters for factory women to emphasize that they were different from the earlier, upper-class, factory women. However, it is clear that Miwada had a hard time endorsing the contribution of factory women to the construction of the nation-state. She did, however, eventually accept them, grudgingly, as national subjects. Miwada continues: "*Jokō* tend to be crude (*inwai*) in their personalities. As they work all day long away from their parents, they tend to sing vulgar songs and engage in obscene talk. Unless someone teaches them 'women's morality' (*joshi shūshin*), it is natural that they will be confused and tainted with vice" (p. 7). While acknowledging their role as national subjects, Miwada points to the "problem" of factory women.

Indeed, the local newspapers around the turn of the century endlessly reported the "problems" among factory women: their adulteries, unwanted pregnancies, abandonment of illegitimate children, suicide attempts, and deaths. For example, a factory woman named Fusa was reported by *Shinano mainichi shinbun* to have secretly given birth to a baby girl after "having a clandestine affair with So-and-So Nakamura" in the village where she was working.[7] Another newspaper article published in 1901 reported that more than thirty young men who had failed to pass their physical examinations for military conscription had allegedly contracted venereal disease from "factory women in the silk industry."[8] One other article hinted that many factory women would eventually end up in the "dirty land" (*fuketsu-chi*), that is, the world of prostitutes.[9] An article published in *Shinano mainichi shinbun* in 1914 claimed: "If the majority of these factory women are to become wives and mothers of men born in Nagano prefecture, one wonders whether we can reproduce sound and healthy subjects in our prefecture in the future."[10] The headlines of local newspaper articles suggest that the factory women in the silk industry were still represented as women of the demimonde well into the 1920s,[11] for example, "Factory woman at silk spinning factory aborts fetus: Fetus found in factory toilet,"[12] or "Secret rendezvous of a factory woman and a local carpenter disclosed!"[13]

Thus, only a very thin line distinguished factory women from what Miwada called "those who waste time sucking the wealth of others." Comparisons of factory women in Nagano and New York City at the turn of the century may be useful here. Kathy Peiss describes young white working women in New York City between 1880 and 1920 as hard workers who toiled in the city's factories and shops but devoted their evenings to the lively entertainment of the streets, public dance halls, and other popular amusements (1983, 1986). Some of these women were so-called charity girls, who did not accept money in their sexual encounters with men. And some among these "charity girls" slipped in and out of prostitution when unemployed or in need of extra income. Many others, however, "defined themselves against the freer sexuality of their pleasure-seeking sisters, associating 'respectability' firmly with premarital chastity and circumspect behavior" (1983, 83). The middle-class commentators in New York City, however, failed to see the dynamic way in which working-class women defined their sexuality and often ignored the line existing between them and prostitutes.

Let me return to Miwada's comments on factory women. She elevates factory women over prostitutes because factory women "depend upon their own physical labor to make their living" and "usually engage in work suitable for women." For Miwada, their dedication to physical labor, their participation in production, and the "feminine" nature of their work all make them superior to prostitutes. However, they are of humble origins and are away from home—these factors make them vulnerable to "vice." Miwada thus argues that they need "women's morality" without, however, explaining or defining what it is.

Several proprietors of silk spinning factories in Nagano seem to have agreed with Miwada. However, they were much more interested in the immediate impact of "women's morality" on the women's productivity than in "morality" itself. For example, two employers in the silk industry in Okaya suggested in 1878 the importance of teaching factory women "women's morality," as the "majority of them were from a lower-than-middle class" (quoted by Kōzu 1974, 362–363). Otherwise, they argued, their employees would produce silk thread of poor quality and "endlessly complain about the scantiness and inequality of their wages" (quoted by Kōzu 1974, 361).[14] Another employer claimed that he provided elementary education for his employees at night and argued in 1902 that he "would continue to do so for the sake not only of factory women but also of his own profits" (quoted by Ōkouchi 1971, 581). "Women's morality" was not the only term that these employers used. One referred to the "things of which women should always be reminded" (*joshi kokoroe*).[15] The Regulation for the Employment of Factory Workers, drafted by a group of silk spinning factory owners in Nagano and approved by the prefectural governor in 1888, used "female virtue" (*futoku*). But if "women's morality" would greatly increase factory women's productivity, what were its contents? Was its counterpart, "men's morality," not conceivable?

Rokumonsen Silk Spinning Factory, for example, tried to teach its women employees "Japanese language" (*kokugo*), "algebra" (*sanjutsu*), "sewing" (*saihō*), "physical exercise" (*taisō*), and "educational songs" (*shōka*) under the rubric of "women's morality."[16] However, Rokumonsen Silk Spinning Factory was one of the few factories in Nagano to offer such general education to its employees.[17] Furthermore, an article published in a local newspaper disclosed that the classes at Rokumonsen were in session only from November to April (when many factory women went home), and "no classes were held last year [in 1914] owing to the reduction of production."[18]

In the previous chapter, I have described how nationalist discourse sought the "morality" of *komori* in their putative ability to become surrogate mothers. Those children raised by *komori* who knew the "scientific method of child rearing" were believed to be valuable national assets. Unlike *komori*, who worked close to the home environment, most factory women worked away from home. The role of surrogate mothers is not applicable to factory women, although the latter worked in a "feminine" branch of industry. And yet, the following examples of nationalist discourse describe rural or factory women as "mothers" in their relation to silkworms, silk thread, and silk cloth. For example, writing in 1906, local teacher Kobayashi Tomojirō claimed that a woman should wake up when "silkworm babies" (*sanji*) wake up and go to sleep when they go to sleep (1906, 13). He further stated that the "life of a family depends on the delicate body of a woman," while the "life of a nation depends on the slender arms of women" (p. 14). Kobayashi thus argues that a woman should support her family as well as the nation. A physiocrat, Inada Masatane, claimed that the silk spinning industry demanded the motherlike devotion of a woman and that, since the time when Japan was founded, only "our nation's women" (*waga-kuni no joshi*) could produce such fine silk thread and cloth (1917). Another physiocrat, Ishida Magotarō, argued that the soft, delicate, and snowlike white bodies of silkworms would demand the care, affection, patience, and tolerance of the mother (quoted by Inada 1917, 104–107).[19] Here, we must pay close attention to such adjectives as "delicate (bodies)" and "slender (arms)." The image of a woman with a "delicate" body and "slender" arms calls to mind an urban upper- or middle-class woman. Why did Kobayashi and others use these adjectives?

This set of nationalist discourses began to appear in the early twentieth century after the Sino-Japanese and Russo-Japanese wars, and became ubiquitous after World War I. I see certain resonances between this set of discourses and the ideology of *kokutai*, which began to take shape in the 1880s (see Miyake 1991, 270). According to the ideology of *kokutai*, Japan constitutes one homogeneous space for a single extended family with the emperor as its supreme and patriarchal head; and the emperor is supposed to offer his unconditional affection to his subjects.[20] This relationship should not be based on the Western notion of right and obligation, or the Eastern (Chinese) notion of domination and submission, but on the truly Japanese notion of harmony. However, women are not direct subjects of the emperor but are integrated into this extended national family only through their fathers, husbands, and sons. Thus, their role is to "give birth to the descendants of their ancestors and to nurture them as Japanese nationals who will serve the emperor" (Monbushō 1941, 86).

The ideology of *kokutai* deliberately confuses productive and reproductive work performed by women. Women are asked to practice endurance, submission, sacrifice, industriousness, and self-reliance—qualities "equally valuable in industrial development as in the presentation of the household" (Nolte and Hastings 1991, 165). Historian Miyake Yoshiko argues: "By examining this interaction [of productive and reproductive works] we can see how women's housework, stemming from their reproductive roles, provided the basis for reproducing the social relations of the capitalist mode of production" (1991, 269).

I believe that "women's morality" is what makes factory women into respectable members in and of Japan, now perceived as the "family-nation" (*kazoku kokka*). Such members not only produce raw silk, silk thread, and silk cloth, but also reproduce the "social relations of the capitalist mode of production," either by themselves offering labor or by giving birth to sources of cheap labor. Thus, factory women who produced more silk thread than others were specifically acknowledged publicly for their contribution to Japan.[21] Their patriotism was also hailed. On October 9, 1894, two months after the eruption of the war between Japan and China, the local newspaper *Shinano mainichi shinbun* printed on an extra four pages the names of 2,013 silk factory women in Nagano who contributed a portion of their wages to the Japanese military. The poorer the patriots were, the better the national subjects they became.

At the time of the Sino-Japanese War, the factory women's contributions were only in money. The local media continuously reported the situation on the battlefront, but never that of the families back home whose members were conscripted (Morosawa 1969b, 9–10). The Russo-Japanese War dramatically changed the manner in which the news media reported the war situation: a variety of "fine episodes" regarding women back home in the Nagano countryside were published in the local newspapers as exemplars of national subjects. Among them were the factory women who helped their families in the absence of fathers, husbands, and sons (pp. 7–11). These factory women were no longer promiscuous women but respectable national subjects.

Tsurumi introduces two textbooks written for factory women in the textile industry in the early twentieth century, *Shūshin kunwa kōjo no kagami* (Moral discourses: A mirror for factory women) and *Jokō tokuhon* (Factory women's reader). Both textbooks describe Japan as the greatest *kuni* and factory women as "soldiers of peace" contributing to the glory of the *kuni* along with male soldiers. The silk industry factories used not only textbooks but "company songs" to propagate nationalism and patriotism among factory women (Tsurumi 1990, chap. 5). One such song represents the toil of a factory woman as a source of blessings for her self, her family, and the nation (p. 93).[22] She was thus firmly integrated into the national space as a worker, yet she always subordinated herself to the patriarchal figures of her father, husband, son, employer, and emperor.

FACTORY WOMEN AND THE DISCOURSE OF SOCIAL REFORMERS

However, there is a contradiction inherent in the ideology of *kokutai* that emerges only if we take into account a working woman's body. For a working woman, toiling for the nation undermines her health; it becomes more difficult for her to play a reproductive role. Using the discursive power of *kokutai* and "women's morality," employers in the silk industry in Nagano refused to acknowledge this contradiction. For those considered "social reformers," however, this contradiction became a problem. Social reformers did not constitute one homogeneous group; rather they included individuals of such different backgrounds as "progressive" bureaucrats and journalists, "paternalistic" employers and factory supervisors, medical doctors, scholars, socialists, Christians, and women activists. Nevertheless, all of them had one thing in common: they treated factory women as an object to be analyzed. Their good intentions notwithstanding, they did not listen to the factory women's voices.

One such social reformer, the hygienics authority Ishihara Osamu, wrote an article, "Eisei-gaku jō yori mitaru jokō no genkyō" (The current conditions of factory women seen from the perspective of hygienics), and delivered a lecture, "Jokō to kekkaku" (Factory women and tuberculosis), in 1913, warning that the "degraded condition of health among factory women will decrease their productivity, block industrial development, decrease the birth rate, and jeopardize the health of the newborn. Hence, it will greatly threaten the prosperity of our country (*kokka*)" (1970a, 81).[23] "Factory women" in his lecture refers to the approximately 190,000 women in the silk spinning industry, 80,000 in the cotton spinning industry, and 130,000 in the cotton weaving industry in the early twentieth century.[24] Many of these factory women suffered from tuberculosis, for which a cure did not then exist. Ishihara further argued that the tuberculosis germs would multiply in the unsanitary conditions of the countryside after factory women returned home. He was thus concerned not only with the fates of factory women but with the fate of the nation, as these women could not possibly give birth to healthy children. Ishihara concluded his lecture by comparing "soldiers of peace" with the soldiers killed in the Russo-Japanese War: "I do not know how Japanese citizens (*kokumin*) will be able to reward those who have been killed in the war of peace. Indeed, you should shed tears for the fate of factory women, which is indeed miserable. Even though they are mere factory women (*yahari karera jokō to iedomo*), they are our important compatriots" (1970b, 196). He thus asked the audience not to look down on factory women of humble origins but to be sympathetic to them as "our patriots."

Ishihara was by no means the first person publicly to declare a reformist discourse. More than a decade before he began his visits to the countryside, the Home Ministry had established the Factory Survey Office.[25] The (usually temporary) employees of this office made an investigation of the working conditions at various textile mills throughout Japan and published *Shokkō jijō* (Factory workers' conditions) in 1903. And yet, *Shokkō jijō* was not widely circulated until the end of World War II. The Home Ministry and the Ministry of Justice worried about the social and political consequences of its publication within Japan; they feared the spread of leftist thought especially among factory workers. Furthermore, the Ministry of Foreign Affairs feared the negative impression of Japan it might give to foreigners (Ōkouchi 1971, 17). Even so, the authors of *Shokkō jijō* did reveal the pitiful working conditions at textile mills employing more than ten laborers (we can only imagine the conditions of those mills employing fewer than ten). As for the conditions of silk spinning factories, they reported the prevalence of child labor, unsanitary conditions of work places detrimental to factory women's health, long shifts that occasionally reached eighteen hours a day, a widely used system of punishments in the form of wage extraction and physical torture exercised on the bodies of unproductive factory women, pigstylike dormitories with food of the lowest quality, and finally, a variety of diseases from which factory women suffered (Ōkouchi 1971, 125–159; see also Yokoyama 1949, 165–177).[26] These social reformers eventually led the government to promulgate the Factory Law in 1911 (Kagoyama 1970, 4).

Social reformers also included both prominent and not-so-prominent socialists and communists. In this respect, as in Europe, nationalism "reached out to liberalism, conservatism, and socialism; it advocated both tolerance and repression, peace and war—whatever served its purpose"(Mosse 1985, 9).[27] Interestingly, the socialist nationalist discourse was also gendered. For example, writing about the factory women at a cotton textile mill near Tokyo, socialist Hirasawa Keiichi commented in 1916:

> Observing the almost magicianlike dexterity of the hands of factory women, I thought that only *women* (*onna*) could undertake this kind of work. I also intuitively felt that only *Japanese women* (*Nippon no onna*), not Western women, could. The *Japanese woman* (*Nippon no fujin*), who identifies sewing with the female vocation, is already destined to develop the dexterity of her hands from the time she is in her mother's womb. (quoted by Akamatsu 1977, 232; emphasis mine).[28]

I note an interesting progression of his description of factory women. Factory women are first identified as "women," defined by gender alone. "Women" then becomes "Japanese women" and then "the Japanese woman," defined by gender and nationality. Hirasawa, following his "intuition," presented "the Japanese woman" as a natural category and a cultural superior to the category of "the Western woman." He elevated factory women to the abstract level of "the Japanese woman" who would represent Japan to the outside world. He defines the culture of factory women not only for them but for the nation-state of Japan.

Hosoi Wakizō was both a socialist activist and a worker at a cotton spinning factory. Together with his wife and her fellow factory women, he personally experienced the harsh working conditions of a textile mill. Hosoi, however, saw factory women as a category of women for his observation and investigation. Thus, he writes: "It is extremely difficult to study the psychology of factory women. But I have lived with them from dawn to sunset. I have observed their daily life, collected various data including their songs, studied their physiology from a medical perspective, and tried to clarify the relationship between their physiology and psychology" (1954, 324). His *Jokō aishi* (The pitiful history of factory women), which was published a month before his death in 1925, at the age of twenty-nine, represented his long-term research on factory women.

In this monumental work, Hosoi contrasts another category of "women" (*fujin*) with "factory women" (*jokō*). He describes the latter as a group of women "whose culture is very retarded . . . and who have more or less the psychology of uncivilized savages" (1954, 325). He thus tries to elevate the status of "factory women" to be as close as possible to that of "women" (ibid.).[29] Hosoi's utopian vision of socialist Japan can be realized when "factory women" are included in the category of "women." In such a society, he writes,

> the government should make it an obligation for every unmarried woman to work for the production of cloth. If all of the twenty-five million young women work, there will be no need to ask sick women or women with children to work, nor will there be any necessity for them to work for ten or twelve hours a day for five or ten years. If every youthful and vibrant woman worked for only four or five hours a day for one or two years, only on the days when she felt fine, Japan could produce a sufficient amount of cloth. (p. 400)

For Hosoi, "all of the twenty-five million young women" constituted the "mother body of Japan" (*Nippon no botai*) carrying the important obligation of bearing and raising children after marriage (p. 399). Thus, Hosoi did not acknowledge the category of the working mother (see Riley 1988, 16).

Hosoi criticizes what he calls the "callousness" of factory women to their own exploitation. On this point, Miriam Silverberg states: "Hosoi is critical of the blindness of the women to the systematic nature of their exploitation in the factory and decries the overwhelming evidence of their inability to focus on the issue of working conditions when they do go on strike" (1990, 107). When factory women go on strike, Hosoi writes, they behave like girls fretting aimlessly to their sweethearts (1954, 363). He does point out twenty-four strikes at cotton textile mills that took place between 1915 and 1923 but refuses to see any "cultural significance" (*bunka-teki igi*) in them.

I see here certain commonalties between Hosoi and labor organizers in the early twentieth century as well as labor historians of our time who have ignored women's role in the history of Japanese labor movements. Male unionists regarded factory women as "unorganizable." They characterized them as "too attached to the family, too young, too filial, and too impermanent a part of the work force to undertake the historic mission of workers in a labor movement" (Sievers 1983, 79). They also objected to being represented at meetings of the International Labor Organization by women until as late as 1920 (p. 211, n. 47). Even the Marxist intellectual Hasegawa Kōichi has claimed that the collective action taken by factory women was merely "accidental," "emotional," and "not modern"; it erupted like fireworks when one least expected it but died out quickly; this was because of the "emotional nature unique to women" (*josei tokuyū no kanshō*) (quoted in Akamatsu 1977, 462, 465, 466).[30] Much later, a labor historian argued that "even deplorable working conditions gave rise to no movements of protest" because of the "ignorant young girls for whom a factory job was only a short interlude in their lives" (Ōkouchi 1958, 20).[31]

To the contrary, Japan's very first labor strike, which occurred at the Amamiya Silk Mill in Kōfu in 1886, was organized solely by women.[32] This particular strike produced at least four more strikes in 1886 in the Kōfu area alone and later among both silk and cotton factory women throughout Japan. Sievers argues that, by 1897, when socialists organized the Association for the Promotion of Labor Unions, "Japanese women had been confronting management for more than a decade with demands for better working conditions and higher wages, and had backed those demands up by refusing to return to work until they had won concessions" (1983, 79). By the mid 1920s, the frequency of labor strikes in which women participated, either alone or with men, increased dramatically in both the silk and the cotton spinning industries (Hasegawa 1931, quoted in Akamatsu 1977, 465). Hosoi did criticize his contemporary male labor unionists for their contempt of factory women and sympathized with women workers who were placed in deplorable working conditions. However, it is unclear to me whether Hosoi wanted factory women to be awakened as laborers conscious of their class positions. Rather, Hosoi's critique seems to be directed at Japanese capitalism, which made even sick women and women with children work outside their homes. He wanted them to return to their homes and become mothers or, even better, "good wives and wise mothers." From his critical viewpoint, Hosoi noted the tendency of factory women to "destroy" their family lives by returning to work after marriage (1954, 342).[33]

What about women activists? How did they perceive factory women? Late-nineteenth-century Japanese women activists did not directly deal with the issue of factory women, but they were seriously concerned with the institution of prostitution and the lives of prostitutes. These early female social reformers were largely urban middle-class intellectuals influenced by Christian educators. Endowed with a superior education, they were critical of certain female roles, namely, those of concubines and prostitutes, and of those men who frequented pleasure quarters or had concubines (see Sievers 1983, chap. 5; Garon 1993; Fujime 1994). In collaboration with male Christian purists, they launched their crusade against prostitution, which they understood to be a system of slavery and a violation of human rights. In brief, they wanted to "modernize the sexual mores of the populace along the lines of contemporary British and American societies" and to confine sexual relations solely to the institution of marriage (Garon 1993, 719). Once working women became prostitutes or were tricked into prostitution, these women activists took on the task of rehabilitating their sexual mores.[34] Early-twentieth-century women activists, however, were more directly concerned with the lives of working women. They participated in the so-called motherhood protection debates (*bosei hogo ronsō*), which began in 1918 and lasted until the early 1930s.[35]

In the history of Western feminism, there has been a constant tension between those feminists who assert femininity as the primary vehicle of women's oppression and those who criticize the devaluation of feminine roles and virtues by an overly authoritarian masculine culture. The former try to deny the social construction known as "Woman," "woman," or "women," while the latter try to define the essential female nature (see, for example, Chodorow 1978; Rosaldo 1980; O'Brien 1981, 1989; Hartsock 1985; Smith 1987, 1990; Moore 1988; Riley 1988; Scott 1988; and Young 1990). The motherhood protection debates in early-twentieth-century Japan are characterized by a similar, perhaps more complicated, tension among several women activists. The debates, which took place largely in print, began in 1918 between Yamada Waka and Yamakawa Kikue on the question "What is woman's true nature?"[36] Here I will focus on the discourse of another woman activist, who exchanged views on motherhood protection with several contemporary feminists.[37]

Hiratsuka Raichō was the founder of the Bluestockings, originally a group of literary women, which later became much more than a literary association.[38] In 1911, she launched the first issue of the group's journal, *Seitō* (Bluestocking), with this opening phrase: "In the beginning, woman was the sun." I characterize Raichō as a feminist who tried to restore what she thought had been lost in early-twentieth-century Japanese capitalism, namely, feminine virtues. Influenced greatly by the Swedish feminist Ellen Key, Raichō discovered those lost virtues in motherhood. She elucidated the negative impacts of the industrial revolution and the general development of Japanese capitalism on the lives of (working) women. In 1916, she wrote: "We are not to be liberated from being 'women'; as 'women' we must be liberated" (quoted and translated in Tsurumi 1995, 5–6; see also Nishikawa 1985, 167).[39] For Raichō, women's liberation entailed, more than anything else, the protection of motherhood, the motherhood of both single and married working women. Unlike Hosoi, for whom the category "working mothers" did not exist, she clearly acknowledged it. Raichō, along with some male social reformers, demanded that society and the state act to protect motherhood, and she devoted most of her life to securing protective legislation—the Factory Law—for mothers and children.[40]

Tsurumi does not assess positively the social reformers' efforts that culminated in this particular law.

> Their major interest in pushing for legislation to improve conditions in the factories was in healthy industries, not healthy workers. Yet unlike other state officials and most of the business commu-

nity, they believed that short-run profits gained from hazardous working conditions would in the long run cost the nation too much in diminished efficiency on the part of weakened workers, who might also produce sickly offspring.[41] (1990, 6)

Raichō may not have been interested in healthy industries. Yet she always acknowledged motherhood's service to the state and to society. She advocated the state protection of motherhood because she valued feminine virtues, that is, women's biological contribution, in bearing and raising children, to Japan. This is why another feminist, Yamakawa Kikue, criticized Raichō's thought as just another version of "the good wife and wise mother" ideology (see Tsurumi 1995, 7). In the end, Raichō upheld the dominant gender ideology of her time.

This quite heterogeneous group of social reformers had one thing in common: they dealt with factory women or working women as a category of women to investigate. They described the bodies of factory women as promiscuous. They described the sexual behavior of factory women as problematical. They saw a gulf between working-class and upper- and middle-class women in terms of their morality and sexuality.

Sangari and Vaid state the following regarding a similar social reform movement in India: "The history of reform—whether colonial or indigenous or nationalist—undertaken by men and by women does not seem very inspiring, freighted as it is with many kinds of patriarchal assumptions" (1989, 18). Indian nationalism divided the "world of social institutions and practices into two domains—the material and the spiritual" (Chatterjee 1993b, 6). The material was the domain of the economy, statecraft, science, and technology. It was also "typically the domain of the male" (p. 120). The spiritual domain had to bear the essential marks of Indian cultural identity. Indian nationalists included "women" in this category, women who had proper dress, eating habits, social demeanor, and religiosity (Chatterjee 1989, 629; 1993b, 6–9, chaps. 6 and 7). Thus, social reformers aimed to reform women and place them into this spiritual domain.

According to Sangari and Vaid, the Indian social reform movement was a "modernizing" one. It merely tried to "modernize" patriarchal modes of regulating women, providing a more "liberal space" for middle-class women only. They envisage another movement, which they call a "democratizing" movement. The latter tries to "change, to whatever degree, both the base (the sexual division of labour in production and property relations) and the ideologies of a specific patriarchal formation" (1989, 19). I believe that the social reform movement in early-twentieth-century Japan was also a "modernizing" movement, which did not change the base or the ideologies. How, then, did factory women perceive themselves and assert their subjectivities?

THE VOICES OF FACTORY WOMEN

Local historians and folklorists, while not paying much attention to the voices of *komori*, attempted to collect the memories of elderly, retired silk factory women workers as best they could. I would like to add to their rich sources the words of silk reelers "spoken at a time when they were working in or running away from the Meiji mills" (Tsurumi 1990, 5). I have said that social reformers viewed "factory women" as an object of analysis. They also collected the narratives of factory women. For example, the appendix of *Shokkō jijō* is a collection of interviews with factory women conducted by temporary hired personnel of the Ministry of Agriculture and Commerce, as well as interviews with factory owners and managers in the silk and cotton industries. I do not know whether they recorded the women's voices as they spoke. That I can find hardly any dialect in the transcriptions may indicate that their narratives were significantly edited by the interviewers. But we can still enter the world of their work through their voices as collected in this appendix.

The factory women in Nagano whose voices I heard myself worked in the 1930s and 1940s, after the silk industry had peaked in its importance to the development of Japanese capitalism. Ryūsui Silk Plant is the only silk spinning factory left in the region of southern Nagano. Furthermore, the number of farming households that raise silkworms has dwindled to a single digit. But the silk industry is still an important part of the memories of many women. Men remember too, but largely "through" women. "Silkworms made tremendous noises at night [while eating mulberry leaves]," said one of my neighbors. But he did not wake up. It was his wife or his mother, probably both, who woke up to feed the silkworms more mulberry leaves. Hiroko's mother worked at a "big silk spinning factory" in Okaya before she married. Even after her marriage, she continued to work at a local small-scale silk spinning factory. She died a few years before

I first arrived Tabata in 1984. But two small pieces of silk cloth of light purple and indigo blue, which her daughter gave me upon my departure to the United States, are more than enough to remind me of the importance of silk spinning in the past of rural women in Nagano.

As was the case for *komori*, in addition to their narratives we have the verses of factory women's songs. The custom of singing while spinning or weaving seems to have had a long tradition. In 1852, an owner of a silk-weaving workshop issued the following statement with the purpose of admonishing weavers for singing while working: "As for songs, I do not strictly prohibit them. However, you should sing them in low voices. Those ballads about the people in this village and the rumors about the master or other songs that are uncomfortable to listen to you must not sing" (quoted in Akamatsu 1977, 55).[42] He further claimed that if weavers were weaving with all their hearts, they "naturally" would not sing. Modern silk spinners and weavers apparently took over this custom of singing while working. They sang:

> *I so often cut silk thread.*
> *I should not sing songs [but concentrate on my work].*
> *I apologize, my master.*
> *But we simply make up all the songs.*
> *So please don't mind them.[43]*
> —*(quoted in Akamatsu 1977, 231)*

The language of factory women's songs, like *komori*'s songs, portrays their thoughts and emotions in a vivid manner. But let me begin with the narratives of factory women and former factory women.

At one meeting of the women's group held in 1984, the women decided to write and then read to each other their experiences at silk spinning factories. An eighty-two-year-old woman wrote:

> We woke up at six, ate breakfast, and started spinning at eight. For each of our three meals, we took turns between the workers of the mill's First Building and those of the Second Building. We were always fed with rice, soup, pickles, and a dish of either fish or cooked vegetables. While we worked, we always felt the gaze of our foreman (*kenban*). We were not supposed to talk [while working or eating]. If we sang, *kenban* shouted at us not to. . . . But I feel my life at the mill was less wretched than what was reported in *Ah, Nomugi touge* (Ah, Nomugi path).

In the book she mentions, local historian Yamamoto Shigemi recorded the following narrative of a former factory woman born in 1882. She went to work in Nagano from Hida, now Gifu prefecture. She crossed the Nomugi path with her friends, all of whom were recruited by the manager of a silk spinning factory:

> From morning, while it was still dark, we worked in the lamplit factory till ten at night. After work, we hardly had the strength to stand on our feet. When we worked late into the night, they occasionally gave us a roasted sweet potato. We then had to do our washing, fix our hair, and so on. By then it would be eleven o'clock. There was no heat even in the winter, and so we had to sleep huddled together. Several of the girls ran back to Hida.[44] (Yamamoto 1977, 176)

Factory work was regulated and regimented in precise manners. At least in the beginning of the Meiji period, the idea that work began and ended at precise times was novel in the Nagano countryside. Factory owners and managers could deliberately make their employees work longer by setting the clock wrong. Furthermore, rural women and men worked into the night after long hours of arduous labor in the fields and did not distinguish clearly between "life" and "work."[45] The above narratives suggest that factory women had incorporated the notion of time into their work life by the turn of the century. Even so, rural women accepted the idea of the night shift without much difficulty. This may be why the Factory Law did not prohibit the labor of women and children at night until 1929.

Another local historian, Hosokawa Osamu, recorded in 1978 the following narrative of an eighty-four-year-old former factory woman, describing the living conditions in her dormitory:

> The room in the dormitory was without closets. More factory women were crammed into it than the number of *tatami* (mats) in the room. Every two of us shared a thin mattress and blanket. In winter, we had to hug each other to warm our bodies. There were fleas and mosquitoes. There were lice even in winter. You could really call it a "pigsty." (Hosokawa 1982, 199–200)

The conditions at work places and dormitories were indeed miserable, and they were conducive to the development of various diseases (see Hane 1982, 189–193). High humidity in silk-reeling rooms was considered important for a quality product. "Steam rose from various artificial sources and quickly condensed into moisture on the ceiling, to fall like rain on the workers below" (Sievers 1983, 77). Many silk factory women, who were exposed to constant fluctuations in temperature and humidity, developed tuberculosis. Overworked and undernourished, others contracted beriberi, peritonitis, or other gastrointestinal diseases.

Many factory women ran away from the miserable conditions (and, I believe, many more wanted to run away than actually did). An annual turnover rate of 50 percent was typical of Meiji textile mills (Sievers 1983, 65; Hane 1982, 190). Those who left transferred to other employers or sought alternative employment, and the number of such women steadily increased in the 1920s. Yamamoto repeats the folk wisdom of the silk-producing region: "The day may come when the cock ceases to crow but never the day when factory girls stop running away" (1977, 97, quoted and translated in Tsurumi 1990, 90). Indeed, even after the business community recognized the importance of a stable work force for production, silk factory owners and managers had to make every effort to prevent these walkouts. The appendix of *Shokkō jijō* contains the following narrative of a factory manager of a silk mill in Nagano: "If we give freedom [to factory women], we may have to shut down silk spinning factories not only in the Suwa region [in Nagano] but also throughout Japan, and [such closings of factories] will block the development of this particular industry. This is why the factory owner had to put them on the second floor of the dormitory and lock them up to prevent them from running away" (quoted in Ōkouchi 1971, 580).

The working conditions at silk spinning factories do not seem to have changed much even after the enactment of the Factory Law. This legislation "placed a twelve-hour limit—including a one-hour rest period—per workday on women and on youngsters under the age of fifteen, and fixed the minimum employment age at twelve" or ten for light work (Hane 1982, 183). However, a member of the women's group in Ina, who worked at a silk mill in Okaya until 1936, said:

> When I began my work at the mill, we worked from five in the morning to five, or even six, in the evening. We ate while working. There was no time for resting after the meal. I was so happy when I heard of the Factory Law, because I heard that the first and the sixteenth of each month would be holidays and that we would not have to work more than eight hours a day. But they were all wrong! We worked for ten or twelve hours anyway. There were no holidays after all.

She is wrong about the stipulations of the Factory Law, but what is important is that she did not see any change after the law was enacted. In fact, the Factory Law allowed employers to exceed the twelve-hour limit by two hours when necessary. Furthermore, it allowed an "additional hour's extension in the busy season, which covered one hundred twenty days a year" (Hane 1982, 183). This means factory women often worked for fourteen or fifteen hours even when their employers abided by the law.

If factory women were lucky enough to stay healthy and returned home, the working conditions back home were equally or even more arduous. Socialist reformer Nakanishi Inosuke compared the working conditions of farming women engaging in sericulture and silk factory women in Nagano. His study, published in 1927, indicates the following: factory women worked for eleven hours a day while farming women worked for eighteen hours; an average factory woman earned about one *yen* and fifty *sen* a day, while an average farming woman earned only about thirty-eight *sen* a day.[46] Nakanishi reports that the food offered to factory women at dormitories resembled pig food, but that factory women could regularly eat beef, salted fish, seaweed, bean curd, vegetables, and miso soup. Farming women, Nakanishi argues, hardly ate any of these. Furthermore, farming men tended to drink a large amount of sake and to smoke considerably, which cost farming households. Thus, farming women were "in the most miserable conditions" (quoted by Akamatsu 1977, 277–282).[47]

A sixty-year-old woman, discussing her work in the past, said in 1984:

> About "honorable silkworms" (*o-kaiko-sama*)?[48] Well, I can only recall the hard and busy days. To raise silkworms did not require physical strength, so it was considered to be women's work. My mother-in-law watched over silkworms while taking care of my children. My job was to walk over to the mulberry fields, pick mulberry leaves, and carry them home on my back [in a basket]. Once or twice, I was caught in torrential rain. I went into a nearby hut and fell asleep, because I had been sewing till past midnight the night before.

Another seventy-nine-year-old woman in the same group said:

> I felt pain around my stomach while I was picking mulberry leaves under the scorching sun of midsummer. I noticed my contractions had finally begun, but this happened during the busiest season of the year when the silkworms woke up four times a day! I had to pick mulberry leaves. I finished picking enough of them and carried

them home on my back. I then went to the nearby river to fetch a bucketful of water for cooking. I worked hard despite the pain from the contractions. I was aware of the leak of [amniotic] water, but somehow I could not stop working.

Thus, women participated in the entire process of silk thread production in the Nagano countryside. For many factory women, home was not a place to rest but to continue working in often more miserable conditions than in silk spinning factories.

Hane argues that this may be the reason why some former factory workers do not describe the working conditions in the mills as harsh. He argues: "Many said they preferred factory work to farm work in their home villages. The girls who were left behind in the villages looked with envy upon the girls who were sent off to the city factories. On occasion, Hida girls even ran away from home to seek work in the silk filatures of Okaya" (1982, 180). At one group meeting, Kyōko, who grew up in a village in the 1930s, said: "I adored my next door neighbor's daughter [who occasionally came home from the silk spinning factory where she worked]. Everything she was wearing was nice, quite different from what we village girls were wearing in those days." Indeed, the money that some factory women brought back was more than a landless farmer's income for the entire year (Yamamoto 1977, 331). And some factory women made their parents rich enough to buy rice paddies. But they were exceptional, and most still owed the company a substantial debt at the end of the year (Hane 1982, 177).[49]

Sakura Takuji, a socialist activist from Nagano, was aware of the harsh working conditions in the fields and factories. He thus tried to form labor unions among factory women at several silk mills. In 1927, Sakura reported on a factory in Nagano where the owner invited a Christian minister to lecture to factory women before their annual departure for home. The following is an excerpt from an interview Sakura conducted with one woman worker at this mill:

We were often told [by the minister]: "the factory women of the silk industry are noble, because you are the treasure of our country; Japan would be ruined without you, because the silk industry constitutes the foundation of the Japanese economy; work hard until your body crumbles to pieces, keeping in mind that you have a sacred vocation; those of you who constantly change your workplace are good-for-nothing; and God always helps those of you who work hard and endure even the worst pain without complaining."

Each time we were thus lectured, I tried to understand him and to work hard. I did not move to any other factory. But I have recently begun to doubt the sincerity of the words of this minister. If spinning is such a sacred vocation, [the factory owner and managers] should do something good for us. (Sakura 1981, 48–49)

Told that they were the treasure of the company and the nation, some factory women demanded to be treated as such. They sang:

> Don't sneer at us,
> Calling us "factory women, factory women"!
> Factory women are
> Treasure chests for the company.[50]
> —(Yamamoto 1977, 375, quoted and translated in
>   Tsurumi 1990, 97)

In this ballad, the singers emphasized factory women's confidence and pride as producers, not as victims of a patriarchal society. They also expressed indirectly their superiority over their male coworkers, who watched over women workers but did not produce anything for Japan. This ballad suggests that factory women were eager to accept the position of national subjects if they were treated accordingly.

The following song also expresses factory women's pride and confidence as producers. In addition, it expresses their protest against male supervisors' exploitation of them. A man named Katsutaro was terribly feared in Nagano, as he had committed a series of murders out of the belief that the livers of the freshly murdered would cure people suffering from tuberculosis (Yamamoto 1977, 142–148). He must have had loved ones suffering from tuberculosis. In this respect, Katsutaro might have protested with factory women against the company (or even Japanese capitalism); instead, he killed his neighbors. Ironically, it was a factory woman named Iwataru Kiku who was reported to have twisted the testicles of this notorious murderer in 1908. The silk factory women in Nagano quickly made her into their heroine in their song:

> Don't scornfully say,
> "Factory women, factory women."
> Iwataru Kiku is
> A real factory woman.
>
> Iwataru Kiku is a shining
> Model of a factory woman.

*Let's wrench the balls
of the hateful men.*

*Mr. Overseer, Mr. Supervisor,
You'd better watch out!
There is the example
of Iwataru Kiku.*

*Who dares to say that
Factory women are weak?
Factory women are the
Only ones who create wealth.[51]
—(Yamamoto 1977, 148–149, quoted and translated in
  Tsurumi 1990, 197)*

In this song, the testicles of Katsutaro become the "balls of the hateful men," including overseers, supervisors, and all men who dare to say factory women are weak.

Like the songs of *komori*, the songs of factory women were harshly condemned in nationalist discourse because of the vulgarity of their style and the crudeness of their language. Hosoi lamented that the factory women he was in contact with chose to compose songs (*kouta, zokka*) to discuss their thoughts.[52] Hosoi relied on this to point out not only the "close relationship between women (*josei*) and song," but also the "low level of education of factory women" (1954, 326).

As Hosoi suggested, everything, from bodily pain in the work place to love, from homesickness to capitalism, and from food to religion became themes of factory women's ballads. About the food served at the dormitories, the factory women of a silk mill in Nagano sang:

*We are not grasshoppers,
But we are always fed squash.
With such food,
How can we spin a lot of thread? —(Katō 1955, 42)*

Katō Sōichi, who recorded this ballad, wrote that factory women also danced to this song at the summer Bon festival.[53] In this song, we can again note factory women's pride as the nation's producers and their protest against their actual treatment.

The following song, often called the "Prison Lament," seems to have been sung widely among the factory women in the textile industry:

Factory work is prison work.
All it lacks are iron chains.
More than a caged bird, more than a prison,
Dormitory life is hateful.
The factory is hell, the manager a demon.
The restless floorwalker a wheel of fire.
Like the money in my employment contract,
I remain sealed away.
If a male worker makes eyes at you,
You end up losing your shirt.
How I wish the dormitory would be washed away,
The factory burned down,
And the gatekeeper die of cholera!
At six in the morning I wear a devil's face,
At six in the evening, a smiling face.
I want wings to escape from here,
To fly as far as those distant shores.
Neither spinning maids nor slops,
Are promoted or kept for long.[54]

Those who exploited factory women included, in their own words, the "manager," the "restless floorwalker," the "male worker," and the "gatekeeper." They were "demons," and the factory was a living "hell." Factory women did not usually sing this song, for example, in its entirety. The complete version is the creation of scholars who have collected and analyzed the spinners' songs. Factory women apparently chose and sang any part of the song that reflected their thoughts and emotions at a specific time of day. They were completely free to change the lyrics of a song or to repeat one or two lines of a particular song.

Although Hosoi was critical of the blindness of factory women to the systemic nature of their exploitation, the following song suggests that they were in fact quite conscious of their position within the class society of Japan.

To kill a factory woman
You don't need a knife,
You just strangle her
With the weight and denier of the thread.[55]
—(Katō 1955, 39)

If we compare the above song with those in which factory women asserted their subjectivities as national subjects, this song suggests that factory women, who might have been proud of themselves as producers, also knew they were the oppressed within society.

The songs that were considered the most "vulgar" were verses in which factory women discussed sex and love.

> *My sweetheart spins the machine.*
> *I spin the thread and my mind,*
> *Worrying about what he thinks of me.*
> —*(Yamamoto 1977, 373)*

> *Listen to what factory women say while asleep,*
> *They say they want to eat plums,*
> *And to make love with a good-looking man.*
> —*(Yamamoto 1977, 374)*

When factory women faced men who might sexually exploit them, their songs became suddenly defensive.

> *Those who whisper sweet words in your ears will*
>   *trick you,*
> *Will rob you of money, and will abandon you.*

> *Don't lose your head over a man at the factory.*
> *You will be abandoned in the end,*
> *Like the tea leaves,*
> *Which are always discarded,*
> *after being used.*
> —*(Yamamoto 1977, 372)*

The following songs, however, suggest that factory women could transform their defensive attitudes into harsh contempt of male workers.

> *We hate male workers in our company.*
> *They are not smart or rich and are good for nothing.*
> *All they have are debts and lovers.*
> *If you visit them at home,*
> *They do not even have lids on their kettles.*
> —*(Yamamoto 1977, 371)*

> *What do male workers do*
> *behind the machine?*
> *They pick lice*
> *from their worn-out undershirts.*

In these songs, factory women cast objective eyes on their male coworkers: they describe them as poor, exploited workers just like themselves; but, compared to factory women, they caricature the factory men as "good for nothing."

"Women's morality" apparently did not deprive factory women of their ability to compose songs. In their songs and narratives, the rural women in Nagano described the minute details of their everyday lives as factory women: the conditions in which they worked, how long they worked, what they ate, and how they slept. They resorted to a variety of metaphors to express their thoughts and emotions: their minds were like "machines," always rotating around their expectations and worries; they were like "caged birds" or "prisoners without iron chains," unable to behave as they wished; and their bodies were like "tea leaves," discarded after being exploited. In their songs and narratives, they expressed not only their frustrations, powerlessness, and resignation as spinners and weavers under poor working conditions, but also their pride, confidence, and defiance as national subjects who could produce silk thread and cloth for Japan.

Thus, singing served a dual purpose: while it boosted women's morale, thereby increasing factory production, it also rallied women together when strikes occurred. Hane introduces a shorter version of the "Prison Lament" as a labor song: the women who attended the rally at Yamaichi Silk Plant in Okaya sang it in 1927 (1982, 196; see also Akamatsu 1977, 401–402). In songs, they protested the lack of medical facilities for factory women, the poor quality of food at their dormitories, and general working conditions. Indeed, we cannot ignore the increasing number of women who became active in the 1920s in labor movements in both the silk and the cotton industries. Unlike the urban middle-class women reformers, these women were of the working class and were themselves factory women. In the few decades since the first strike launched by women in 1886 at Amamiya Silk Mill, the number of women labor activists had increased significantly.[56]

This brief history of the labor movement among factory women in Japan suggests the need to conceptualize resistance as a process that is often long and drawn out. Thus, historian Barbara Fields proposes: "*Resistance* does not refer only to the fight that individuals, or collections of them, put up at any given time against those trying to impose on them. It refers also to the historical outcome of the struggle that has gone before, perhaps long enough before to have been hallowed by custom or formalized in law" (1990, 103; emphasis in original).

Resistance and history are inseparable concepts. Resistance is continuously and variously experienced by those who resist and who thus transform the nature of their resistance.

But Masayo's comments at a group meeting in Nagano suggest something else. She spun silk thread for the production of parachutes for the imperial army in the 1940s. "All the women in my factory," she said, "sang military songs (*gunka*) to uplift our spirits." Military songs were not factory women's creations. The mass media, then tightly controlled by the state, taught military songs to these women. When were factory women's songs replaced by military songs? Masayo could not answer my question. "It just gradually happened," said Masayo. She took it for granted that she should sing military songs while spinning silk thread for the benefit of the nation (*o-kuni no tame ni*). She was not scolded but encouraged to sing. "Military songs suited my patriotic spirit because of their forceful tunes," she commented. The period during which women's spinning and weaving songs were replaced by military songs was short compared to the centuries in which rural women had been singing spinning and weaving songs before the war. And yet, Masayo's comments suggest that factory women could be quite active as national subjects.

What about factory women's attempts to commit suicide? Were they only a costly and passive way to deal with miserable working conditions, cruel punishments, illegitimate pregnancies, and incurable diseases? Or were they an "implied protest against both the mill owners who exploited them and the parents who had put them there" (Sievers 1983, 78)? All we know for sure is that factory women did compose pensive songs about suicide.[57]

Even though you spin thread of poor quality
[and therefore will be punished],
Don't go to Benten-oki [of Lake Suwa].
When you put stones in your kimono sleeves [to
*   commit suicide],*
you feel more depressed.
—(Yamamoto 1977, 377)

Alas!
My body will eventually become,
bait for corbiculas (shijimi) in Lake Suwa.
—(Yamamoto 1977, 377)

Yamamoto writes that there were several "noted spots" for silk factory women in Nagano to commit suicide. Hence they simply changed
the name of the spot, which might be a lake, a river, or a railroad cross-
ing. These songs suggest that factory women perceived their own subjectivities and bodies ultimately as their own, not of the company or
of the nation, and took responsibility for their final destiny.

Chapter 5

The Countryside and the City 1: Yanagita Kunio and Japanese Native Ethnology

I have argued that the silk industry was a central feature of Japanese nationalism from the very beginning of the Meiji period. Even after the 1880s, silk factory women were national subjects, while constantly being monitored for their "women's morality" and their sexuality. What was their status when the silk industry declined in the 1920s? To answer this question, I must depend on the formulation of "the country(side) and the city."[1] This is because certain nationalist discourses during this period manipulated this dichotomy in order to keep the factory women in the silk industry as national subjects: those who returned to the countryside upon losing their jobs remained national subjects, while those who migrated to the city (to work in the manufacturing or service industries) lost their status.

In this and following chapters, I will focus on the discourses of Japanese folklore studies or native ethnology (*Nihon minzoku-gaku*) and of agrarianism as two important components of Japanese nationalism in the 1920s through 1940s.[2] Both relied on the division between the countryside and the city. Both favored the countryside and its women over the city and its women. Since the early twentieth century, rural women in Nagano had to face a dramatic increase in their work load because of economic recessions and a series of wars that caused shortages of male labor. Yet the reader will not hear their voices in this chapter and the next one, for the discourses of Japanese native ethnology and agrarianism spoke for them, suppressing their voices.

The Country and the City is the title of a book by literary critic Raymond Williams.[3] According to Williams, "the country and the city are changing historical realities, both in themselves and in their interrelations" (1973, 289). In England, the country became "subsidiary, and knew that it was subsidiary," in its relationship to the city in the late nineteenth and early twentieth centuries (p. 248). The general industrial and financial development in the city completely overshadowed life in the country. Although "our social experience is not only of the country and the city," it is significant that "the ideas and the images of country and city retain their great force" even to this day (p. 289). And it is always in a period of exceptional change in the rural economy, such as the late nineteenth and early twentieth centuries in England, that people reflect on the relationship between the country and the city (p. 291).[4]

Likewise, many intellectuals in 1920s Japan were struck by the images of the countryside and the city. Prominent among them was folklorist Yanagita Kunio (1875–1962). Indeed, he published a book with a title almost identical to Williams', *Toshi to nōson* (The city and the country) in 1929, when the countryside in Japan became "subsidiary" in his own eyes.[5] "A new question should be posed frankly. First of all, the ruination of the countryside (*nōson*) is wrong" (Yanagita 1962d, 256). Yanagita criticized not so much the ruination of the countryside as the "sacrifices it was being forced to make for an entirely new kind of social order based on urbanization and massive industrialization" (Harootunian 1990, 100). For Yanagita, urbanization and massive industrialization, which the Meiji state had mobilized, caused the ruination of the countryside. They triggered the migration of farmers to the city. They made it difficult for farmers to find marriage partners in the countryside. And they further impoverished farmers with the ever-increasing need for cash to purchase the products of industrial capitalism. Consequently, Yanagita and his students had to find a "resolution of the question of social determinacy—the principles of social cohesion, if the survivors of the past were not to be subdated by capitalism and its theory of social relationships" (Harootunian 1990, 100). For them, such a resolution was the agrarian mode of economic and cultural production.

In her article "The Transformation of Rural Society, 1900–1950" (1988), historian Ann Waswo brilliantly captures the moments of decline in rural Japan. With the sudden end to the post–World War I economic boom, on the one hand, crop prices began to fall in 1920 and fluctuated unpredictably at lower levels for the next several years (1988, 583). On the other hand, local tax burdens continued to increase. Farmers of middling and lower status were most affected by such an economic shock. This shock was more pronounced in Nagano prefecture than in other prefectures, because the majority of farmers depended on sericulture for cash income.[6] Because of the gradual decline and the fluctuation in the price of raw silk, their income declined accordingly. This process culminated with the world depression, which hit Japan in the late 1920s and early 1930s. The price of silk cocoons "dropped by forty-seven percent between September 1929 and September 1930," devastating the roughly two million farm households throughout Japan. Rice prices also plummeted, and the indebtedness of farm households increased markedly (Waswo 1988, 596). In addition, the return of thousands of unemployed workers from the city to the countryside worsened economic conditions.

The migration from the countryside to the city had begun much earlier than the 1920s. According to a survey conducted by the social reformer Ishihara in 1910, for example, 120,000 female factory workers of both the silk and the cotton industries from various villages in twenty-eight prefectures did not return home. Ishihara claims that the majority of those who remained in the city drifted from one job to another until they were compelled to take up prostitution owing to economic need or faltering health. Of the 80,000 who returned home, 13,000 were seriously ill, primarily of tuberculosis (1970a; 1970b; see also Sievers 1983, 85).

In Nagano, however, the exodus of rural women to the city seems not to have alarmed local journalists until much later, with the sudden decline of the price of silk cocoons in 1929 and 1930. By the early 1930s, many of the factory women whose voices we listened to in the previous chapter had lost their jobs. Many returned home, knowing that their families (which had relied on their income) were economically devastated. Others did not return, having been lured by the charm of the city, which had prospered in the economic boom during World War I. Thus, a local newspaper reported a "stream of young men and women heading to towns, abandoning their villages" in 1930.[7] The majority of these women, according to the same article, ended up working as domestic servants in the provincial towns within Nagano or in metropolitan cities. Another local newspaper article, published in 1929, lamented: "Alas! A stream of rural women leaving for the pleasure quarters to sell their own bodies!"[8] This indeed portrays the plight of rural women who were deprived of employment at silk mills and became nuisances to their families. Another newspaper article reported the "sale" of young women by a pimp to the pleasure quarters in the port cities in Echigo (now Niigata prefecture),[9] and another indicated that "90 percent of bar, cafe, and restaurant waitresses working in the provincial town of Matsumoto in Nagano were former factory women who had recently arrived in the town from their villages."[10]

The results of the national census (*kokusei chōsa*) of 1930, the first such nationwide census in Japan, supports what I have locally observed. According to the census, approximately 60 percent of the "women gainfully employed" (*joshi yūgyō-sha*) were still engaged in agriculture. Slightly less than 50 percent of the rest were employed in manufacturing, mostly in the textile industry. The rest were employed in the commercial and service sectors (see Ōshima 1982, 2). These figures, however, merely represent a static reading of census results taken at one point in history. Fortunately, economic historians have undertaken dynamic readings of the same census results: many of those employed in the silk industry either returned to their home villages or moved to the city to be absorbed in manufacturing, notably cotton, industries or in the commercial and service industries; but those employed in the commercial and service sectors had increased dramatically since World War I (Ōkouchi 1952; Ōkouchi and Sumiya 1955; Makino 1980). Restated, beginning in the late 1920s, there was a substantial flow of the female labor force from the manufacturing to the commercial and service sectors.

In the previous chapter, I described how their employers in silk spinning factories tried to teach female workers "women's morality" in order to prevent them from falling into "dirty land," and I mentioned that social reformers did not object to such an idea. By the late 1920s, however, many of the women apparently had fallen into "dirty land"; the image of factory women as promiscuous and undutiful became at least the statistical reality in the eyes of employers and social reformers. It is in this specific context that the division between the countryside and the city emerges in the discourse of Japanese nationalism. In it, factory women no longer appear as national subjects, as they have been replaced by *nōson fujin*.

Nōson fujin (or *nōka fujin* or *inaka fujin*) were "farming women" in the strict sense of the term. Factory women in the silk industry were also rural women; they not only spun and wove silk at modern factories but picked mulberry leaves in the fields and tended silkworms at home. However, *nōson fujin* as new national subjects had to be exclusively and explicitly farming women. Furthermore, farming women appearing in the nationalist discourse of the 1920s and 1930s were almost always "mothers." In a very common pattern of the life cycle of Nagano rural women, a silk mill girl who had lost her job returned home, was married off by her patriarchal father, and became the wife of an impoverished farmer. Thus, the emergence of an exclusively and explicitly farming woman as a national subject coincided with what Yanagita called the "ruination of the countryside."

The ruination of the countryside was deplored not only by Yanagita but by self-cultivating farmers. I refer to these landowning or large-scale tenant farmers who farmed their own or rented land as "middling farmers" (*chū-nō*).[11] Like Yanagita, they harshly criticized the national economy that, in their view, had risen with the development and expansion of industrial capitalism, as the economic foundation of agriculture had eroded. The middling farmers maintained the system of family farming: they became neither landlords nor landless laborers; they remained self-cultivating farmers who relied on family labor.[12] Not only did the middling farmers criticize the economy based in the city, they lamented the decline of "traditional" agriculture by self-cultivating households. In the end, they embraced the view that self-cultivating farm households would reproduce the essential values of Japanese culture. I would describe their ideology as *nōhon shugi*—the doctrine of agriculture as the essence.[13] Translations for *nōhon shugi* range from "agrarianism" or "agrarian fundamentalism" to "agrarian nationalism" (see Havens 1974, chap. 1). Since these farmer-ideologues also sought the Japanese "principles of social cohesion" in agrarian modes of economic and cultural production, "agrarian nationalism" may be as accurate as other translations (Harootunian 1990, 100).[14]

GENDER, NATIONALISM, AND JAPANESE NATIVE ETHNOLOGY

In an article published in 1990, Uli Linke reveals the origin of folklore studies with both subtlety and originality. He argues that "folklore research in Germany, Great Britain, and China came into being as a logical extension of 'nation building,' a process in which the knowledge of the various populations was deemed essential to the formation of the new state" (1990, 142). He thus emphasizes the importance and need of understanding folklore as "forms of power and knowledge."[15] In this section, I explore Linke's thesis of folklore as a logical extension of "nation building" in the context in which Japanese folklore studies or native ethnology emerged and was established as a new discipline of the social sciences in the early twentieth century.[16]

However, I have another, no less important agenda in mind. Folklorists as well as those interested in the history of folklore studies have conceptualized various populations, whose knowledge was deemed essential to the formation of the new state as gender-neutral populations. They have described those people, who have always resided in the countryside, as the "common folk," the "vulgar folk," the "abiding folk," "simple peasants," or the "rural population," but they have rarely considered them as populations in which men and women live interdependently. It may not be appropriate to criticize nineteenth-century scholars of folklore for their lack of interest in gender. But why have contemporary commentators of folklore studies failed adequately to question the gender neutrality of a term like "rural population"? Have they simply assumed, as nineteenth-century folklorists apparently did, that it was always men who determined the way of life and that women always obeyed men's dictates among the "simple folk"? Or, does it not make any sense at all to address the question of gender, since the "common folk" is, after all, an "imagined" population that folklorists eventually used as a metonym for the nation?

Yanagita called the "common folk" in Japan "*jōmin,*" and began to use that term frequently in his writing during the early 1930s. Yanagita occupies a special position in the discipline of Japanese native ethnology. During his lifetime of more than eighty years, Yanagita wrote "so much of his own that he was obliged to publish under pseudonyms." Furthermore, the "close to one hundred books and one thousand articles" by Yanagita have been reprinted continuously since the time of their original publication (Dorson 1975, x). *Teihon Yanagita Kunio-shū* (Standard edition of the complete works of Yanagita Kunio; hereafter *Teihon*), published in the early 1960s, totals thirty-six volumes. Commentaries on Yanagita's texts by later scholars, who are appropriately called "Yanagita scholars," continue to be published to this day. In other words, although Yanagita's students have also published a number of monographs, they have made it their primary concern to comment, both critically and uncritically, on the voluminous works by Yanagita as well as the key concepts proposed by him, including "*jōmin.*"

Although the term "*jōmin,*" a combination of "*jō*" (ordinary) and "*min*" (people), is clearly a gender-neutral term, what distinguishes

Yanagita from his students and later commentators on Japanese native ethnology is that he constantly referred to the "power of women" (*imo no chikara*) or the "work of women" (*onna no hataraki*). Thus, he clearly focused on rural women in early-twentieth-century Japan. Miyata Noboru, a contemporary commentator on Japanese native ethnology and himself a folklorist, identifies Yanagita as an early liberator of women, asserting that his "progressive" view of the "power of women" during "such an early period as the Taishō era" (1912–1926) was in no way outmoded in the 1980s (1987, epilogue; see also Miyata 1983). But was Yanagita truly a pioneer in the cause of the liberation of commoner women in Japan? My view is that Yanagita was not a liberator of working women and that his ideas were by no means progressive. To make this argument, I will first historicize Yangita's concept of *jōmin* in his own writing, reconceptualizing it as a gendered notion. I will then ask the following two questions that have been egregiously neglected in the field of folklore in Japan: what is the meaning of Yanagita's term "power of women," and how did Yanagita and his students conceptualize this power in light of their task of nation building?[17] I will eventually argue that Yanagita elevated the status of rural women to that of Japanese women, but that in that process he suppressed their own voices. Note the two roles of gender here. Gender relates to the relationship Yanagita constructed between men and women among the common folk. It is also at issue in the relationship I perceive between Yanagita, the "paternal gentleman from above" in E. P. Thompson's words, and his female subjects (1978, 249).

LOWLAND WOMEN AND MOUNTAIN GODS

If *jōmin* did not frequently appear in Yanagita's writing until the early 1930s, on what kinds of populations did Yanagita focus before this time?[18] *Tōno monogatari* (The tales of Tōno),[19] published in 1910, is a collection of legends and lore that Yanagita recorded as they were told to him by Tōno storyteller Sasaki Kizen.[20] In the preface to *Tōno monogatari*, Yanagita wrote: "In the mountain villages of Japan, in areas yet deeper into the mountains than Tōno, there must be countless other legends about mountain gods and *yamabito*. I wish these legends could also be heard for they would not only make us who live in the lowlands shudder, but would also provide a fresh start like *The Tales of Tōno*" (Yanagita 1963e, 5; 1975, 5).[21]

In this passage, Yanagita makes a spatial contrast between the mountains and the lowlands and classifies people residing on the archipelagoes of Japan into *yamabito*, the mountain people, and *heichi-jin*, those who live in the lowlands, including himself. In his *Yamabito-kō* (Thoughts on the mountain people), published in 1917, Yanagita asserted that the mountain people were the true natives of Japan (1963f).[22] Rather like the native American Indians, the mountain people were not of a single tribe, but of several (p. 172). According to Yanagita, the mountain people were eventually conquered by a "foreign" tribe, whose leader was the ancestor of the Japanese emperor. Mountain people did not become extinct, Yanagita argues, but successfully assimilated themselves into this "foreign"—Japanese—tribe. The "foreign" tribe preferred living in the lowlands in order to cultivate rice, a technology they introduced to Japan (p. 177). Yet the mountain people survived in the oral traditions of folk tales recounted by successive generations of lowland people.[23] In *Yamabito-kō*, Yanagita uses the term "*jōmin*" only once, where he argues that the "majority of those who lived in the mountains descended to the lowlands (*sato*) and mingled with *jōmin*, while the rest remained deep in the mountains and acquired the name '*yamabito*'" (p. 177). Here, Yanagita conceptualizes *heichi-jin* (lowland people) or *jōmin* (ordinary people) solely in relation to *yamabito* (mountain people).

Tōno monogatari depicts women among both the mountain and the lowland people. The mountain woman is always "tall" and "fascinating," with "long black hair trailing behind her" and a beautifully "white" face. She occasionally appears alone, but she also appears together with a mountain man or small children. She may also carry a supernatural power. The protagonist of one of the many folk tales Yanagita collected and recorded, Ōiko (meaning "big woman"), is one such woman. One day, she meets a man who is on his way to the capital to become a mighty sumo wrestler. He tries to tease her, but she hits him and defeats him in a fight. The man thus decides to stay with her at her house deep in the mountains in order to train himself. Ōiko makes rice balls for him every day for three weeks. The rice balls she cooks are too hard for him to bite initially, but in the third week, the man is finally able to eat them. He eventually becomes a very famous sumo wrestler in the capital (Yanagita 1964g, 113–115; see also Miyata 1987, 35). This is a story in which a mountain woman offers her power to a lowland man, who then becomes famous for his power.

In *Tōno monogatari*, sedentary lowland women often become victims of mountain men, while lowland men, although much less frequently, also become victims of mountain women.[24] The lowland women are suddenly kidnaped and hidden by mountain men, by whom they bear (usually many) children. These lowland women are always depicted as strong enough to remain in the mountains for the rest of their lives, together with their husbands, mountain men who devour their own children. One tale reads as follows:

> The daughter of a peasant from Kamigō village went into the mountains to gather chestnuts one day and never returned. Her family, thinking she had died, conducted a funeral ceremony using the girl's pillow as a symbol for her. Two or three years passed. One day a man from the village went hunting on the lower part of Mt. Gōyō and unexpectedly came across the girl in a cave which was concealed by large rocks. They were both surprised and when he asked why she was living there, she replied, "I came to the mountain to gather nuts and was carried off by a dreadful man who brought me here. I have thought of escaping but haven't had a chance."
>
> He asked, "What does he look like?"
>
> "To me he looks like any ordinary person but he is very tall and the color of his eyes is somewhat threatening. I have had several children, but he says that the children don't resemble him and are not his. They are perhaps eaten or killed, but in any case they are all taken off somewhere." . . .
>
> It is said the hunter was frightened and returned home. More than twenty years have passed since then. (Yanagita 1963e, 13; 1975, 15–16)

This tale and many others emphasize the close relationship between lowland women and the mountains.

In the same text, Yanagita writes, "In Japan, as in other countries, women and children playing outside at dusk often disappear in mysterious ways" (1963e, 14; 1975, 16). The lowland people revere the mountains as the space in which mountain gods and mountain people live, but it is somehow always "women and children" whom these mountain gods and mountain people kidnap and hide. In his *Yama no jinsei* (Life in the mountains), published in 1925, Yanagita further elaborates his thesis on the relationship between lowland women and the mountains (1963g, 68).

> The majority of lowland women who fled into the mountains were those who became insane after childbirth. This fact may indeed

open up a question of larger significance. There are many stories in Japan in which women who belonged to age-old shrines as shamans (*miko*) gave birth to sacred sons. These shamans were respected precisely because they were the mothers of sacred children. These stories are similar to the story of Virgin Mary. If women are born with such a tendency [to go mad after childbirth and run off into the mountains], this could be considered one universal explanation for the genesis of religions across many cultures. (Yanagita 1963g, 68–69, my translation)

He adds the following commentary to the above passage. "Obviously, women never hid themselves in the mountains because they were weary of this world. It was quite apparent in everyone's eyes that these women ran into the mountains because they had become insane" (p. 68).[25] He thus implies that men, as rational beings, do hide themselves in the mountains because of their world-weariness, but that women, as irrational beings, do so for biological reasons. In the end, Yanagita even identifies the entire category of lowland women with mountain gods (or goddesses) by citing examples from various regions in Japan in which housewives themselves are called "mountain gods" (*yama no kami*) (pp. 119–126).

Later scholars of Yanagita and Japanese native ethnology have pointed out that Yanagita abandoned his interest in the mountain people sometime before the 1930s. *Yama no jinsei* is the last comprehensive publication in which Yanagita dealt with the mountain people and their relationship to the lowland people (see Akasaka 1991, chap. 3). Afterwards, Yanagita shifted his focus to the lowland people, whom he named "*heimin*," "*minkan*," "*shomin*," "*minshu*," and "*jōmin*," all of which can be translated as "common folk."[26] Meanwhile, the term "*heichi-jin*," lowland people, disappeared in Yanagita's writing, presumably because he had coined the term solely for its use in relation to mountain people (see ibid.). Referring to this shift in Yanagita's interests, Akasaka Norio claims that Yanagita abandoned his early perspective of Japanese culture as an amalgam of distinct cultures. He also argues that, with this particular shift, Yanagita established native ethnology as *ikkoku minzoku-gaku*, "one nation" or "national" native ethnology, by ignoring the lives of the marginal (*shūhen*) (Akasaka 1991, 36, 268; see Yanagita 1964e, 339–357).[27] Thus, Yanagita began to conceptualize native ethnology as an essentially "Japanese" discipline, contrasting it with (social) anthropology. He understood the latter as the study of alien tribes by scholars of

developed societies. For him, "anthropology" was a discipline imported from the West (Yanagita 1964k).

With British anthropologist James Frazer in mind, Yanagita once
wrote:

> Among us, a little fact of our everyday life still tells us a lot about
> our own past in the most vivid manner. All of these facts that sur-
> round us and survive in us are too numerous to be called "survivals"
> or "vestiges." It is impossible for a cultured Japanese to live his
> everyday life without being conscious of them. In many instances,
> merely pondering these facts constitutes the art of collection, clas-
> sification, and comparison. We cannot hope to encounter the kind
> of situation we enjoy in Japan in other countries. That any new dis-
> cipline should necessarily follow the path of the white people is our
> mortifying experience of mere imitation. (1964e, 355)

I see in this quote Yanagita's unmistakable pride in Japan.

The appearance of *jōmin* in Japanese native ethnology constitutes
the most important moment in Yanagita and his students' enterprise
of "nation building." I believe this is because the term "*jōmin*" is a
homogenized concept, referring to "lowland people" in the absence
of "mountain people." Hence *jōmin* could and did become "Japanese."
Here too the "power of lowland women," now reconceptualized as
the "power of *jōmin* women," emerges. How did Yanagita perceive
such power for his task of nation building? Let me now turn to
another text in which Yanagita discusses the "power of women" in a
now homogenized and "imagined" context of Japan.

THE POWER OF WOMEN AND JAPANESE
NATIVE ETHNOLOGY

"Imo no chikara" (The power of women) is the title of an essay
Yanagita published in 1925. He later added eleven more essays on
women and a new preface and published them in the format of a
single volume in 1940. Yanagita begins this essay with several changes
he observed when he returned to his home village after thirty years
or so of residence in the metropolis. One such change Yanagita
describes is in the general sentiment of the villagers: "I do not know
about other regions, but I feel people have become somewhat gentler
here" (1964b, 10). He also notes a change in child-rearing practices:

"Parents have recently adopted the custom of treating children as an important asset" (ibid.).[28] Of one other change, Yanagita writes: "One thing that struck me is the increasing intimacy between older brothers and younger sisters. As older brothers grow, they rely more and more on their younger sisters. This phenomenon has become quite ordinary among people, but was not known before. Since I have observed this for the first time in my life, I do not know how to explain this particular phenomenon" (ibid.). In "The Power of Women," Yanagita attempts to seek an explanation for this increasing intimacy between (older) brothers and (younger) sisters. He does not necessarily reject the idea of a "phase of women's liberation" (*fujin kaihō no ichi katei*), but he does not pursue that line of argument. Instead, Yanagita relies on the idea of women's "special physiology" (*tokushu seiri*), "religious character" (*shūkyō-teki seikaku*), and "emotional nature" (*kandō shiyasui shūsei*), which he regarded as the power specific to Japanese women. In the following passages, Yanagita argues for a power distinctive to "women" (*fujin, josei, fujo, onna*) in the context of Japan.

> As it has been understood in our discipline [of Japanese native ethnology], women (*fujin*) have controlled almost all the principal aspects of the religious festivals and prayers. *In our race*, shamans have always been women (*josei*) in principle. (p. 14; emphasis added)

Of the "special physiology" of Japanese women, he writes:

> There have been many occasions for men, who fight with nature and enemies, to rely on the power of women. This is because women could always offer predictions and ideas to be used by men in their pursuit of war and peace. That [Japanese] people deified the power of women is a consequence of their belief in women's power. As we tend to deal with the sacred separately from the mundane, [Japanese] people of the past were rather afraid of touching the power of women precisely because it was regarded to be sacred. (pp. 14–15)

And, in the following passage, Yanagita writes of the power of women in its relation to production:

> The ideas of our [Japanese] ancestors are quite intriguing. They thought, as women (*onna*) have the power of reproduction, they should naturally ask women to be engaged in this most important task of production, that is, rice planting. (p. 15)

In these quotes, Yanagita discusses the "power of women" in terms of the power of "Japanese" women. Yet he uses the ideas of women's "special physiology," "religious character," "emotional nature," and "power of reproduction" in relation not to the mountain people but to "our race," Yanagita included. How, then, did Yanagita reconceptualize lowland women as "Japanese" women? And, what is the nature of the power Yanagita tried to confer upon Japanese women in the specific historical context of the 1930s and 1940s?

To address these questions, I must briefly discuss the notion of *jōmin* more generally by recasting it as a gender-neutral term.[29] In Yanagita's writings published in the early 1930s, "*jōmin*" meant nonelite sedentary peasants or farmers, excluding those who held power over them as well as those who were below them. In his *Kyōdo seikatsu no kenkyū-hō* (Research methods on the everyday life in the countryside), originally published in 1935, Yanagita defines "*jōmin*" as the majority in the Japanese countryside: they are "really simple peasants" (*goku futsū no hyakushō*) in between the upper class of people with family names[30] and the class including beggars, coopers, or blacksmiths, who only temporarily live in any village but will soon move to other villages (1967, 150–151).[31] These *jōmin* are "poor," caught in the wave of the Great Depression (1964c, 327). Thus, "*jōmin*" still refers to a part rather than the whole of the Japanese and consequently appears to carry the potential to reverse the hierarchical order of the state, which promoted urbanization and industrialization over the nonelite farmers.

If "*jōmin*" refers to the nonelite rural population, its women should logically be nonelite rural women. Wakamori Tarō, one of Yanagita's disciples, argues that "*jōmin* women" (*jōmin josei, jōmin-teki josei*) excludes the small number of elite women in Japanese history and refers to the "nameless" women who never appear in written documents (1975, 154–155). Such "*jōmin* women" seem also to have carried the potential to reverse the hierarchical order of the state over the nonelite rural population. Indeed, in his "Kafu to nōgyō" (The widow and agriculture; 1964f), Yanagita perceived what he thought was the most underprivileged resident of the village—the widow—as the victim of industrialization and modernization. He believed new agricultural technologies, such as the new harvester, had deprived the widow of her cash-earning opportunities, abundant before the mechanization of agriculture (pp. 132–149).[32]

His early formulation of *jōmin* indeed parallels his criticism of contemporary modernist historians who perceived *jōmin* as "countless round pills" (*musū no ganyaku*).

> When one looks at the pictures of famous spots (*meisho*) drawn during the peaceful period or the pictures of the River Festival of Ryōgoku and the Festival of Gion Tenma, the painters have drawn numerous circles with only dots for eyes and mouths or, much later, have simply arranged something like countless round pills and called them "the masses" (*gunshū*). Isn't this an expression of their attitude, which utterly ignores the personality and human feelings of the masses?[33] (Yanagita 1964d, 10)

And yet, as *jōmin* became a synonym for the Japanese people, the concept lost its potential to erode the hierarchical order of the state over the rural population. At the same time, Yanagita abandoned his project of restoring the "personality and human feelings" of *jōmin*. Let's see how Yanagita elevated *jōmin* to the "Japanese" and made the Japanese country folk into a "Japanese identity."

Referring to the interrelationship between the countryside and the city, Yanagita often emphasized the difference between Europe or the West and Japan. In Europe, he argued, the city always antagonized the countryside by symbolically enclosing itself with a wall. In Japan, according to Yanagita, such an antagonistic relationship between the city and the countryside did not exist in the first place, for even when the rural folk moved to another location to build a city, some of them always moved back to the countryside. He also argued in 1931 that, "even legally speaking, no distinction has ever been made between the city and the village. Originally, the city (*machi*) meant a ward (*kukaku*) and referred to a section where houses were concentrated within the village" (1962c, 170). According to Yanagita, city life is a mere metamorphosis of country life in Japan. That assertion provided the logical foundation for him to further assert that the rural folk could metonymically represent Japan to itself and the outside world. "The urban residents too, in the sense that they migrated to the city from the countryside," could be included in the category of rural folk and *jōmin* (Ito 1972, 9). Itō Mikiharu has termed these premises of Yanagita as "urban-rural continuum theory," apparently after Robert Redfield's "folk-urban continuum" (ibid.).

Yanagita thus magically made the cleavage between the country-side and the city disappear. Did he also make the power of state apparatuses disappear? Commenting on this question, historian Irokawa Daikichi argues: "From the time Yanagita established the concept as well as the methodology of *jōmin*, he demonstrated a theoretical weakness in leaving the connection of the state (*kokka*), the emperor (*tennō*), and the masses (*minshū*) unexplored" (1978, 417). I will consider each of these three institutions in turn. Yanagita seems to have given more attention to the emperor than to the state and eventually to have incorporated the Japanese emperor and the imperial family into the category of *jōmin*. Yanagita claimed in 1934, "humbling myself greatly to say so (*osore ooi koto de aruga*)," that the Japanese emperor was also a *jōmin* (1934, 111–112).[34] Indeed, the emperor's ancestor was the leader of a tribe who successfully assimilated mountain people. As an important piece of evidence to support his claim, Yanagita presented the commonalty between the rituals of the Japanese imperial family and rituals performed by the rural population, both transmitted without writing. In a 1928 essay titled "Onie-matsuri [also read Daijō-sai] to kokumin" (The festival of Onie and Japanese national people), Yanagita comments: "In this Grand National Festival performed by His Majesty the emperor, there are innumerable elements [of the ritual] that are commonly found in village autumn festivals, although, of course, the latter are smaller in scale and inferior in rank" (1964h, 374).[35] Yanagita also argued in 1941 that the "festivals of the imperial family are just like those of the little shrines in the village. This strengthens our conviction that, in Japan, the nation (*kokka*) is the extension of each family" (1963c, 503). As the nation simply becomes the "extension of each [*jōmin*'s] family," the state as an institution equipped with enormous power disappears.

The second institution, *kokka*, means the "state," "nation," or "nation-state," depending on the context in which it is used. Nakamura Akira argues that the state in Yanagita's thought constitutes a "natural state," which originated in the permanent settlement of Japanese/*jōmin* on the Japanese archipelagoes (1974, 171–193; see also Yoshimoto 1990, 139). A "natural state" is a state that was "naturally" born out of a human settlement in a specific locality and does not exercise power over its members. In this respect, Yanagita's *kokka* is similar to *kuni*: *kuni* represents the triumph of concealment of power, as does Yanagita's *kokka*. In contrast, Yanagita at times criticized the state when it interfered with the affairs of the rural population. For example, he condemned the state bureaucracy that did not offer official ranks to local Shinto shrines (1964l, 315–396) or interfered in village festivals by deploying the local police (1964i, 399). We have also seen that Yanagita criticized the state as an agent of industrialization and modernization that impoverished the life of the widow.

This apparent contradiction poses a problem for Yanagita scholars. Akasaka, for example, argues that Yanagita's criticism of the state manifests itself only insofar as he thought its power undermined the spiritual (*shinkō*), not the institutional (*seido*), aspect of *jōmin* life (1991). However, as many passages I have quoted from Yanagita's works suggest, he makes only arbitrary distinctions between the spiritual and the institutional. Rather, I believe that *jōmin*, as a concept and a methodology, prevented him from challenging the state's power. In other words, by the 1930s, *jōmin* no longer referred to what Irokawa called "the masses." Yanagita included in *jōmin* every Japanese, encompassing the emperor, the state bureaucrats (Yanagita was a young office holder in the Ministry of Agriculture and Commerce before he became a folklore scholar), the state's or the emperor's subjects, and folklorists themselves.[36] He thus could no longer place himself in a location from which he could challenge the power of the state. Victor Koschmann, correctly I believe, points out that Japanese native ethnology established itself only after the state, the "emperor system," and the bureaucratic system were already preeminent (1985, 160), but it "remained, ironically, not only somewhat similar to that regime, but conceptually dependent upon it" (p. 162).

In *Kyōdo seikatsu no kenkyū-ho*, Yanagita addressed three "problems" faced by *jōmin*/Japanese. The first was the popularization of an education that taught *jōmin* the value of civilization based in the city. The second was the difficulty of finding a marriage partner among *jōmin*, owing to the disintegration of such traditional institutions as the young men's and women's groups. Third, and related to the second, was the problem of *jōmin*, especially *jōmin* women, enraptured by the charm of the city, running away from the countryside (Yanagita 1964c, 327). Yanagita, however, never asked why *jōmin* were confronted with these "problems." He simply urged his contemporaries, that is, *jōmin*/Japanese, to go back to an unspecified past when *jōmin* did not know them.

It is of particular interest here that Yanagita rarely used such terms as "landlords" (*jinushi*) or "tenants" (*kosaku*) in his own writings. Akamatsu, perhaps the only folklorist who criticized Yanagita's native ethnology in the 1930s and has continued to do so to this day, points out that, "Saishū techō," a manual containing a hundred entries for research topics compiled by Yanagita for students of Japanese native ethnology, does not include these terms at all (1991, 51).[37] "*Jōmin*," then, lacks any notion of class and, according to Akamatsu, any notion of discrimination. Indeed, if "*jōmin*" is conterminous with "Japanese" nationals, how can it imply either of these notions?[38]

Even though "*jōmin*" is a gender-neutral term, women, left in the countryside, became the major labor force by the early twentieth century. With the Manchurian Incident (1931) and the China Incident (1937), increasing numbers of able-bodied rural men were conscripted by the imperial army (see Chapter 7). Yanagita was clearly aware of this fact when he wrote in 1926 that, now that "Japanese men must increasingly think about the faraway land," Japanese women should maintain the "serenity" and "beauty" of the *jōmin* world (1962e, 17). It was not that women were left by themselves and freed from patriarchal authorities during the wartime period. Elsewhere Yanagita still describes the *jōmin* world as one in which "men are stronger than women, women customarily obey men, and fathers are thought to be more important than mothers" (1964e, 323). The departure of men did not change the patriarchal nature of rural society. This is why Maruoka Hideko, who worked for the national headquarters of the agricultural cooperatives, emphasized not the power of rural women but their fatigue, faltering health, high rates of stillbirths and miscarriages, and poverty (1948). In the Japanese countryside, according to Maruoka, women were but a "labor force" and did not hold any power at all. If so, what kinds of power did Yanagita confer upon *jōmin* women?

In the preface of a new version of *Imo no chikara* published in 1940, Yanagita argues that *jōmin* "could accumulate their parents' experiences in their minds, even though they themselves were not taught how to read and write" (1964b, 4). Society in general, Yanagita continues, tends to despise such *jōmin* because of their lack of formal education. But, says Yanagita, it is these *jōmin* who inherit and bequeath oral traditions to coming generations. More important for my argument, Yanagita perceived *jōmin* women as better storytellers and purveyors of oral traditions than men.[39]

Yanagita further elaborates this point in his essay *Josei to minkan denshō* (Women and oral traditions), published in 1932 (1962a). He argues that written history covers only a portion of the past, because the history of ordinary people has been unwritten; men, who are always busy, have avoided recording the history of ordinary people, thinking others might do it for them; women can undertake such a job more easily than men, for they can "naturally" read the minds of ordinary people better than men; hence, in several foreign countries, women are taking over the field of folklore from men (1962a, 317–320).[40] For Yanagita, *jōmin* are "unlettered" people and therefore more "authentic" than "lettered" elites (Ivy 1988, chap. 3). *Jōmin* women are even more "unlettered" for Yanagita than *jōmin* men. Interestingly, in these two texts on women, Yanagita reinstates *jōmin* as a part, not the whole, of the Japanese population, that is, those who are not taught how to read and write. Yanagita then elevates unlettered *jōmin* women over lettered *jōmin* men. And yet, the former become a metonym for Japan, because, for Yanagita, it is they who make the national continuity possible.

Yanagita published a very short, one-page article, titled "Tokkō seishin o hagukumu mono" (Those who nurture the spirits of kamikaze), only five months before Japan was defeated in World War II. I quote it here in its entirety, for it represents most vividly to me Yanagita's understanding of the power of *jōmin*/Japanese women.

> In Japan, brave soldiers appear continuously in history. They are not a particular chosen few among the majority, as anybody is resolved to sacrifice himself when such a time comes. Otherwise, their stories would be the biographies of only a handful of individuals. The bravery of these men indeed constitutes a part of the Japanese national character.
>
> Reading the old histories of wars, I find many examples in which so many men were killed in local battles that their communities risked extinction. But there is no evidence whatsoever that the next generation of young men became timid because of such mass killings. These men believed that the women who had been left behind had power (*chikara*). They believed that, with this power, the women could raise their descendants to be brave soldiers like their fathers. We now find innumerable examples of such power among women.
>
> Women's work (*shokubun*) has increased enormously both within and outside Japan. In addition, their sufferings are tremendous. But women are already raising the generation to come. We really must thank them deeply.
>
> The situation of each family, however, is different. There are families in which women have adequate power, but there also are

families in which they still lack power. I want women to have broader minds and to participate in the plan to raise even evacuee children to be brave soldiers. The morality of mother citizens (*haha to iu kokumin*) should still be cultivated in this difficult time.[41] (1964m, 497)

Yanagita apparently accepted the state's war policies. But it is more important for me that he did not entertain the slightest doubt about the power of Japanese women, who he believed would comfort the soldiers and tell their brave stories to subsequent generations.

Furthermore, the "power of women" consists not only of women's ability to transmit the past orally to subsequent generations. Yanagita seems to have believed that such power also originated in women's *hataraki*. For example, he cites the power of a housewife in a family of fifteen or twenty, who took care of not only her children, husband, and parents-in-law, but all the other employees of the house. He admires her work and power, although he never broaches the question of how she felt about her enormous task (1963a, 271–290). Yanagita also cites the power of a mother who committed suicide together with her children. Instead of asking what forced her to kill herself and her children, Yanagita emphasizes her power which could dictate even the fate of her own children (1964f, 190). Furthermore, for Yanagita, a woman's power increased if her husband was away fighting on the battlefield.

Even more interesting is that *jōmin* women never suffered discrimination directed against themselves. Yanagita argued that the institution of young men's and women's groups found in almost every village throughout the Japanese countryside in the recent past taught *jōmin* the "techniques of love" (*ren'ai gijutsu*): the young village women who gathered in the young women's group every night worked communally, sewing, weaving, or making rope, and talked about the village men and their future partners; this was the "most harmless way for them to know the world" (1963b, 296). Yanagita, however, ignored the possibility that, under those circumstances, only men might have had the right to choose their mates and that women could only passively accept men's marriage proposals.[42] In *Meiji Taishō-shi sesō-hen* (Social conditions during the Meiji and Taishō periods; 1963b), he criticized the state for transforming the traditional young men's and women's groups (*wakamono-yado, musume-yado*) into young men's and women's associations (*seinen-dan, joshi seinen-dan*).[43] The associations, according to Yanagita, were the products of state interference in the world of *jōmin;* instead of teaching the "techniques of love," young men's and women's associations taught their members the political ideologies of the state. However, Yanagita urged the reader only to understand, restore, and return to a historically unspecified *jōmin* past, without engaging in a critical discussion of the presence of the state's power in the countryside.

Yanagita also demonstrates his conservative notion of the power of women in his interpretation of the marriage system in Japan. In *Mukoiri-kō* (Thoughts on the matrilocal marriage), published in 1929, and again in 1948 in a larger essay with that title (1963d, 152–203), Yanagita argued that the marriage system in Japan had always been patrilocal and patrilineal.[44] Even though it was reported in various regions that the bridegroom lived with the bride's family for a certain period of time, eventually the bride always moved to the groom's household; the custom of a groom living in his bride's household indicates that a woman's labor was crucial to her own household and, according to Yanagita, never suggests the vestiges of a matrilocal and matrilineal marriage system in Japan (see Murakami 1977). Yanagita thus completely ignored the works of his contemporary, the historian Takamure Itsue, who demonstrated that the marriage system in Japan was matrilocal and matrilineal until about the fourteenth century, now the dominant interpretation (see, for example, Wakita 1993).[45]

Of special interest to students of nationalism is Yanagita's embarrassment over and criticism of Tamura Nao'omi's *The Japanese Bride*, which disclosed the unwillingness of many Japanese women to obey their fathers and brothers under the prewar patriarchal family system. Yanagita writes:

> When I was a student, the now infamous "incident of *The Japanese Bride*" surprised Japanese society. A Christian priest named Tamura Nao'omi published a book and argued that many Japanese women were forcefully married off by their fathers and brothers. He argued that there was no freedom for women to choose their partners. . . . Our common sense would tell us that such an incident should not have occurred in the first place. Even a small animal has such a freedom [to choose one's mate]. (Yanagita 1963d, 158)

In insisting on the freedom of Japanese women to choose their marriage partners, Yanagita apparently had in mind the custom of young men's and women's groups in rural Japan. I have already claimed that rural women did not always exercise such a freedom. Equating

Japanese women with rural/*jōmin* women, Yanagita asserted otherwise by suppressing the voices of rural women while elevating them as national signifiers.[46]

Furthermore, Yanagita depicted the space in which these *jōmin* women lived as a place of beauty and serenity, free from tragic events. Describing spring in the snowy countryside of Japan, Yanagita wrote of "the mound of reddish earth shining in the sun, the color of the azalea mingling with dwarf pine trees, the shimmer of the heated air of the wheat field where a skylark raises her chicks, dandelions and violets growing on the stone wall in the village, and the purple color of wisteria in the forests of gods" (1962e, 9). It is striking that he had depicted the world of lowland people in a starkly different way in *Tōno monogatari*, as a world afflicted with poverty, famine, murder, and incest. In about fifteen years, Yanagita had transformed this near-grotesque world into an elysian one. In his collection of photographs of everyday life in the countryside of northern Japan, we see only smiling faces of women (Yanagita and Miki 1944). "Tidy" (*seiso*), "simple and beautiful" (*kanso-bi*), "fresh" (*shinsen*), and "colorful" (*shikisai-teki*) are the most common adjectives used to describe the life of rural women in this region.

What of the women who still belonged to the Shinto shrines as *miko* or shamans in early-twentieth-century rural Japan? Yes, they still held power, because, in Yanagita's view, women had a "special physiology," "emotional character," and "reproductive ability" to become shamans (1964b). Yanagita also thought that such shamans gave a certain cohesiveness to the village community; and, since Yanagita had extended the rural space to the entire space of Japan through his construction of *jōmin*, shamans should also give a certain cohesiveness to the nation-state of Japan. But Yanagita never described these shamans as historical subjects. Yoshimoto Takaaki claims in his *Kyōdō gensō-ron* (Communal imaginary) that no shaman appears in Yanagita's texts as a protagonist (1968, 92–108). Neither Yanagita nor any of the tales he collected offers an explanation of the conditions under which a specific woman has become a shaman. Rather, according to Yoshimoto, the female shaman always appears as a mediator and places herself as a partner of the community, which is conceptualized as a male sexual being. She is thus parallel to the figure of a lowland woman who wanders into the mountains because of her "special physiology" and becomes a mountain man or mountain god's wife. Yoshimoto implicitly compares the shaman in Yanagita's texts with another kind of shaman. The latter is pan-human and is able to identify her imagination with that of the whole community. The gender of such a shaman is thus irrelevant. In contrast, the shaman in Yanagita's texts is subordinated to the interests of the patriarchal community. Before the interests of the community, she carries only the power to repeat the past.

In an essay titled *Josei to bunka* (Women and culture), published in 1942, Yanagita writes:

> I have always paid close attention to how women use the term "culture." I now feel that, in the recent past, some women clearly misunderstood its significance. For example, at a recent gathering of young women, all of whom are well educated, one woman told me that she had thought about abandoning the old culture of Japan and creating a new one. She also told me that she now felt it was impossible to do so and was confused about what to do next. Although I should not criticize her because she had already given up her idea of creating a new Japanese culture, we all should be alarmed at the fact that she once had believed in such a possibility. (1970, 211)

Yanagita goes on to say that "abandoning old culture is tantamount to bidding farewell to one's parents, aunts, and sisters. . . . How could a woman ever consider such a possibility?" (ibid.). Thus, Yanagita never offered Japanese women the power to create a new culture.

In this chapter, I have tried to explore the meaning of Yanagita's "power of women" by reconstructing *jōmin* as a gendered concept. It is true that Yanagita has often been described as a "scholar of resistance." This is perhaps so, if we highlight his early interest in the space of the mountains or his early formulation of *jōmin* as a nonelite rural population. However, I have tried to demonstrate that his scholarship of resistance was only possible because he denied rural women their voices.[47] And when the *jōmin* world became the "imagined community" of the nation-state of Japan, Yanagita asked *jōmin*/Japanese women to exercise their power, remembering, telling, and retelling the facts of their everyday lives to subsequent generations. The *jōmin* world extended from the snowy countryside of the north to the southernmost island of Okinawa and even to the Japanese colonies to which *jōmin* migrated to create new villages (the nexus of Japanese native ethnology and colonialism, however, is a separate issue, deserving greater attention than I can devote to it within the scope of my current research).[48]

Chapter 6

The Countryside and the City 2: Agrarianism among Nagano Middling Farmers

anagita left thousands of books and articles on his perceptions of rural women and his vision of nation building. Did the middling farmers in Nagano also leave us their writings? In 1990, I visited Ueda Hakubutsukan (Ueda History Museum), located on the compound of Ueda Castle Park. Ueda, which became an administrative city in southern Nagano in 1919, was first developed as a castle town in the sixteenth century. Since then it has served as a commercial center, surrounded by numerous villages, many of which have now been incorporated into the city itself. At the museum, I found piles of old newspapers published in the thirty villages surrounding Ueda during the 1920s and 1930s.

Generically called *sonpō* or *jihō*, these are newspapers published by a group of local youths, called *seinenkai* or *seinendan*, in each village.[1] Table 5 lists the titles of these newspapers, most named after their own villages, and the date of first publication.[2] By the end of the 1940s, all of these groups of local youths had stopped the publication of their village newspapers, owing to the scarcity of paper and the increasing ideological control by the government during the wartime period.[3] In one small column at the bottom of the last page of *Urazato sonpō*, published in 1922, one finds the following editorial statement: "You may contribute an article on any topic to this village newspaper, not only on local politics and economy but on your inner thoughts. The deadline is the fifteenth of every month. Please keep and file all the newspapers delivered to you, as such a file will constitute the

TABLE 5

JIHŌ OR *SONPŌ* IN UEDA AND ITS VICINITY

Title of *Jihō* or *Sonpō*	Date of Initial Publication
Ebōshi no hana (later called *Motohara*)	1919
Shiojiri	1919
Aoki	1921
Urazato	1921
Kangawa	1923
Nishi Shioda	1923
Takeishi	1923
Toyotomi	1923
Izumida	1924
Kamishina	1924
Kanō	1924
Muroga	1924
Naka Shioda	1924
Nishiuchi	1924
Osa-mura	1924
Shiokawa	1924
Yazu	1924
Fujiyama	1925
Higashi Shioda	1925
Kawabe	1925
Wada	1925
Yoda-mura	1925
Agata-mura	1926
Bessho	1926
Shigeno	1927
Tonoshiro	1927
Daimon	1928
Maruko	1928
Nagase	1928
Nagakubo	1929

Source: Kanō Masanao has published a similar table (see Kanō 1973, 98–99). I created this table independently, using information provided by the Ueda History Museum.

important history of our village."[4] It is in these village newspapers published between 1919 and 1940 that I attempted to explore middling farmers' perceptions of rural women in their task of nation building.[5]

I will call their discourse "agrarianism," using its broadest definition: agrarianism reproduces "society's (not merely farmers') ambivalent relation to industrialization, urbanization and centralization" (Vlastos 1994, 2–3). Indeed, agrarianism was advocated by socially and ideologically diverse groups. Although my focus here is on the agrarianism promoted by Nagano middling farmers, their discourse is not uniform and it changes over time between 1919 and 1940. I reject the classification of agrarianism into "traditional" and "popular" varieties (see, for example, Havens 1974; Waswo 1988, 589). According to this classification, traditional agrarianism prevailed in the early Meiji period in northeastern Japan, where large-scale landowners were concentrated. These landowners, together with the state's bureaucrats, promoted it with the goal of commercializing agriculture and gaining higher profits. Popular agrarianism prevailed in the 1920s and 1930s in southwestern Japan, where small-scale self-cultivating farmers were concentrated. These middling farmers advanced popular agrarianism to improve their economic, political, and social status, which had been eroded with the development of industrial capitalism. In contrast with traditional agrarianism, popular agrarianism implies the absence of state involvement in rural affairs.

The agrarianism I will present here, even though it was advocated by middling farmers in the 1920s and 1930s, was by no means "popular." The state was heavily involved in promoting it. The deterioration of rural conditions invited the state to penetrate further into the countryside, a process that had already begun in the late nineteenth century with the state reform of land taxation and local administration. It tightened its grip on the countryside by issuing a series of laws in order to increase agricultural output at the turn of the century. The state also assaulted vestiges of village autonomy by encouraging farmers to participate in a nationwide movement that was nonetheless called the Local Improvement Movement (*chihō kairyō undō*). Furthermore, facing a rise of tenant disputes, the state attempted to suppress so-called dangerous thought of socialism, communism, and anarchism among the village youth, while offering "alternatives" in order to lessen their grievances.[6] Waswo argues that the state's penetration encouraged not only "centrifugal" forces within the village that increasingly mobilized farmers for national goals, but "centripetal" forces, which created the desire for communal autonomy among farmers (1988, 557–558).

What was the nature of the local youth groups that published the newspapers? According to Waswo, a local youth group was the product of both "centrifugal" and "centripetal" forces. That is, the young men's groups (*wakamonogumi*) that existed in each rural community during the Tokugawa period were revived in the mid-1890s by the farmers themselves. Their functions were related to everyday life, such as "patrol duty to protect the community from fire or theft, labor services on communal land, and participation in festivals at the local shrine." From 1905 onward, the Home Ministry, working in concert with the Ministry of Education, tried to mobilize the young men's groups in local improvement causes. The Home Ministry also gave, in Waswo's words, "a new, more modern name" to the young men's group, *"seinenkai"* or *"seinendan,"* local youth group or corps (p. 573).

Although Waswo argues that membership became almost standardized throughout Japan by 1915, beginning when a young man finished elementary school and ending when he reached the age of twenty (p. 574), the membership of the local youth groups in the villages in the vicinity of Ueda deviated from this norm. For example, the members of a local youth group in the village of Urazato were male residents between the ages of fifteen and thirty. In 1922, there were 484 members, 162 of whom resided outside the village and were not active members.[7] This does not mean that all 322 local members were actively involved in the publication of the village newspaper. In reality, members had to pay a variety of fees to become active members of the group, for example, 25 yen for joining or leaving the group, 30 yen for attending its once-a-year general meeting, 50 yen for attending a five-day lecture series, 80 yen for joining sports clubs, and so forth.[8] Those who could pay these fees were largely middling farmers, that is, landowning farmers and large-scale tenant farmers. They were thus situated, according to historian Suzuki Masayuki, one rank below the rank of "local government officials, teachers, Shinto priests, and Buddhist monks," but above the majority of small-scale farmers and tenants (1977, 19).

As the exposure to education must have varied almost directly with economic status, the active members of the local youth groups were also more educated than others, many of whom were graduates of second-rate agricultural schools. They actively used their skills in reading and writing, acquired in the Meiji compulsory educational system. They were also significantly influenced by what the state described as "dangerous thought." In all thirty villages, the active members of the local youth groups built village libraries in the early 1920s, purchased Marxian literature, and invited urban-based liberal intellectuals as guest speakers (see also Kanō 1973, 129; Nakamura 1978, 214, 217). The village newspapers periodically published lists of books purchased by the libraries. One such list includes *Marx zenshū* (The complete works of Marx), *Shakai shisō-shi kenkyū* (The study of social intellectual history) by Kawai Eijirō, and *Shakai kaizō no genri* (The principles of social reconstruction) by John Russell, along with dozens of literary works by such writers as Arishima Takeo and Mushakōji Saneatsu.[9] The term *"Marukus booi"* (Marx boy), used in a positive or a negative sense, also appeared occasionally in the village newspapers. Historian Aoki Keiichirō (1964) reports the existence of numerous study groups among farmers in Nagano, who read *Kaizō* (Reconstruction), a popular journal of urban liberalism, and other proletarian literature in the 1920s and 1930s (see also Suzuki 1977, 7; Nakamura 1978, 217). Taking the village of Urazato as an example, only about sixty men were actively involved in the publication of the village newspapers, editing, soliciting articles from other residents, personally contributing to articles, and distributing newspapers.[10] Many of them were eager to learn leftist thought in order to "reconstruct the countryside" (*nōson kaizō*), yet they were cognizant of their position as national subjects of modern Japan.

What were the main purposes for publishing village newspapers? The inaugural issue of *Ebōshi no hana*, published in 1919, succinctly summarizes them.[11] The first is to publish all information regarding the self-government (*jichi*) of the village, including information coming from the state, such as the dates of examinations for military conscription and the payment of national and local taxes. The second is to provide an open forum for all village residents to exchange freely their own, uncensored views. But another purpose stated in the same issue contradicts the second goal. It is to prevent "dangerous thought" among the village youth and to make them as useful as possible for the construction and expansion of the nation-state of Japan. Thus, we can recognize both of what Waswo calls "centrifugal" and "centripetal" forces within the countryside in various articles published in the village newspapers.

Did the village newspapers offer the opportunity for open debate to rural women? *Urazato sonpō* in 1922 has an interesting illustration

FIGURE 3. The figure of a woman holding a pen, which appeared in *Urazato sonpō*, May 15, 1922. (Reprinted with the permission of Urazato Sonpō Fukkoku Jikkō Iinkai)

that is relevant to my inquiry. It is an illustration of a woman naked from the waist up, with long, black, somewhat curly hair, holding a pen.[12] Did this represent the desire of the members of the local youth group to have women contribute their writings to the village newspapers? Indeed, in *Urazato sonpō* of 1932, I found the following: "I lament that no woman has contributed a single article so far this year to this village newspaper. How should we interpret this reality? Women should not forget this important means of making their thoughts publicly known. I really would like to know the woman's world."[13] An earlier article, published in 1923, says the following: "When we offered a class on ethics [to the members of the youth group] one icy cold night, we saw two women listening to the lecture intently from outside the classroom window. We were so moved by their eagerness to learn, that we immediately sent a letter of invitation [to the next class on ethics] to the women alumni."[14] The article does not state which school the women alumni belonged to; it may have been the elementary school, which, by 1923, offered six years of compulsory education to both boys and girls. Indeed, though only very sporadically does one find articles written by women in the village newspapers, almost all of these articles seem to have been specifically chosen by the editors in accordance with their own views.

For example, there is an article titled "A Young Woman's Cry" published in *Ebōshi no hana* in 1921 by a woman who identifies herself as M.Y.[15] Much later, I spotted another article, written by a woman who uses only her first name of Keiko as her pen name.[16] Both articles present a rather conservative view of rural women. Using a horticultural metaphor for the nation of Japan, both M.Y. and Keiko argue that rural women should be proud of themselves as they nurture the roots of plants flourishing in the city. Keiko then writes: "It is now time for us rural women to gain and use knowledge not only for consumption but for production. Work that is suitable for women, such as tending vegetable and fruit gardens, taking care of domestic animals, or growing plants and flowers, is piling up in front of our eyes."

Did these middling farmers, like Yanagita, confer upon rural women a "power" so that the latter could participate in the task of nation-building? My answer is a definite yes, but we must note that middling farmers did so by alternately denying it to urban women. Stated differently, we cannot understand middling farmers' representation of rural women's power without understanding their negative portrayal of urban women. For example, in 1928, a man named Suzuki Saburō, who lived somewhere in the Japanese countryside, sent a letter to a journal called *Ie no hikari* (The light of home).[17] In it, he wrote:

> I occasionally meet a woman who has cut her hair very short and makes up her face with rouge, lipstick, and an eyebrow pencil. But when I scrutinize her clothes, I find them not to match her hair style and make-up. She seems to be satisfied with herself only because she can catch the attention of others. I find her modern [*modan*], but my feeling toward her is one of contempt. She lacks something to be truly modern [*modan*].[18]

Suzuki Saburō describes the image of the urban Modern Girl, a "glittering, decadent, middle-class consumer who, through her clothing, smoking, and drinking, flaunt[ed] tradition" in the 1920s (Silverberg 1991, 239). Using the term *"modan"* (modern), he conveys the idea of a person who might have moved to the city and occasionally come home to her village or, even without moving to the city, might simply have been influenced by the image of the urban Modern Girl. It is interesting that a man, most probably a farmer, dissatisfied with the modernity originating in the city, was actively searching for the "truly modern" woman in the midst of the Japanese countryside. He thus equates "modernity" with urban women and "true modernity" with rural women. He affirms the latter but denies the former. He concludes his letter, "If I were to be called a Modern Boy, I would like to be called a 'truly modern' boy (*makoto no modan booi*)."[19]

"TRUE MODERNITY," "TRUE CULTURE," AND GENDER IN THE NAGANO COUNTRYSIDE

How and what, then, did these middling farmers write about gender? This question entails another, regarding the kind of power they conferred upon rural women. I note that they almost always wrote about this topic in its relation to "modernity" or, more specifically, "true modernity,"[20] or to "culture" or, more specifically, "true culture" (*makoto no bunka*). Some scholars observe in the Taishō period what they do not observe in the previous Meiji period, namely, the emergence of the notion of "culture" (Minami 1965; Harootunian 1974a, 1974b; Roden 1990).[21] Thus, historian Minami Hiroshi even argues that the Japanese term for culture, "*bunka*," is itself a product of the Taishō period (1965).[22] These scholars, however, make their argument largely referring to the city. Since the writers of the village newspapers refer to "true culture" as something superior to (urban) culture, I must first discuss the connotations of the term "culture" as it is discussed by these scholars.

I have already introduced Roden, who characterizes Meiji Japan along with Victorian England, postbellum America, and Wilhelmian Germany as civilizations of character (1990). "Civilization" refers to a "basically material realm that embraced the institutions of state and technology of the machine age" (p. 40). Meiji Japan, however, built civilization by sacrificing the "cultural life" (*bunka seikatsu*) of each individual man and woman. To the contrary, in the Taishō era the individual Japanese restored his or her cultural life, largely through the so-called cultural industries (*bunka sangyō*) evident in the new communication media represented by radios, photographs, phonographs, and so forth. "Culture," then, refers to a "basically spiritual realm that embraced literature and the arts." Culture springs from the inner spirit of every person and is "indistinguishable from personality or the qualities of being over doing, feeling over accomplishment, and madness over reason" (p. 40). Restated, one's "cultural life" springs not so much from one's character as from one's natural and often irrational personality. Thus, even the clear division of labor by gender became blurred in the Taishō period; there emerged masculine women, independent and self-confident, as well as feminine men, dependent, fragile, and indecisive.

The writers for the village newspapers, however, argued that the Japanese countryside had never observed the emergence of civilization. They claimed instead that civilization had always been the product of the city, but that it had infiltrated the countryside and eroded its economic foundations. One contributor writes in 1924 that farmers no longer drink clean water from the nearby brook but drink "soda" brought from the city, a sign of civilization's encroaching presence in the countryside.[23] Here, I must stress the effects on these middling farmers, of the Great Kanto Earthquake, which hit the Tokyo metropolitan area and killed more than a hundred thousand urban residents in 1923. It is not that these farmers embraced a rosy image of the city before 1923. Their attitudes toward the city and its civilization before 1923 can best be described as ambivalent. For example, a young male resident of Urazato contributed an article, titled "For My Friends," to his village newspaper in 1923, about six months before the Great Kanto Earthquake:

> These days, many village youths are talking about "the city." The term seems to carry a sweet charm. The shadow of smoke covering the sky, the clamoring sound of engines, the horde of urban laborers, the trains, and the busy tempo of life of the urbanites. How the atmosphere of the city has seized the hearts of the village youth! I think it is by all means possible that they, bored with the monotonous life of the countryside, will run for the city. The city is stimulating like strong wine![24]

The author, though ultimately criticizing those who leave for the city, here attempts to understand the urban charm captivating the minds of many local youths.

Another contributor, also writing before the Great Kanto Earthquake, proclaims: "We should not prevent the local youth from leaving for the city as long as they do so with firm decisions in accordance with their own ideal future visions. Nor can we stop impoverished tenant farmers from leaving for the city as long as they aim to improve their economic lot."[25] What mattered to these writers was their perceived reality in which the "countryside was left alone with

its twelfth- or thirteenth-century customs while the city was monop-
olizing the civilization of the new age."[26] At least before 1923, these
writers' attitudes toward urban civilization was ambivalent, displaying both criticism and envy.

I further note in these articles published before the earthquake a
silence on the problem of rural women leaving for the city. Although
many village newspapers offer statistical data on the numbers of
local men residing outside their natal villages, they are conspicuous-
ly silent on the same data for women. However, the majority of
Modern Girls, whose glittering urban consumer image masked their
true identities as female wage workers, moved from the countryside
to the city in order to assist their families back home (Silverberg
1991; see also Ōshima 1982).[27] For example, in 1917, 176 men and
160 women left Motohara. In 1921, 104 men and 188 women left.[28]
These figures do not tell us the migrants' destinations and may
include women who moved to other villages upon marrying.
However, the number of women who moved to Motohara in 1921
was only sixty-six. Thus, the figures of 160 and 188 women who left
the village in 1917 and 1921 do at least indicate that a significant
number of women migrated to the city every year. Indeed, even a year
after the Great Kanto Earthquake, 206 men and 232 women left
Motohara.[29] Much later, around 1929 and 1930, the rate of migration
from this village to the city began to decrease, not because of the
earthquake but primarily because of the "poverty that had spread by
then into the city itself" (Kanō 1973, 105). One must wait, however,
until the postearthquake period to read the criticism leveled against
the exodus of rural women to the city.

After the Great Kanto Earthquake, culture is mentioned in a
variety of articles published in the village newspapers. Such culture
should be simultaneously "rural" (*nōson bunka*), "regional" (*chihō
bunka*), "true" or "genuine" (*makoto no bunka*), and "modern"
(*kindaiteki bunka*). Such culture could be constructed only in the
countryside by the rural population. This "rural" and "true" culture, then, differs markedly from the "urban" culture of the same
period, which was "indistinguishable from personality" (Roden 1990,
40). Although I find certain commonalties between "rural/true" culture and Meiji urban civilization, the writers for the village newspapers present their culture as the complete antithesis of urban and
material-based civilization. When urban "culture" is mentioned in
the village newspapers, it is specifically marked as "so-called" (*iwayu-
ru*) or "mundane" (*futsū no*) culture.[30] The local youth group of the

village of Urazato, for example, invited a speaker in 1924. Called a
"critic of civilization" (*bunmei hihyōka*), he apparently gave a public
speech on the decline of Roman civilization and the turmoil (in the
First World War) of Western civilization.[31] Of course, the rural
youth knew that they could construct culture only when they could
improve the rural economy. Hence, in the village newspapers, the
three terms "*nōson shinkō*" (the improvement of the rural economy),
"*nōson kaizō*" (the reconstruction of the rural life), and "*nōson bunka*"
(rural culture) almost always appear together. And the middling
farmers always presented their views on gender in relation to these
three notions.

In the following passages from two village newspaper articles on
gender relationships, although the editors seem to parley two very
different messages about gender, they in fact present a very similar
view.

> Until today, Japanese society has always been a male-centered soci-
> ety (*danshi no shakai*). It was Japanese men's will and knowledge that
> created every institution and system of this society and it was their
> power that improved them. Rural Japan in particular has so far been
> a patriarchal world, where there has been no opportunity for
> women to use their will and knowledge. Now that Japanese are suf-
> focated in this male-oriented society, I must ask the following
> questions. Does this signify the limit of men's knowledge and
> power? Does the present ruination of the countryside mean the
> exhaustion of rural men's knowledge and power? If so, we desper-
> ately need the great power of rural women, which has long been
> forgotten, for the development of our society and the reconstruc-
> tion of rural Japan. . . . Indeed, the recent activities of the Urazato
> women's association surprise us all. They have had a series of class-
> es in order to improve home economy (*kasei*) and female morality
> (*futoku*). They have already had ten classes about dyeing and weav-
> ing. When we reflect upon this awakening consciousness of rural
> women, we envisage the bright future of this village. Recently, the
> village government appointed the leaders of women's associations
> to be the leaders of the "movement for improving the quality of
> everyday life" (*seikatsu kaizen undō*). These women will thus make
> efforts for the self-government of our village along with men. At
> the meetings, they have already presented very logical opinions
> about which we men have hardly thought. While the ruination of
> the countryside has been loudly discussed throughout Japan, the
> awakening consciousness of these women gives us hope. Today,
> when the civilization supported by men does not have a way out,

these rural women suggest a future path for us to take to improve our society.[32]

Men and women are and should be inherently different. Modern civilization, however, is about to lose sight of this important difference. Essentially speaking (*honshitsu-teki ni*), women do not need suffrage. We must regard it simply as a means to rescue women from their present misery. . . . As long as modern civilization progresses, we, men and women, will never be able to save the Japanese countryside. We can rescue the countryside in the "cultured society" (*bunka no shakai*), which can be constructed only after the fall of civilization.[33]

The author of the second quote endorses the innate difference between genders but claims that "modern civilization" is "about to lose sight of this important difference." He also argues that women's participation in politics will not save women. After men rescue women from their present misery, however, he seems to demand that women contribute to the construction of a "cultured society." The earlier quote sounds much more liberal, yet what the author observes in his village, far from the emergence of politically active women, is the emergence of women who still firmly know their own, gender-specific duties. This author too asks women to play a certain role in the self-government of the village. It seems to me that the key issue connecting these two quotes is the "movement for improving the quality of everyday life."

In *Urazato sonpō*, the term "*seikatsu kaizen*" appears for the first time in 1922,[34] although an article published in 1923 claims that the movement had already been discussed in Urazato in the late Tokugawa period.[35] From June of 1922, *Urazato sonpō* repeatedly published articles, slogans, and lists of what to do under this movement to remind the reader of the importance of *seikatsu kaizen*. Other village newspapers followed this trend. For example, *Tonoshiro* published in 1931 a "song of economic regeneration" composed specifically for its readers (Kanō 1973, 149–150). It is a counting song, like the one created for *komori* by school teachers (see Chapter 3).

*One, don't complain but work for "economic
　regeneration."
Two, economic depression does not heal by itself,
each one of us must make efforts to heal it.
Three, don't forget our own power,
we must have our own solidarity.*

Four, let's look at this world with candid mind,
there are people who not only earn but save.
Five, don't count on others,
each one of us has to do his or her own best.
Six, don't make any argument about our poverty,
let's just work hard.
Seven, self-sufficiency is the most important in
    anything we do.
Eight, farmers are farmers,
let's live our lives as farmers.
Nine, don't despise minor works,
let's do piecework and side jobs (naishoku, fukugyō).
Ten, let's study and work hard to our own
    satisfaction.[36]

Motohara jihō published a list of tasks in 1925, which urged rural women to (1) use time in the most effective way; (2) curtail unnecessary costs in everyday life; (3) save money for the education of their children; (4) buy daily necessities with cash, not on credit; (5) use public markets; (6) use simple make-up; (7) wear simple clothes; (8) respect work, do side jobs (*fukugyō*), and utilize scraps (*haibutsu riyō*); (9) curtail unnecessary costs of weddings; (10) respect the Shinto-style wedding ceremony; and (11) reserve one day a month as a day of women's volunteer work.[37] In a methodical manner, the list exhorted all women to improve rural life.

To participate in this movement, men were supposed to refrain from drinking and smoking, practices that were thought to destroy the body, brain, and family life of each individual.[38] They were also discouraged from visiting pleasure quarters frequently.[39] But the same articles that indicate the negativity of these practices also indicate that they have been "public secrets" (*kōzen no himitsu*) and "practices that we have tolerated" and will tolerate (*ōme ni mitekita mono*). Thus, although both men and women were supposed to participate in this movement, women were asked to carry out the bulk of the tasks for *seikatsu kaizen*.[40]

Women who were seriously involved in the movement for *seikatsu kaizen* were described as opposite to, or rather as transcending, the urban Modern Girl. One author writes:

Why, Ms. N, do you have to transmogrify yourself with such heavy make-up every morning? . . . When you walk carrying a big bag on the glittering city streets at night, you really look like a monkey. . . .

> Ms. N, I secretly adored you when you were here [in this village] working so diligently picking mulberry leaves, wearing a white cotton apron. Don't you know that the sweat on your forehead sparkled in the sun? A woman's beauty shines only when she works in the countryside.[41]

For this author, only a woman who diligently works in the countryside can create true culture. Returning to the quote I cited earlier from the journal *Ie no hikari*, we could say that this author distinguishes the "so-called Modern Girl" from the "truly modern girl," the former the product of urban or "so-called" culture and the latter the product of rural and "true" culture.

In this respect, it is interesting to note the following poem sent to *Ie no hikari* by an apparently female reader.

> A doll is striding on the street,
> swinging her hip,
> showing her naked arms and chest,
> and carrying an umbrella thicker than her neck.
> She has fat legs and big feet.
> Showing her teeth and giving an amorous glance,
> is she still a "good wife and wise mother"?
> Even when her child complains of a tummy ache,
> she laughs and says it's nothing.
> How detestable and ugly she is![42]

The "so-called Modern Girl" is transformed into an ugly, fat woman in this poem; she is also antimotherhood and cannot act as a "good wife and wise mother."

Ms. N and the "doll" in the above poem may have physically moved to the city and become the Modern Girl. But the Modern Girl seems also to have been present in the countryside, owing to the urbanization of rural areas. Thus, one author describes "contemporary rural women" as "snakes" and argues that "they are not true women. Their bodies may be those of women, but their souls are certainly not." This transformation precludes the possibility of "true love" (*makoto no ren'ai*) in the countryside.[43] Another writes disapprovingly about village girls who use parasols to protect their skin from the sunlight and leave the elderly to take care of farming.[44] Another writer laments the recent phenomenon in which rural women prefer men of blue-whitish skin color and slender arms; some women describe such men as "high collar" (*hai kara*), meaning "modern," but they are in fact half-sick men (*hanbyōnin*).[45] As for the activities of the village women's associations, one author disapproves of them when the members invite a woman suffragist but approves when they hold meetings for *seikatsu kaizen*.[46]

The "truly modern" woman is not the "traditional" woman of the feudal period. She could "wear pretty clothes and put on make-up if not excessively heavy." In fact, if she does not, she is "accepting the stereotypical idea of the farmer being stupid."[47] She should not be the kind of woman who "won't read books once she is married and won't search for beauty and truth." The "traditional" woman is surrounded by a "traditional" husband and parents-in-law who, even if she tries to search for beauty and truth, will suppress her desire. Such a woman "won't bring a spring breeze to her family."[48] A "truly modern" woman "dances to the tunes of Western music" yet "takes care of her family, believes in Shintoism, worships her ancestors, and won't ask for money for this or that gadget."[49] The "truly modern" woman is also "scientific"; she accepts the principles of "eugenics" when choosing her marriage partner,[50] and she appreciates lectures on "hygiene, food and nutrition, and scientific child-rearing practices."[51] Furthermore, the "truly modern" woman does not stay at home like urban upper- and middle-class women. The beauty of the "truly modern" woman originates from physical work in the healthy, wholesome environment of the countryside. The "truly modern" woman thus needs "day-care facilities." A village assemblyman in Urazato argued in 1925 that there were 686 babies and toddlers in his village and that the village would be deprived of the labor of their mothers and siblings because of the lack of day-care facilities. He therefore contended that day-care facilities would make it possible for "truly modern" women to work and produce more.[52]

In the discursive space of the village newspapers, then, the figure of a "truly modern" woman in the "truly cultural" countryside finally emerges, capturing the sense of modernity of the middling and educated farmers who wrote to these papers. Their sense of modernity certainly competed with urban modernity. It even transcended urban modernity, which these middling farmers regarded as the product of material civilization. These men then invited rural women to work along with them in order to realize the self-government of the village and to construct what they considered a truly rural culture.

Still, these middling farmers clearly preserved their patriarchal power over rural women. Acknowledging the "essential" difference between men and women, they rejected the possibility for rural women to participate in politics. They asked instead that women shoulder the major responsibility for the *seikatsu kaizen* movement. Without questioning the nature of rural women's labor, the middling farmers in the vicinity of Ueda asked women to produce and save more and to improve the rural economy. Of course, women may have accepted, perhaps selectively, the modern elements discussed in the village newspapers. They must have welcomed village day-care facilities to the extent that those facilities eased their labor (see Chapter 7). But we also must note that the village assemblyman of Urazato regarded the day-care facilities as a means to increase the productivity of women and even children (the toddlers' siblings). As the village newspapers rarely contain the voices of rural women, I must conclude that "true modernity" is strictly a male and a patriarchal version of modernity.

Furthermore, rural modernity did not resist the state's power. *Seikatsu kaizen* was a product of "centrifugal" and "centripetal" forces within the village: while the local youth group promoted it for the goal of self-government, the state also actively promoted it from the beginning of the twentieth century under various slogans, such as "*chihō kairyō undo*," "*seikatsu kaizen undo*," "*keizai kōsei*" (economic regeneration), and "*jiriki kōsei*" (self-regeneration). By appealing to the "traditional" sense of frugality and diligence among the rural population, especially among women, the state aimed at improving the rural economy, while being dependent on it for tax revenues and human resources. This "traditional" sense of frugality and diligence became integral to the sense of modernity among the middling farmers, which they then inscribed onto rural women.

The nature of agrarianism in prewar Japan is still a focus of scholarly debate.[53] Most recently, Vlastos has argued: "The notion that farming alone reproduces essential national culture appeared comparatively late, at the end of the nineteenth century. It is, in other words, a case of modern invented tradition" (1994, 2).[54] Furthermore, Vlastos argues, agrarianism is a "double-voiced discourse: contained within the furious, apocalyptic polemic was a healing vision of reconstituted harmony and social cohesion" (p. 3). For example, a farmer named Kitagawa Tarokichi argues in *Kangawa jihō* in 1927 that farmers should construct a "classless society" (*mukaikyū no shakai*):

Those of you who work like horses under the golden civilization of the city, you were once our brothers who lived in this countryside but moved to the city, weren't you? Please return to our village as soon as possible. After you return, let's build our community together and work for ourselves. We do not hate capitalists, but we do hate capitalism. We do not admire such cultures as the Russian one that were created by the proletarian dictatorship. We want a classless society in which everybody works in return for not money but life!"[55]

Kitagawa's discourse indeed contains the "furious, apocalyptic polemic" and a "healing vision of reconstituted harmony and social cohesion." His discourse is neither left nor right, Marxist nor fascist.

Yet, he speaks only to "brothers." With respect to gender, "the philosophical foundations of populist agrarianism were social conservative" (Vlastos 1994, 25). The Nagano middling farmers did confer power upon rural women, but this power was merely the reflection of these middling farmers' patriarchal vision of their relationship to their fellow women. In this respect, I see a clear parallel between Yanagita and these farmers: Yanagita asked rural women to remember the past and bequeath its "tradition" through storytelling to the next generation; the Nagano middling farmers asked their fellow women to produce and save more, that is, to improve but not change the status quo. If Yanagita was a cultural patriarch, I would describe the Nagano middling farmers as economic patriarchs.[56] Their "true modernity" parallels Yanagita's "tradition."

To further stress the conservative nature of agrarianism with respect to gender, I will cite the works of several nationally recognized ideologues of agrarianism. For example, Yamazaki Nobukichi argues in *Ie no hikari* that the four most important tasks to be fulfilled in any human society are the administration of the citizens' morality (*shūshin*), households (*saika*), the nation (*chikoku*), and world peace (*hei-tenka*) (1925, 16). And he argues that school teachers (to control the people's morality), politicians (to govern the nation), and diplomats (to attain world peace) should fulfill three of these four important tasks, but that each individual citizen must administer his or her own household. According to Yamazaki, it is in this domain that a woman's role as a wife and a mother is crucial. He then classifies Japanese wives, as if grading sumo wrestlers, into "good" and "bad" ones.[57] The right side of his chart is for "good" wives, the best of whom is the wife who "accepts every suggestion of her husband." The second best is the chaste and virtuous wife. The third is the wife who teaches proper manners to her children. The fourth helps out the household business; the fifth always cleans up the house; the sixth does not care about how she looks, and so forth. Yamazaki actually expects every woman to be a combination of all these qualities. The left side of the chart is for "bad" wives; the worst is a "deeply jealous" wife, followed by the wife who sews incompetently and the wife who does not clean up the breakfast table until noon. The fourth does not change filthy pillow cases; the fifth wants to buy fashionable kimono, and so on. The leftmost part of the chart is a column reserved for the "supreme champion" of a bad wife: the wife who is disturbed by this very classification chart (quoted in Adachi 1960, 66). Who classified rural women in Japan into such a hierarchy? Yamazaki, who exercised his enormous patriarchal power over them.

Tokutomi Ichirō (Sohō) conflated an ideal image of the "best wife/woman," as depicted by Yamazaki, from his own mother, who was a farming woman (1932). For him, his mother represented Japan itself; rural women like his mother would save Japan. Here, we can overlap the image of his mother with that of numerous rural women who daily participated in the movement for *seikatsu kaizen* to save Japan. Tokutomi, then, is not only an agrarianist but a nationalist. Vicente Rafael argues that the relationship between nationalists/patriots and the nation as the mother is at best ambivalent (1990). Focusing on José Rizal (1861–1896), a Filipino nationalist under Spanish rule, Rafael traverses the process in which the relationship between Rizal and the Philippines shifted not only to that between a lover and his woman but one between a father and the female other under his patriarchal authority. Likewise, when Tokutomi depicts his mother, and by extension Japan, he does so not as her son but as a patriarchal figure over his female other.

In concluding this chapter, let me examine briefly the history of Western modernism. David Harvey interprets the mid–nineteenth century as a watershed, when the optimism brought by the notion of universal rationality was shaken. This transition was largeley triggered by new technologies that greatly affected Europeans' sense of space and time. The construction of railroads; the invention of the radio, the telegraph, the bicycle, the automobile, the airplane, cinema, and photography; the technical and organizational innovations in production; the emergence of corporate management; and the massive investment in colonialism all radically transformed Europeans' sense of space. Harvey states: "En route, the world's spaces were deterritorialized, stripped of their preceding significations, and then reterritorialized according to the convenience of colonial and imperial administration" (1989, 264).

What interests Harvey, however, are the counter forces sweeping through Europe against the expansion and therefore the growing abstraction of the space. Following Heidegger, scholars of Western modernism express this dialectic in terms of the tension between Becoming and Being. Being always has its inherent power to make it emerge (Heidegger 1959, 102). Being is permanent, always identical, and already there (p. 202). However, Heidegger argues, Becoming is by no means unimportant: it represents power that may dominate and bewitch Being (p. 203). Scholars of modernism express this same dialectic in terms of the tension between universalism, internationalism, or imperialism, on the one hand, and particularlism, nationalism, or exceptionalism, on the other (see, for example, Kern 1983; Schorske 1981); or, as Harvey does, in terms of the tension between space and place. The search for a place, then, signifies a return to Being, the original or the authentic location, the location from which the conquest of space—Becoming—began. Hence, one common explanation given to Nazism's rise in Germany is the Nazis' wish for the Aryan race to search and claim its own place, depicted predominantly as rural. When the countryside became "subsidiary, and knew that it was subsidiary" in mid-nineteenth-century Europe (Williams 1973, 243), it began to carry the potential of becoming a metonym for the entire nation-state.

The sense of rural modernity shared among the middling farmers in Nagano carried with it the potential to become "Japanese" modernity, as they imagined the countryside to be the origin of the authentic Japan. However, their sense of modernity was a male and patriarchal one in which rural women were asked to labor to fulfill patriarchal goals in order to create a true rural culture. In such a culture, rural women were asked not to participate in politics but to play a very specific role to "improve the quality of everyday life." Meanwhile, Japan began an active imperial expansion in the 1930s. Harvey argues, quite correctly, that modernity carries with it the potential for "creative destruction and destructive creation" (1989, 17). Rural modernity in Japan was created by farmers who sought to destroy urban modernity in order to realize a profarming nation-state. When the state actively began to coopt this rural modernity into a greater Japanese modernity to fulfill imperial desires, these farmers increasingly left for the battlefields of Asia. In the end, they could not fulfill their patriarchal wish but left women in the countryside to meet the ever-increasing demand of the state to produce both material and human resources. How, then, did women interpret their fellow farmers' sense of modernity?

Chapter 7

The Wartime Period

In the previous two chapters, I argued that students of Japanese native ethnology as well as Nagano middling farmers tried to imagine a national community by identifying agrarian life as a "principle of social cohesion." In order to do so, they relied heavily on the discursive category of "rural women." However, they spoke for rural women without allowing them to speak themselves. My goal in this chapter is to elucidate rural women's voices from the past and in their memories. Before attempting to do so, I will ask the following question: Was the Japanese countryside in the early twentieth century "authentically Japanese," "traditional," "truly modern," or "truly cultural," as Japanese folklore scholars and Nagano middling farmers claimed it to be?

MODERNITY AND RURAL WOMEN, 1925–1945

In both the history and the anthropology of Japan, the countryside is almost always regarded as "traditional," irrespective of the historical context. Indeed, the association of the countryside with the "traditional" seems to be almost universal. Here, I will focus only on the Japanese countryside in the 1920s through 1940s. Historian Katō Shūichi argues that the rural Japanese in the 1920s were quite alien to urban modernity, which he characterizes by the spread of mass media and mass education and the potential for mass participation in politics. Instead, Katō argues, the rural Japanese cherished the traditional values of loyalty and the obedience of lower to higher. The rural Japanese thus developed an inferiority complex vis-à-vis urban elites. The only place they were fit to try their luck was in the imperial army. The complex of the rural Japanese was "finally to find its outlet in ugly uniforms and hysterical outbursts of anti-intellectualism" (1974, 229). Yamamoto Akira goes a bit further and argues that "modernism," which developed in the city after World War I, did not reach the countryside at all (1976, 328; see also Maruyama 1969). Unlike Yanagita and the Nagano middling farmers, these scholars do not praise but castigate the countryside and its culture.

However, Wigen presents a rather different picture of the Japanese countryside in the 1920s. She says of Shimoina county in southern Nagano, "Fueled by strong markets for timber and silk, the county's population had grown nearly 30% since the turn of the century, and the net value of local goods and services had grown even faster; most residents now had access to schools, banks, electricity, and improved roads or cableways" (1995, 222). If "schools, banks, electricity, and improved roads or cableways" are the signs of modernity, Shimoina certainly became modern by the 1920s. And by this process of modernization Shimoina was increasingly incorporated into the centralized state and global market. Shimoina was designated as a meaningful unit in the new administrative hierarchy in the early Meiji period; it was also granted electoral representation in Nagano prefecture; since then, Shimoina county's citizens secured development funds from prefectural and national coffers, while the government raised the land tax to finance the nation's industrialization and imperial expansion. Clearly, there were significant regional differences in rural Japan. Generally speaking, the southwestern part of Japan became more modernized than the northeastern part. It is misleading simply to say the Japanese countryside in the 1920s was "traditional."

The everyday life of rural women was also "modernized" by this time, as shown in the women's magazines that reached the countryside. *Ie no hikari* was a magazine for the entire family. Here, let me focus only on those volumes published in the prewar period. In a single volume, one found sections for male members of the family (mainly concerning national politics and economy as well as agricultural technology and know-how), female members, and children.[1] However, the editors of *Ie no hikari* seem to have accepted the idea that the family was primarily a female domain: the section for women was proportionally larger than the other sections. The section for women consisted of two parts. A few articles and lectures contributed by national ideologues of agrarianism were normally placed in the beginning of the magazine (the article by Yamazaki Nobukichi that I cited in Chapter 6 is in this part). A variety of articles on topics such as "how to knit warm and soft underwear," "a week's menu during the busy farming season," "how to make restaurant dishes at home," "proper exercises during pregnancy," "a caution for mothers with toddlers," and "how to make home herbal medicines" followed toward the end of the magazine.

In her critical reading of *Ie no hikari*, Itagaki Kuniko divides the prewar years of the magazine's publication into three different periods (Itagaki 1978, 1992). The first, between 1925 and 1929, is the period in which rural women were reminded of the importance of their position in the "movement to improve the quality of everyday life." Various articles published in this period also talk about the ruination of the Japanese rural economy. These articles, however, do not explore the cause of rural poverty. Instead, they simply focus on its consequence, the low standard of living in the countryside. Thus, the articles exhort rural women to improve their daily living conditions without offering much practical advice. Instead, the figure of an ideal rural woman is presented: a Danish rural woman who speaks various foreign languages, plays piano, and talks about politics, yet tends cows and horses, and works in the fields during the day (Itagaki 1978, 314).

In the second period (1930–1937), *Ie no hikari* articles do offer rural women more detailed and concrete information about how to improve the quality of everyday life. In addition, we can directly hear the voices of rural women as they tried to implement such information in their own lives. They also share their thoughts about marriage. A journalist from the *Ie no hikari* editorial office interviewed nine rural women in Wakayama prefecture in the early 1930s.[2] What follows are some of their words.

Woman 1: I do not think it is right that parents decide the partner of their daughter without even consulting her.

Woman 2: We should stop competing among ourselves for the most extravagant wedding ceremony.

Woman 3: I do not like those go-betweens who lie a lot simply because they would like to succeed in making matches.

Woman 1: I would like to know more about the personality of my future husband.

Woman 2: I would like to know more about his health.

Woman 3: I think it would be ideal if we could exchange medical records [in order to know whether he has a venereal disease].

Woman 2: But a doctor I know told me that medical records are utterly unreliable.

From the women's conversations, Itagaki also reveals their urgent wish to read newspapers, have "holidays," spend more time with their children, improve their relationships with their mothers-in-law, and so forth. Itagaki, however, points out that these rural women could improve the quality of their everyday life only in the context of a patriarchal family. Even though *Ie no hikari* introduced its female reader to a new style of work clothes, a wife normally did not have the economic power to buy the material. Or, even though *Ie no hikari* offered her a new dish to try, she could not do so, either because she was busy working in the fields or because her mother-in-law decided on the menu for dinner.

In the third period (1937–1945), Itagaki notes, *Ie no hikari* demanded that rural women improve the standard of living in the context not of a family but of a community. Various articles published in this period urged female readers to step outside their households, to contribute their labor to the state's war efforts. Furthermore, *Ie no hikari* asked rural women to work, sell, purchase, save, and take care of their children *communally*, all in hopes of raising rural women's productivity. The problem *Ie no hikari* discussed in the first period, the ruination of the countryside, was not resolved. Yet *Ie no hikari* asked rural women to increase their productivity so Japan could win the war.

Finally, Itagaki argues that rural women developed, throughout these three periods, their own sense of modernity, which she calls *nōson-teki modanizumu* or "rural modernism." "Rural modernism" is "communal" (*kyōdōshugi-teki*) aiming at "self-sufficiency" (*jikyūjisoku-teki*) (1992, 288). Even though "rural modernism" was coopted by the state by the third period, we must distinguish "rural modernism" from "true modernism" advocated by Nagano middling farmers in village newspapers. While the former is quite practical, the latter is ideological. Itagaki's argument makes me wonder whether rural women in early-twentieth-century Japan were the embodiment of Japanese "tradition."

THE WARTIME PERIOD AND NAGANO RURAL WOMEN

At women's group meetings, members often lumped together the 1920s, 1930s, and 1940s as the "wartime period" (*senji-chū*). When I began participating in these meetings, I did not understand what "war" they were talking about. I had a knowledge of History, which I had learned at school while growing up in Japan, but I did not know these women's histories. When they spoke of the "wartime period," all I could think of was the chronology of events: a Manchurian incident of 1931, a China incident of 1937, the Japanese navy's attack on Pearl Harbor in 1941, and the end of World War II in 1945. The rural women in Nagano did not experience the wartime period as a succession of events, but as a drawn-out process. Their wartime period began earlier than 1931, with the years of economic depression, and it ended later than 1945, with the continuing lack of material resources in the countryside after 1945.[3]

Although I cannot tell how "accurate" their memories are, the rural women in Nagano still have very vivid memories of the wartime period. They are always eager, almost excited, to tell to each other how devastating their wartime experiences were. Their eagerness is expressed in the name of one women's group, Sensō Keiken o Tsutaeru Haha no Kai, the "Association of Mothers Who Impart Their Wartime Experiences to Subsequent Generations," a group of women who are specifically interested in narrating their memories of the wartime period. The rural women in Nagano talk about such devastating experiences today not only because they cannot forget them even if they want to, but because they do not want to repeat them. Their narratives often amount to "confessions" of very personal matters. I believe this is because, first, the burden of the past on each individual is so heavy that she is now willing to release it in company with other members of her group; second, she is also willing to construct a collective memory of the wartime period by sharing her private memories with others.

Throughout my fieldwork, I was struck by the women's use of the first-person plural whenever they talked about their wartime experiences. I first thought that "we" referred to the members of the group. But I gradually realized that "we" in fact referred to several generations of rural women who, as the major wartime work force, shared similar experiences of isolation in the village. Then, they were small girls, adolescent girls, or young housewives. Now, they live in an excessively affluent society. When they narrate their wartime experiences, either they are without an audience or they are the audience themselves. When I joined these groups, there were many times when they talked to me, explaining what had happened during the war, for they assumed my ignorance of their experiences. When my presence became familiar to them, they began to talk once again among themselves, which compelled me often to interrupt their discussion. But before attending to the contemporary Nagano women's memories, let me try to hear their mothers or their grandmothers, who might have left their voices in the very context of the wartime period.

Claudia Koonz, a historian who explored the question of how women in 1930s Germany brought Nazi beliefs home, argues:

> German women varied in both support and opposition, as victims and perpetrators. Even the blindest fanatics and crassest opportunists could on occasion protest a specific policy or take a great risk to protect a friend. The staunchest skeptics of Hitler's rule might comply with certain directives. Archives had (as they always had) broken up the monoliths with which I had begun my work. No one woman conformed to either the passive-docile or the heartless-brutish model. (1987, 12)

Koonz describes German women under Nazi rule as complicated human beings: they supported and opposed Hitler's rule both consciously and unconsciously. She thus rejects the notion of a "typical Nazi woman" (ibid.).

But Koonz asks the following question: "Where, I asked myself, did the spirit of resistance live if not among women? Somewhere within that society saturated with terror, someone must have preserved a humane tradition" (p. 16). Regarding the spirit of resistance, then, Koonz privileges women over men, not because of her inability to find it among men, but because of her near desperation that, if she cannot find it among women, she cannot possibly find it anywhere. It is not that Koonz essentializes the nature of "women" but that she is aware of the different manners of involvement in the war according to gender: "men and women remained separated by function, personality, and responsibilities" (p. 16). Unlike Nazi-occupied countries during World War II, Germany inspired little military resistance. Women simply used their age-old skills to "survive emotionally," and for these Nazi women, to "resist" meant first of all to survive emotionally. Like women in 1930s Germany, Nagano rural women in the 1930s and 1940s "varied in both support and opposition, as victims and perpetrators." But, like Koonz, I too would like to ask, "Where did the spirit of resistance live if not among rural women?" What follows are the voices of Nagano rural women that I searched for in newspaper articles, letters they wrote, and records of women's associations.

On the day of *Niiname-sai* (an imperial ritual in which the Japanese emperor shares with the spirits of his ancestors the rice harvested for the first time each year) in 1938, sixteen women's associations were chosen by the Nagano prefectural government as the "associations that had contributed the most to the construction of the 'new imperial village' (*kōkoku nōson*)."[4] "New imperial village" was a name bestowed on any village that was considered by the state to have a potential to serve as the foundation of the Japanese empire. After all, every village in Japan had to be and was a "new imperial village." This meritorious name suggests that the countryside became a part not only of the national polity but of the Japanese empire. One of these sixteen women's associations was in the village of Kawaji, where I joined the group the "Association of Mothers Who Impart Their Wartime Experiences to Subsequent Generations"; it was chosen because the members delivered promptly to the village authorities 10 percent more rope than they were expected to deliver, for they "communally worked, forgetting to sleep."[5] The leader of this association, a woman named Imai Ume, was reported to have said the following to a local newspaper reporter:

> Even when we confront the enormous amount of work, we can do it easily if we work together. If I work alone or with just one neighbor, I find it very difficult to accomplish anything. Working communally is really wonderful. Increases in agricultural production, in the quota of food to be delivered, and in our saving are the three goals we must attain. However hard these goals seem to be, we are determined to accomplish them by working together.[6]

Imai Ume tried to work communally to increase agricultural production and to save, to improve the quality not so much of her own life as of the life of everyone in her village, nation, and the Japanese empire.[7]

Rural women eagerly responded to the state's requests for not only "more production" but also "more babies," under the official slogan "propagate and multiply" (*umeyo fuyaseyo*). Here, we should note that certain nationalist discourses represented rural women as having better reproductive abilities than urban women, thereby providing Japan with the "finest military and labor forces."[8] For example, Kawakami Hajime, an ideologue of agrarianism who later gained scholarly fame as a Marxist, believed in the close relationship between the robustness of the female body and intimate human relationships in the countryside, on the one hand, and a sound national army, on the other (1977, chap. 2; see also Havens 1974, 117).[9] Kawakami believed that a woman living in the hygienic and wholesome environment of the countryside could bear more children than an urban woman. He also believed that, as rural women raised their sons in this wholesome environment, their sons would become stronger soldiers, creating a stronger army. Using statistical data from Japan and Europe, Kawakami demonstrated that the birth rate was significantly higher, while the infant mortality rate was significantly lower, in the countryside than in the city (1977, 114).[10]

The state acknowledged and praised those villages where a significant number of women gave birth to many children. When the policy of increasing the Japanese population to one hundred million by 1960 was implemented, a local journalist set out on an expedition to explore the "secrets of fecundity" in the villages of Nagano. He found a sound and wholesome environment, good food, long winters, abundant ultraviolet rays, early marriages, and frequent bathings, but the grim reality of a high infant mortality rate was deliberately underreported. He concluded his report by writing that "there was not even one 'degenerate' (*deki-soko-nai*) born so far, in this village where 'marriages among close kin' (*shinzoku kekkon*) were frequent."[11] Most of the women reported in his articles were married to eldest sons, the successors to the household heads, who were spared from military conscription until the final phase of the war. In other words, these women were most likely living in patriarchal stem-families. Even though the reporter did not mention their working conditions, we can imagine their hard labor in the fields and at home.

Furthermore, after 1939, mothers who had more than two sons killed in the war were annually recognized by the Japanese imperial household. These mothers were appropriately called "honorable mothers of the militarist state" (*gunkoku homare no haha*). Kamakura Toyo, in the village of Wada in Nagano, was one of the "honorable" mothers. According to a local newspaper article published in 1942, she raised five children all by herself after her husband died of illness in 1920. She then lost her three sons and one son-in-law in China. She is quoted as having told a reporter the following:

> As we were landless peasants, I went out to work as a day laborer carrying baggage of various sorts. In those days, an able man could earn 25 *sen* a day. A woman could get only 15 *sen* even if she carried eighteen *kan* of charcoal on a muddy steep mountain path. The most able woman could earn 20 *sen* a day at most, but as I had to

raise five children alone, I competed with men and always earned 25 *sen* a day. . . . Now that four of my children have dyed the soil of China red with their own blood, I feel most honorable as a mother of our imperial nation.[12]

How could she feel "honorable" for the loss of her children, whom she raised through such hardship? She might actually have thought otherwise, that is, she might have wanted to criticize the state that "killed" her three sons and one son-in-law. Newspaper articles during the wartime period could not have possibly have reported such other voices of Kamakura Toyo even if she had them. However, it is hard to believe that the reporter totally rewrote what she had said. She might have wanted recognition for her services not only to her own family but to the nation as she conformed to the state's expectations of rural women as national subjects. Speculation aside, I find in her narrative precisely what Yanagita called the "power of women." It is the power Kamakura Toyo exercised to raise her family after her husband had died. It is also the power she exercised to contribute to the nation. Yanagita would have been delighted in listening to her voice. He would not have speculated, as I did, on the other voices of Kamakura Toyo.

Perhaps more praised than the "honorable mothers of the militarist state" were those women who left for Manchuria, the northeast region of China. In the early 1930s, when anti-imperialist and nationalist movements were raging in China and the Western imperial powers were withdrawing from China, Japan sought more direct political control of that country. In 1931, a group in the Japanese imperial army blew up a stretch of the Manchurian railway and accused the Chinese of the crime. Immediately after the incident, the army took South Manchuria and, after having seized the entire region in 1932, established Manchukuo, the "Nation of Manchuria."[13] Japan cut off Chinese migration to Manchuria and encouraged Japanese settlement. The goals of the settlement were, first, to increase overall agricultural output in the empire and, second, to solve the problem of land scarcity and overpopulation in the Japanese countryside.[14]

Between 1932 and 1945, Nagano prefecture sent the largest number of peasant settlers to Manchuria.[15] The reason may be twofold. First, poverty prevailed in the sericulture zones in Japan, including Nagano, by the late 1920s. The second reason is the representation in the state's discourse of Manchuria as a "dreamland," to which rural men and women were constantly exposed: "Please, everyone, for the sake of the future happiness of your family and for the sake of the future of your own children, think about farming in Manchuria as a way of life that will always reward you for your hard labor."[16] Responding to such a call, Nagano rural men and women left, dreaming of a new life in a foreign land. There is a clear contradiction between the above quotation and the discourses I have presented in Chapters 5 and 6. The Japanese countryside appears as a hopeless place here, while Yanagita and the Nagano middling farmers presented it as the most cultured. Yanagita solved such a contradiction by interpreting the Japanese migration as an extension of the *jōmin* world (see p. 136). Such a solution, however, remained partial, as the migration did not solve the problem of the ruination of the Japanese countryside.

The women who migrated to Manchuria were mostly the brides of Japanese peasant settlers, called, rather romantically, "brides on the continent" (*tairiku no hanayome*). Prior to her departure, Yokozeki Mitsue, for example, attended a training center founded by the state that aimed at making trainees into "superior" national subjects. She recalls a line of the song she and other trainees—all women—sang every morning: "Let us die at the feet of the emperor, for we shall never regret such deaths" (Yokozeki 1990, 65). The "feet of the emperor" is a metaphor for Manchuria, a place far from where the emperor lives. The state then married off these women to peasant settlers whom they had never met.

Another woman, Sumiko, moved to Manchuria with her mother to join her brother. Once she was in Manchuria, the head of her brother's settlement arranged a marriage for her. Another woman sent a letter to the editor of her village newspaper, a passage of which reads: "Together with friends, I arrived here this spring, but we do not miss Japan at all. The weather is very comfortable; there is not even a single mosquito in summer. We can grow any crop and the food is of superb quality. You must send more and more 'brides of the continent' to Manchuria."[17] These women were clearly national subjects, willing to contribute not only their labor but themselves for the expansion of Japanese empire.[18]

Let me return from Manchuria to Japan proper. My neighbor Noriko, who was born in 1918, volunteered to work at the Mitsubishi Munitions Factory, near Nagoya. She said she often walked between her dormitory and the factory building with a futon mattress over her head or around her body for fear of being bombed. "The warning siren for air raids no longer worked toward the end of the war," said

Noriko. She daily saw heaps of corpses, but "did not have the slightest thought of criticizing the army, the state, or, much less, the emperor."

These munitions factories were located in the city, along the shores of the Pacific Ocean. In the final years of the war, the state relocated young women from the countryside to the city as "volunteer workers." This action of the state surely contradicted the discourse of Japanese native ethnology, which depicted only farming women as "authentic" national subjects. This contradiction was hardly resolved by statements like the following from the then prime minister and military commander Tōjō Hideki. A Diet man in 1943 asked, "Are not the villages of Imperial Japan being endangered by the absorption of their labor power in the armament industries?" Tōjō answered:

> This is a point that truly worries me. On the one hand, I want at all costs to maintain the population of the villages at forty percent of the total population. I believe that the foundation of Japan lies in giving importance to agriculture. On the other hand, it is undeniable that [armament] industry is being expanded, chiefly because of the war. It is extremely hard to reconcile these two factors. However difficult it may be, I am determined to maintain the population of the villages at forty percent. But production must be increased. A harmony must be created by degrees between the two requirements. But, in creating this harmony, care must be taken to avoid making havoc of the Japanese family system.[19] (quoted in Halliday 1975, 138–139; his translation)

For Tōjō, as for Yanagita and ideologues of agrarianism, rural populations should epitomize authentic Japanese values. Hence "care must be taken" not to disrupt the ratio of the rural population to the urban population in Japan. Such care involved recruiting only "young unmarried women," not "mothers," as the major labor force in the city. Compared to Germany or the United States, the mobilization of married women, and even of unmarried women, in manufacturing industries in Japan was surely less significant.[20] Nevertheless, it is clear that Tōjō was caught between diametrically opposed demands of the Japanese empire: to recruit more women workers in the manufacturing industries in the city and to maintain the "Japanese family system" that he still identified with the rural way of life.

Rural women worked not only as volunteers at munitions factories but as store clerks, train station employees, or conductors in the city because, toward the end of the war, the state could no longer find an adequate number of men for these occupations. Whether we can call such a mobilization young unmarried women's "emancipation" is debatable. After all, they were forced to work in the absence of men. They were not paid properly or fed adequately. They were told to endure for the emperor and the men in combat. These women were asked to serve Japan in order to be "emancipated." Tōjō's ambivalence notwithstanding, I agree with Havens, who argues that "war was a time for rulers to reaffirm accepted symbols and conventions, not a time for redefining them" (1975, 933).

Several women in Nagano expressed their desire to leave for the battlefield. The following letter and an additional four letters were published by the educational affairs bureau of the Nagano prefectural government and the military headquarters of the Matsumoto regiment in 1932. Except for one, which was written by a married couple, they were written by young single women. They addressed their letters to the commander of the Matsumoto military regiment and were reported to have written them "with their own blood" (*kessho tangan*).

> I feel very sorry to hear of the horrible Manchurian Incident reported in the newspaper. I try to comfort my pounding heart and wait for the moment when women will be drafted for the war. According to yesterday's paper, it was bitterly cold in Manchuria and there were many dying soldiers. As a Japanese woman (*Nippon joshi*), I cannot ignore their fates. I would like to go there and serve our soldiers but do not know the way to do so. I thought it rather rude to address this letter directly to you, but I will ask you to make arrangements for me so that I can work in the land of Manchuria. (quoted in Morosawa 1969b, 274)

Can we identify this author with the Modern Girl, who acted more like a man in the 1920s urban scene? Perhaps, no. While the Modern Girl could be a revolutionary, this woman expresses her desire to serve the nation.

In Germany under Nazism, Mosse argues: "The exaggerated respect for masculinity not only forced women into passivity but also gave them bodies that should be sporting and earnest, tough and brave" (1985, 179–180). This is why, as in Japan of the same period, women became train station employees, conductors in the city, or tough workers in the armament industry. But, Mosse continues: "Here a so-called manly deportment was difficult to reconcile with the professed ideal of femininity. Yet, the division of labor had still to be kept intact" (p. 180). The author of the above letter might have been drafted as a nurse, but never as a soldier. The state was always careful when it had to alter the division of labor by gender.

Meanwhile, the mayor of Urazato created a variety of organizations for "self-regeneration" in his village. They were an association for young men (*seinen-kai*), an association for unmarried women (*shojo-kai*), an association for married men in the prime of manhood between the ages of twenty-six and forty (*sangyō kumiai seinen renmei*), and an association for married women (*shufu-kai*). By the 1940s, the first three associations had dissolved by themselves, and an increasing number of men headed for the battlefield. Young single women left for the city as volunteer workers. Meanwhile, the association for married women became an integral part of two nationwide women's patriotic organizations, which later merged into one. They sent off and welcomed soldiers and sailors, comforted wounded ones, and helped out families who lost their major source of labor to the front. They contributed money, rice, and, in the words of one Nagano woman, "even the metal handles of drawers of chests" to the Japanese military. They also bore "healthy" children, protected them from "dangerous thought," and raised them as strong soldiers (Nagano-ken-shi Kankō-kai 1987, 811–940).

Among all these voices of compliance of Nagano rural women, we can also hear the voice of the "spirit of resistance." For example, statistics published during the wartime period show that, among 6,386 female graduates of all the middle schools in Nagano prefecture in 1944, only 2,206 (34 percent) indicated their desire to work at munitions factories. The rest did not want to.[21] Furthermore, since women would be spared from working as volunteers if they were to marry, an increasing number of young women filed "false" matrimonies (Aoki 1987, 289). Among their teachers, some strongly but not openly criticized the patriotic spirit of their own students. Ikegami Aiko finally gave up her wish to work at an arsenal after her teacher repeatedly told her not to go. She later wrote that she could not appreciate her teacher's courage until the war ended (quoted in Aoki 1987, 290). My neighbor Noriko told me that her parents were "very angry when they discovered the school's decision to send her to the Mitsubishi Munitions Factory instead of letting her go home to help with farming" (the daughters of farming households were exempted from working in the city if they personally engaged in farming). When the air raids on the Mitsubishi Munitions Factory became intense, some of her school teachers ordered their students to go home, ignoring orders from state and factory authorities. In

1988, during my field research, Noriko and others who were once volunteer workers at Mitsubishi honored these teachers at their school reunion.

In the village of Suye, Wiswell reports the following scene of village women welcoming the soldiers' return in the late 1930s:

> After lunch the hamlet women gathered in several different houses to dress up. They wore school girls' skirts and middies, kimono turned inside out, soldiers' uniforms, firemen's uniforms, and all kinds of men's clothing—pants, coats and hats. . . . They generally acted in complete accordance with their presumed sex, making passes at all the girls and women. The girls squealed loudly and jumped off the road into the fields to avoid being pinched on the buttocks. One old lady got hold of a young woman, and later a man, and held them against the walls imitating the movements of intercourse. The crowd roared with laughter, while the poor victims ran away as fast as they could when released. (Smith and Wiswell 1982, 80)

Like the rural women in Nagano, the women in the village of Suye were organized into the national women's association and were supposed to show their patriotism. Welcoming the soldiers' return should have been a solemn occasion. But in Suye, it was a happy, noisy, merry-making occasion where women reversed the order of gender. Using symbolic expressions, these women seem to have demonstrated their resistance against the political order imposed on them (Nolte 1983). Yanagita would have been quite shocked at such a scene.

In 1942, the Ministry of Education issued *Senji katei kyōiku seido yōkō*, "Guidelines for Home Education during Wartime." These guidelines were popularly called "Ie no michi," the "Way of the Family" (Dower 1986, 280), and women, children, and the elderly who were left at home were supposed to follow them.[22] "Family life should be a life beyond the boundaries of a family, and the children of a family should not be the children of a particular family alone, but the heirs of this imperial nation (*kōkoku no kōkei*). Each family should raise its children as such" (quoted in Morosawa 1969a, 273). This passage shatters the analytic distinction anthropologists often make between the public and the private domains in order to understand the nature of family.[23] And yet, listening to the voices of Nagano rural women, I felt that between these women and the state there was something, a kind of "buffer zone," that the state could not possibly penetrate, even if it tried hard to do so.

REMEMBERING THE WARTIME PERIOD

I begin this section with the narrative of Eiko, who returned from the city of Osaka to her home village of Kawaji in 1940 with her husband. They returned to the countryside not because the city represented the vice of civilization but because they thought it would be much safer to live in the countryside. They had also predicted, in the very near future, a food shortage in the city. Eiko used "farming households" (*nōka*) and "nonfarming households" (*hi-nōka*) to distinguish the countryside and the city. *Hi-nōka*, however, does not always refer to the city. In this category, Eiko included the households of school teachers and policemen, who lived in the countryside but did not grow food. She commented: "I indeed felt sorry for people of nonfarming households. The rumor spread that they were eating anything, including grass growing by the roadside. Having heard those rumors, I truly felt thankful that I was born into a farming family."

At another group meeting, Tomiko also acknowledged the merits of living in the countryside. She was then in her teens and was "always hungry," but she always had something to eat "until the situation got really bad toward the end of the war." Tomiko admitted that she could not eat white rice in broad daylight, for "if the village headman caught sight of me eating it, he would have called me an 'unpatriotic citizen' (*hikoku-min*)"; rice was for soldiers and not for those on the home front. But Tomiko's family could hide white rice somewhere and eat it at night in the pitch darkness. The countryside was thus good, because there was food, while the city was bad because there was no food.

When a large number of urban residents began to evacuate to rural Nagano, material conditions in the village "got really bad." Toshiko, then a young bride marrying into a rather well-to-do landowning farmer's household, said at the group meeting:

> The village government official told us to accept several evacuees from the city. We told him we would accept two or three of them, as we then had a small detached house. But a family of seven came—the wife of Colonel Kawasaki and her six children, the oldest of whom was twenty years old, I believe. I was quite shocked when I saw them. They stayed with us until the fall of 1945. We also had our relative's grandmother and her friend [who had evacuated from the city] occupying one room of our house. . . . I really felt sorry for them. Even though we did not have much to eat, we shared all the vegetables from our garden with them. The detached

house had its own kitchen, but I ended up sharing our meals with them anyway. . . . Mrs. Kawasaki was very good at embroidering. She embroidered the sash of my daughter's kimono. So, there were some good things too.

Toshiko's family, I think, was rather exceptional. Most families in her village lacked resources even for themselves, especially in the final years of the war.

Mieko commented at the same meeting:

After my husband had gone [into the army], our first son was born. I heard the news of the end of the war while he was sucking my sweating breasts. I had not heard from my husband since his departure. And when we did not have much left to eat, my sister-in-law evacuated from Tokyo to stay with us with her children. In the fall, my brother-in-law came back from Manchuria. And then, another sister-in-law, who was widowed, came home with her children. Instead of war, we faced the threat of starvation.

She described herself as a "beast trying to protect its child" in the household she was married into; she was the only "alien" (*yoso mono*) in the household of her parents-in-law, which suddenly expanded because of the return of their three children. Mieko could not help but think that the "return of her husband might make conditions much worse."

The members of the "Association of Mothers Who Impart Their Wartime Experiences to Subsequent Generations" published a booklet in 1977 titled *Ishoku ni matsuwaru haha-tachi no sensō taiken* (The wartime experiences of our mothers: Concerning clothes and food). Most of the participants were adolescent girls in the 1930s and 1940s. Their memories, which are contained in this book, are mostly of their mothers, who tried to make their children's lives as comfortable as possible. They ate acacia, cicadas, locusts, dragonflies, grasses, tree roots, and "half a piece of one single fish rationed for all of us on the morning of the New Year" (Kawaji Fujin-kai 1977, 147). They carried school bags made of cardboard or bamboo sheath and wore sandals made of an old tire. Young mothers remembered making diapers out of a single worn-out kimono. An acute sense of material deprivation and their mothers' efforts to ameliorate it resonate in this book.

However little they had, some remember that they shared their resources with the soldiers stationed in their villages. Kimi said at a group meeting:

A group of soldiers arrived at our village's elementary school. When they had free time, they took walks in the village. One day when we were working in the fields, two soldiers came and asked us for a cup of tea. As my husband had been drafted, I felt sorry for them and invited them to our house. . . . Although we never ate white steamed rice, I cooked rice, which I had set aside, for them. The two soldiers told me again and again, "delicious, delicious," and thanked me deeply.

After this incident, the same soldiers began to visit Kimi more often. She always cooked something "special" for them, something she and her family did not eat. "But you did not have much to eat yourself," I offered. "No, and my father-in-law once criticized me, saying that I was too good-natured. But I felt I had to treat them this way, as they were fighting for us. Their wives must have been anxiously waiting for their return, as I was then waiting for my husband's return," said Kimi.

While listening to Kimi, I could not help but notice a nostalgic tone in her narrative: she affirms her relation with the soldiers as good and warm, hardly the kind of relationships one would experience today. Like Kimi, Eiko also reminisces:

We now have all the food and clothes we want. We drive to the big grocery store and buy a lot of food to keep it in the refrigerator for days and weeks. We see mountains of clothes piled up at the stores for "bargain sales," and the young people take this for granted. There are so many scenes in television programs in which the characters waste food, throwing it or stepping on it. My grandchildren laugh, watching such scenes. For us who cannot forget our wartime experiences, there is something wrong with all this.

Indeed, contemporary life in the Nagano countryside is rather like suburban life in the United States. Each family has at least one car; the grocery store is bigger than its counterpart in the city, with adequate space for parking; and a housewife goes less frequently to but buys more at the store than the urban housewife. Eiko does not drive; her daughter-in-law drives her to the grocery store, where she says she is always overwhelmed by the excess of goods. Her past experiences seem to have provided Eiko with a yardstick to measure the conditions of the present.

Another member contrasted "commercialized," "expensive," and "glittering" contemporary wedding ceremonies and receptions with her "plain" one.

The village government gave each adult resident tickets worth one hundred points to buy clothes. We paid, for example, ten points for a wash towel, fifty points for a summer cotton kimono, and so forth. A would-be bride could carry an extra seven hundred points. But I used them all to buy fabric to make bedding. My relatives shared their tickets with me, and I could finally manage to buy two kimono to prepare my trousseau. Young people today do not understand what we did. They simply laugh, listening to our stories.

These are the memories of those who survived the difficult wartime period and are no longer under the patriarchal power of their parents-in-law. However, being nostalgic about the past is not the same as wishing to repeat past experiences. They are quite different. As I will argue in the next chapter, the contemporary discourse of Japanese nationalism confuses them, almost to the point of affirming rural women's experiences in the wartime period.

The postwar voices of the rural women in Nagano are also the voices of guilt. In speaking and writing about their memories, they often juxtapose two separate time frames. What they thought and what they think are often totally incongruous, and the incongruity poses a serious problem for these women to face and, if possible, to resolve. Arai Takako, who, as a young unmarried student, applied for the position of volunteer worker at the munitions factory, wrote:

My father was too old to be conscripted and my brother was only an elementary school student. There was no one in my immediate family who could serve our nation (*o-kuni no tame ni*). When my teacher asked the class whether we would want to work at the Toyokawa Naval Arsenal, I immediately raised my hand, even before consulting my parents. . . . Only after we had lost the war did I realize for the first time in my life how enormous and horrible the power of education was. It made me totally blind to the reality of life. I do not know why I thought it was important to work at the arsenal. (quoted in Aoki 1987, 291)

In this quote, Takako juxtaposes her wartime and postwartime thoughts. They are incongruous, and she does not know how to reconcile them, except by blaming the "power of education" and expressing her sense of guilt. Takako was one of the few survivors when "2,445 persons, all but 130 of them civilians," were killed in the air raid of the arsenal in 1945 (Havens 1975, 325). She thus feels guilty not only for what she did, but for her friends and coworkers who became victims.

Miharu told the group members the following:

> We were totally mobilized for the purpose of winning the war. We sang such songs as "To realize the peace of East Asia, why should we value our lives?" or "Long live our majesty the emperor, how can we forget the echo of this phrase?" . . . I did not come to myself until the day of destiny. For whom and for what did we lose our families? For whom and for what were our houses burnt down?

"The day of destiny" is August 15, 1945, when the war ended. Her narrative is again a narrative of guilt, remorse, and determination never to repeat the same mistake of believing in the dictates of the state.

According to Theodor Adorno, discussions punctuated with talk of a guilt complex are not to be trusted. He argues that guilt feelings are pathological, inadequate to reality, and that guilt is really no guilt at all, but a device to render a real and terrible past harmless and to transform it into a mere figment of the imagination of those who are affected by it (1986, 117). Is the talk of a guilt complex among these rural women also really no guilt at all? Do they talk of a guilt complex without feeling responsible for what they did? I will return to these questions later.

Some of their narratives suggest that the rural women in Nagano did not share the perception of the "glory" of the Japanese empire. Remembering her hard labor during the wartime period, Fumi said: "I had to work like a madwoman, and yet we did not have enough to eat. No one had enough in those days! I wondered whether Japan was really going to win the war." Fumi had to work like a madwoman because, except for her aging mother-in-law, there was no one else in her family who could farm. She also had to fulfill her obligation of increasing quotas on farm produce deliveries. Another group member, Kiwa, said: "We were told it was honorable to die and it was shameful to show tears. But even though I tried very hard not to cry [when I was notified of the death of my husband], tears poured down and down my cheeks." During the wartime period, Kiwa said, there were many moments when she felt herself to be a truly patriotic citizen. However, on learning of her husband's death, they quickly disappeared.

At another women's group meeting, we intently listened to the story of Yoriko. Yoriko's wedding was quickly arranged just weeks before the departure of her groom to the front. He was a total stranger to her. Two weeks after the wedding, he left. A life with his family—his parents, sisters, and brothers—began. For Yoriko, they were all strangers. She told us how much she missed her own family: "I wanted to go home. All day long, every day, I thought only of that." The members all nodded in sympathy with Yoriko and said that, in those days, families who had sons were eager to find brides for them before their departure.

"Why is that?" I asked.

"Because they strongly felt their sons had to be married before leaving for the battlefield."

"Even though they knew their sons would be leaving soon and might be killed?" I asked.

"That is precisely the reason their parents wished it. 'To make him a man before he dies' was really important in those days."

Another group member, Kisae, jumped into our conversation and said that she truly regretted her marriage when her husband was drafted four months after their wedding; then she found herself pregnant. Surrounded by "strangers," Kisae did not know what to do. When she was resting, she sensed their criticism of her laziness. When she was working, her pregnant body ached.

"To make him a man before he dies" is an interesting phrase. But for whom was this important? For his parents, perhaps more important for his mother than for his father. This phrase, then, represents not only an intergenerational relationship (between parents and sons) but an intragender relationship (between mothers-in-law and brides).

We cannot generalize the family situation in the Nagano countryside during the wartime period. Women who were married to younger sons (and therefore nonsuccessors) did not usually live with their parents-in-law or brothers-in-law, yet they too had to shoulder the burden of labor.[24]

Indeed, I heard numerous narratives of hard labor at the group meetings. Sachi, who was left with her small children after her husband was drafted, said: "I arranged with the village government official that he would send school children to help us. One of my neighbors, who was too old to be drafted, also came to help us. But I had to feed these helpers three times a day! I also had to prepare tea and snacks in between these meals. All this on top of my working in the fields and at home!" During the wartime period, school children were mobilized by the local government as farm helpers. "Evacuee children" (*sokai gakudō*) from the city, living together at the village temple, were also mobilized as farm helpers. Sachi said, "To tell you the truth, these city kids were useless! They did not know what to do and simply stood there." Another group member said: "In addition to tending silkworms, which did not allow me to sleep much, I had to go to the fields, plant rice seedlings, prepare food, wash clothes, bear children, raise them, and clothe them. I took for granted that all these were my duties. All of my neighbors were just like me, working and working without much complaining."

In order to alleviate the problem of a temporary labor shortage in the countryside, the government allocated to each village a certain number of Koreans and Chinese. They were brought from the then Japanese colonies of Korea, Taiwan, and China. For example, the government allocated about 250 Koreans to the village of Yomikaki in Nagano (Takahashi 1976, 371).[25] The land of the three hamlets next to Tabata, I was told, was first tilled by Koreans, who were brought by the Japanese army. My neighbor Noriko told me that they slept at the barracks of the village elementary school and marched every morning to the work site, singing. In reality, they were forced to march and sing Japanese military songs every morning. Noriko also told me that some of these Koreans occasionally came to her house to beg for food and that "they were so grateful when my father gave them corn or other vegetables or fruit." I learned later that all of them had died when their ship was sunk in the Sea of Japan as they were being deported back to Korea after the end of World War II. Historian Kobayashi Kōji maintains that more than 1,500,000 Koreans and 50,000 Chinese were brought to the Japanese countryside and forced to work at over 135 construction sites and mines (1977).[26] Although this indicates the presence of a significant number of non-Japanese in the Japanese countryside during the wartime period, Yanagita and his students never referred to them. Nagano middling farmers ignored them in their village newspapers. Instead, they depicted the countryside as a homogeneous space, the locus of Japanese identity.

In this chapter, I have presented narratives of Nagano rural women about the wartime period. All these narratives suggest that they worked extremely hard not because they held "power" inherent in rural women or because they embodied an authentically Japanese identity, but because they had to survive. They also suggest that these women were publicly recognized precisely because of their labor and hardships. Most of the Nagano rural women accepted such public recognition and then rejected it after the war was over. I agree with Adorno that their guilt feelings are pathological, inadequate to reality. But I do not agree with him that these women render a real and terrible past harmless. The past has remained real and terrible for these women. It is true that I occasionally heard narratives of nostalgia for the past. And I admit that nostalgia often denies the past and that its thrust is "less to preserve the past than to restore it, to bring it back in its original state, as if nothing had happened in the interim" (Anthony Brandt, quoted in Kelly 1986, 614).[27] But these women do not want to experience what they experienced: although they do become nostalgic about certain elements of the past, they never wish to restore them in a context similar to the wartime period. Nor do they wish to wipe the past from memory through nostalgia. Rather, they are trying to hold on to their memories in order to reconsider the past, in which most of them willingly accepted the status of national subject. In the final chapter, I will focus on the postwar period. Since I heard the Nagano rural women's voices in the context of the 1980s and 1990s, I will revisit some of the narratives I have presented in this and earlier chapters.

Chapter 8   The Postwar
            "Democracy" and
            the Post-postwar
            Nationalism

In this chapter, I will divide the postwar period into two periods. I will call the first, from 1945 to the early 1970s, the (immediate) postwar period and the second, from the early 1970s to the present, the post-postwar period. The latter, a rather cumbersome phrase, connotes that the postwar period is not yet over in Japan. This periodization is different from the one used in the *White Paper on Japanese Economy* published in 1976 (Keizai Kikaku-chō 1976). The authors, bureaucrats of the National Institute of Economic Planning, declared that the postwar period (*sengo*) had ended in 1956. That was eleven years after the end of World War II and three years after the end of the Korean War. Indeed, Japan's economic recovery, which had been slow at first, became quite evident in the early 1950s. By the mid-1950s, the Japanese had regained their per capita production levels of the prewar years (Reischauer 1978, 115).

Despite such a declaration, both the government and the mass media continued using the term *"sengo,"* postwar period. And despite the emperor's death in 1989 and a new era name, this term remained intact. In 1995, there were a variety of public gatherings throughout Japan, commemorating the fiftieth anniversary of the end of World War II (*sengo gojū-nen*). In the summer of 1996 in Japan, I read numerous newspaper articles that reprimanded citizens for their forgetfulness of their hardships during the war. Thus, the postwar period continues, despite the economic growth since 1956 that eventually placed Japan ahead of the United States in terms of per capita GNP. I use the early 1970s to divide this protracted postwar period.

I will later elaborate why I have chosen this particular point in time; suffice it to say here that the Nagano rural women began to form various groups in the early 1970s. The women's voices I heard and have presented throughout this book belong to this post-postwar period, which has yet to end.

THE IMMEDIATE POSTWAR NAGANO COUNTRYSIDE

On August 19, 1948, a meeting was held in Iida composed exclusively of about 350 women. Forty years later, Miyoko recounted her memories of "this big event in my life" at a group meeting: "Holding hands with each other, we marched to cheerful band music. I thought we had finally come out of a long and dark life of submission. I felt as if I were traveling in a Western country." The meeting was organized by the regional headquarters of the U.S. Occupation, officially called the Supreme Commander for the Allied Powers (SCAP), to which Japan had surrendered in 1945. The meeting's aim was to teach these women how to introduce "recreation"—square dancing in this case—into their everyday lives.[1]

The women in Nagano began to call this and other series of meetings held by the U.S. Occupation *shon shon undō*. This almost nonsensical Japanese coinage would literally be translated as "-tion, -sion, movement": where "-tion" is the last syllable of "recreation," while "-sion" is the last syllable of "discussion." In addition to square dancing and games, the U.S. Occupation taught these women how to hold "democratic" discussions and advised them always to carry pencils and notepads. Put another way, the U.S. Occupation introduced "recreation" and "discussion" to Japan as the embodiments of "democracy."[2]

It is not that democracy did not exist in prewar Japan.[3] The notion of *minken* (people's rights), which was "rooted in traditions of popular struggle from the feudal period," spread in the city and the countryside immediately after the Meiji Restoration (McCormack and Sugimoto 1986, 11). We have also seen the emergence of the so-called Taishō democracy in the 1910s and 1920s. The publication of village newspapers by youth groups in the vicinity of Ueda is one example that attests to the infiltration of Taishō democracy into the countryside. There are distinctions, however, between these prewar democracies and the postwar democracy. First, in terms of gender, the prewar democracies were what I would describe as "male-oriented" democracies. True, women made certain inroads in the People's Rights Movement. Although the movement first relied on precedent to deny women access to popular rights, some women had become its new and potentially important constituency by the late 1870s (Sievers 1983, 27–28). During the period of Taishō democracy, women suffragists and their supporters pressed for political rights, and an increasing number of working-class women began participating in the male-dominated labor movement (see Chapter 4). However, women were few in comparison to men, and in rural areas such as the Ueda region, women were largely excluded from the youth movement (see Chapter 6). The postwar democracy, in contrast, affected both genders more or less equally. Since it was a direct product of the U.S. Occupation and since every corner of Japan was occupied between 1945 and 1952, the postwar democracy was expected to and did infiltrate the life of every Japanese. Second, the prewar democracies were eventually suppressed: the People's Rights Movement by the constitutional monarchy and the Taishō democracy by the xenophobic atmosphere following the Manchurian Incident of 1931. Yet, the new democracy—which later scholars called the "postwar democracy" (*sengo minshu-shugi*) in order to differentiate it from the prewar democracies—still exists in Japan, though it constantly changes its institutional base.

The passion for democracy was apparently shared widely among the rural women in Nagano in the immediate postwar period. Miyoko used the suffix "*joshi*" to refer to the handful of American women officers of the U.S. Occupation that she met. "*Joshi*" is a term reserved only for highly educated women of some prominence. Democracy, Miyoko thought, enabled these American women to attain such status. But why did the U.S. Occupation hold square dancing classes and many other meetings for women only? Restated, why did the U.S. Occupation emphasize the need for inspiring rural women with democracy? In the immediate postwar period, why did the Occupation try to remake women into, borrowing Miyoko's words, "vanguards of democracy" (*minshu-shugi no senpei*)? True, many men were not yet back home by 1945. Sumiko's husband, who had been detained as a POW by the Soviet army in Siberia, did not come home until 1949. And many were killed in the war. At Miyoko's group meeting, another member said:

> I received a box [from the village government official] that was sup-
> posed to contain my late husband's remains. It was very light and
> made a small sound when he handed it to me. Thinking this was my
> husband, I could not stop crying. I went home, but I became sus-
> picious about whether his remains were truly in the box. I could not
> suppress my urge to open it. When I finally opened it, I discovered
> only a tiny piece of unshaved wood on which there was a red
> rubber stamp mark of *"mitama"* (spirit).

Miyoko told me that, in the immediate postwar period, "war widows"
(*sensō mibōjin*) were everywhere in her village. Still, there were men,
the very young and the very old. Why did the U.S. Occupation not
hold similar meetings for men? After all, wasn't it only men who had
fought? Were men more patriotic and nationalistic than women?
Should men have learned democracy first?

Herbert Passin, a young officer of the U.S. Occupation and later
a historian of modern Japan, claims that the Occupation was aware of
the unique relationship between the Japanese countryside and the military aggression (1990, 116). What is this unique relationship? The
report submitted by the "Committee in Charge of Investigating the
Possibility of Implementing Special Education for Farming Women"
to the Nagano Educational Committee in 1941 offers some clues: "In
the countryside now being ruined by the consumerism brought from
the West, the education of farming women should be considered of
the utmost importance, because it is women who send children to the
frontline, endure all possible ordeals at home as wives and mothers,
and nurture the spirit of sacrifice in their children as female subjects
of the imperial nation" (Nōson Josei Kyōiku Kenkyū Iinkai 1941a,
43–44).[4] In the eyes of the Occupation, then, it was these farming
women who nurtured the spirit of sacrifice in their children and
willingly sent them to the frontline to fight the United States. In the
U.S. Occupation's point of view, farming women were "ignorant,"
because they never questioned what they had taught to their sons.
Consequently, farming women were the first to be reformed.

Miyoko, however, rejected the U.S. Occupation's point of view.
She presented her interpretation to me: "The U.S. Occupation must
have thought that we women, by our own nature, were potentially
more democratic and pacifist than men. This is why they tried to
educate us first. I think they expected us to teach democracy to
men." Miyoko has a firm belief in women's natural disposition to
pacifism and democracy. This itself is not surprising, considering that

the postwar women's movements in Japan have been partly characterized by the activists' belief in women's special ties to pacifism. This belief is based on a biological and circular argument: women give birth; women naturally reject anything that threatens human life; consequently, women avert violence. But, in my view, the U.S. Occupation was particularly interested in reforming *rural* women. So I pressed Miyoko further. "We rural women worked so hard for our country (*o-kuni no tame ni*)," she continued. "But, after all, we were the number one victims [of the war]. We worked beyond our ability, sacrificing our own lives. We also lost many of our loved ones. But this society regarded us rural women as the most backward, feudalistic, ignorant, and superstitious [while we were not]. I think the Occupation knew this and were most sympathetic to us."

Tokie, another member, interrupted our conversation. She too resented the urban Japanese misconception of rural women. She recounted humorously to us the story of her first trip to Tokyo, not long after Japan's surrender. She went as part of the female section of the agricultural cooperative. They visited the Imperial Palace, shopped at a big department store, and strolled on the streets of Ginza. And as they marveled and cringed at the bobbing of the Tokyo Tower elevator, the urban folk laughed. "They must have thought we were genuine country bumpkins. Maybe we were, but they did not have to laugh at us." In their criticism of the urban folk, I sensed the pride Miyoko and Tokie must have felt that they had learned democracy first.

Along with other women over twenty years old in her village, Miyoko was suddenly given suffrage in 1945 and campaigned hard for a woman candidate. In 1951, this woman candidate won a seat in the Nagano prefectural assembly. Miyoko remembered that one of the slogans used by the prefectural government to promote democratic elections was "good government always begins with the voice and the self-determination of women" (*yoi seiji, fujin no koe kara jikaku kara*). In the wartime period, the state denied rural women their own definition of their political role. Now, after the war, the state emphasized the importance of their voice and self-determination for governing the nation.

Historians have demonstrated that the end of the war and the arrival of democracy did not signify an abrupt change in the nature of the Japanese state: the state was democratized, but only to a certain extent. Halliday writes:

The year of the war's end did not mark a transition in terms of a change in the mode of production, but it was a transition from seeking autonomous imperialism to accepting subordinate imperialism in a reorganized world in which the US guaranteed Japanese capitalism the essential medium- to long-term conditions under which it could prosper. And precisely because there was no change in the mode of production, there was no change in the ruling class.[5] (1975, 162)

He goes on to say that big businesses remained intact on the economic front, as the U.S. Occupation purged only 468 people in private economic enterprises. This number constituted less than 1 percent of all purges (p. 169, 179). Furthermore, he argues, a "special nucleus of the Japanese armed forces was preserved by MacArthur's Intelligence chief," which made a complete capitulation on the military front impossible (p. 173). The Occupation also retained the emperor and his imperial institution intact (see also Nakano 1990, 33). Listening to the narratives of Miyoko and Tokie, however, I felt that Halliday's argument regarding the lack of notable change did not apply to the women in the Nagano countryside or to Japanese women in general. Women were suddenly allowed to speak when Japan was occupied (see Gluck 1993, 89). This change must have been greater for rural than for urban women.

When we carefully scrutinize the everyday life of the rural women in Nagano between 1945 and the early 1970s, we find that democracy became a specifically marked vocabulary in certain domains. One such domain is the land on which rural women had worked. The Agrarian Reform (*nōchi kaikaku*), carried out by the U.S. Occupation in collaboration with the Japanese government, made every farmer into a small landholder. Although one of the motives of the U.S. Occupation might have been to help disarm rural protest (Halliday 1975, 190–194), the Agrarian Reform brought to the villages and towns in Nagano the very idea of equality and democracy.

The law stipulated that the state would purchase the following categories of land in Nagano and distribute them among landless farmers: (1) land owned by absentee landlords that had been rented out, (2) land owned by local landlords that had been rented out in excess of 0.8 hectare, and (3) land owned by self-cultivating landlords in excess of 2.3 hectares. In Tabata and its vicinity, more than 150 hectares of land that had belonged to twelve landlords was affected by the Agrarian Reform.

Shigeko, who married a tenant farmer in 1936 at the age of eighteen, told me that before the Agrarian Reform she had to pay thirty-nine bales of rice to her landlord every year. In a bumper crop year, she and her husband normally harvested about fifty-five bales of rice. According to Shigeko, the remaining sixteen bales of rice was not enough to give them the necessary cash income. When she heard the news of the Agrarian Reform, she was so pleased that she would now be able to eat rice harvested on her own land. Much later, when land prices soared, many of these former tenant farmers sold their land. A former landowner, whose land had been confiscated during the reform, told me: "They all now live in palacelike houses, having abandoned agriculture." Equality among farmers might not have lasted long, but for rural women in Nagano, the Agrarian Reform was the earliest and perhaps the most visible representation of democracy.

The second domain comprises several aspects of the everyday life of these rural women. Here, democracy was always accompanied by "rationalization" (*gōrika*). An order "to rationalize this or that" came from above, first from the regional headquarters of the U.S. Occupation and later from the local government. Such orders created the "rationalization movement" among the rural population, where local branches of the agricultural cooperative society served as liaison offices.

The term "*gōrika*" has a wide range of nuances from "efficient," "impersonal," "calculable," "standardized," to "modern," "impartial," "egalitarian," and "democratic" (Kelly 1982, 15–38; 1986, 606, 615, n. 6). In many respects, the rationalization movement was similar to the movement to improve the quality of everyday life in the early twentieth century, but the rationalization movement was directly linked to the U.S. Occupation in particular and to the West in general. The 1920s and 1930s movement to improve the quality of everyday life would not have been possible without the Westernization of Japanese society. But its premise became anti-West over time, and the movement eventually coalesced into the state's efforts to win the war against the West. In both movements, however, it was primarily women who were asked to contribute their labor for the movements' successes.

When the rationalization movement positively changed the everyday lives of the women in Nagano—by making tasks easier for them to do, generating more free time for them, or giving them more power in making decisions—they seem to have readily accepted and complied with the orders. For example, they happily accepted the rationalization of water management. Until then, "water problems" (*mizu no mondai*) had tormented the rural women in Nagano. In a meeting held in the town of Kanae, participants expounded on past frustrations in obtaining water. Aiko said:

> I moved to this town in 1951 and used well water. We used a pump, but it got frozen very easily during winter. If that happened, I had to borrow water from my neighbor who used a well bucket.[6] But each time I borrowed, I felt sorry [as water was so scarce]. I used river water for washing clothes and thawed snow to obtain extra water.

Another woman followed, saying: "I still cannot throw away the water I use to wash my face every morning. I store it in a bucket and use it for watering my plants."

When the Kanae village authorities told the housewives to remodel their kitchens, they tiled their kitchen floors. Shining tiles covering dirt floors represented great improvements, as did clean white sheets on worn-out mattresses. Indeed, the immediate postwar years seem to have generated many symbols of democracy, such as square dancing, games, pencils and notepads, shining tiles, and white sheets. And what the members of various women's groups talked about were not so much the abstract notion of democracy but its tangible symbols.

Furthermore, so-called feudalistic customs had to be corrected under the slogan of rationalization. Saemi decided not to make and put away her mother-in-law's bed, because she was told at a village meeting that the elderly had to attend to their personal needs by themselves to stay healthy. Yumiko decided to rent a wedding gown from the agricultural cooperative office rather than spend a fortune for it. She was told by a cooperative employee to stop publicly displaying her trousseau, an act now considered "feudalistic." She also said that the members of her county's women's association decided not to speak ill of their daughters-in-law or mothers-in-law behind their backs, because it was "feudalistic." It was not that all these "feudalistic" customs disappeared overnight. Some disappeared more quickly, while other customs persisted longer or still persist. However, the rationalization movement gave the rural women in Nagano at least alternatives to traditional ways.

Another term circulated widely in the postwar Nagano countryside along with "democracy" and "rationalization," was "*bunka*," "culture." Note again that a term that was the topic of extensive discussion in the village newspapers in the 1920s and 1930s reappeared after the war ended. Miyoko commented: "The term '*bunka*' was added to almost every possible noun": *bunka seikatsu* (cultural life); *bunka jūtaku* (cultural home); *bunka sai* (cultural festival); *bunka fuku* (cultural clothes); *bunka nabe* (cultural pot); and so forth. Some of these, notably "*bunka jūtaku*," were coined in the 1920s. They reappeared as essential items that promised housewives a "rationalized," "efficient," "standardized," and "modern" way of life. Hence *bunka nabe* was a pot in which one could cook everything from rice to meat, while *bunka fuku* was a dress one could wear on every occasion from a funeral to a wedding reception.

I asked Miyoko whether she knew the difference between the prewar and postwar "cultures." "Really? The term has been with us for many years. I do not remember which is which," said Miyoko. I see in the term "*bunka*" both continuity and rupture between the prewar and postwar periods. Continuity, because, as Gluck argues, the postwar term is one of those words that "described the future in terms of 'the rebirth of the people,' a guaranteed 'cultural livelihood' in a 'cultural nation' (*bunka kokka*) or a 'national culture' (*minzoku bunka*)—all phrases reminiscent of wartime ideology but now couched in the postwar terms of democracy and peace" (1993, 69). And yet, rupture, because the postwar "*bunka*," unlike the prewar one, led the rural women in Nagano to reconsider many of the prewar notions of feminine virtue. The postwar "culture" offered women the freedom to spend time and use resources in their own ways. In this sense, "*bunka*" represented a departure from pre-war Japan.

Another domain subjected to democratization was the rural woman's body. In the wartime period, women were told to give birth to as many children as possible for Japan. They were now told to follow "democratic family planning" (*minshu-teki na kazoku keikaku*). In one village, a public health nurse made what she, and subsequently all the housewives in her village, called the "little box of love" (*ai no kobako*). Handed from one household to another, the box contained packages of condoms and was always handled by the women. In this domain, then, it was indeed women who taught democracy to men. A housewife took one package, inserted a small fee, and handed the box to the housewife next door: the box moved from woman to woman. The public nurse advocated the rhythm method and the use of condoms to avoid unwanted pregnancies. But if they did not work (and indeed they often did not work), she advised them to resort to now "legal" abortions. Setsuko said in 1984 that 60 to 70 percent of the women in her village who were younger than fifty years of age had had at least one abortion. But abortion did not always work out democratically for every woman. A participant in one meeting wrote a short story based on the experience of her close friend who had an abortion and contributed it to the book that the group later published. The following is an excerpt from her story.

> Haru, the bride (*yome*) of a farming family, was already the mother of three children. As her family was engaged in rice production, sericulture, and fruit culture, she had to work all day long every day in the fields throughout the year. When she found herself pregnant again with her fourth child, though it surprised Haru herself, she never expected the objections of her mother-in-law and her husband to her decision to have her baby. "These days, every family has only two children. Three are already too many," said her mother-in-law. She said it so flatly and clearly that Haru hardened her decision and asked her husband for his approval. "In this busy season, we cannot finish anything if you complain about morning sickness and whatnot," replied her husband.
>
> In the dark hospital room, Haru felt warm tears streaming down her cheeks. Suddenly she felt a sharp pain in her abdomen. She recalled the words of her husband, who had said, "Long ago, women used *hōzuki* or jumped down from a high cliff to abort the baby."[7] His every word suggested that Haru should be thankful for having had a safe abortion in a clean hospital.
>
> In the mulberry field where Haru's husband and mother-in-law worked, the sound of picking mulberry leaves echoed. It began to rain, both in the mulberry field and just outside Haru's hospital room window. (Katari-tsugu Ina no Onna Henshū Iinkai 1984, 195)

Could we say that Haru's mother-in-law, who preferred a smaller family, and her husband, who understood the notions of economic calculation and hygiene, were more "rationalized" human beings than Haru? For Haru, however, the rationalization of her everyday life and the democratization of family planning were carried out against her body and her will.

The reasons for abortions varied significantly among the rural women in Nagano. Kazuko said she aborted her third child after witnessing the many hardships her parents had endured while raising their seven children. Another member nodded in approval of

Kazuko's statements and said she had several abortions because of the intolerable morning sickness she had experienced in each of her three pregnancies. Both stressed that their husbands and parents-in-law supported their decisions. Because of the postwar democracy that had legalized abortion, these women made their own decisions. Democracy and rationalization, however these notions were interpreted, thus infiltrated into the life and the body of each rural woman in Nagano.

What happened to Japanese nationalism during the immediate postwar period? According to George Packard, the "pendulum . . . had swung toward absorption of foreign—especially American—culture" and not toward its rejection (1966, 334). One should not forget the role played by leftist intellectuals and individuals, who rejected the subject of nationalism as an evil associated with prewar militarists (p. 337). Ironically, the U.S. Occupation, which suppressed xenophobic ourbursts of nationalism, also suppressed the leftists. In the name of democracy, severe restrictions were placed on workers' rights; leftists in universities, government, and private industries were purged; student strikes were banned; and the leftist union federation was dissolved (Halliday 1975, chaps. 8, 9, and 10). Such repression continued even after Japan regained its formal independence and throughout the period of the Korean War. In addition, one might also argue that people were simply busy recovering from the material devastations resulting from the war and did not have time to ponder the destiny of the nation.

Packard suggests that the Security Treaty Crisis of 1960 marks the beginning of a *new* Japanese nationalism. From 1959 to 1960, Japanese conservative politicians, progressive intellectuals, leftist activists, and students engaged in massive protests against the renewal of a revised version of the U.S.-Japan Security Treaty, which provided for the stationing of U.S. troops and military bases in Japan (Packard 1966; Kosai 1986; Sasaki-Uemura 1993).[8] Stated differently, nationalism reemerged in the Security Treaty Crisis of 1960 when memories of the war had faded into the past (Packard 1966, 338). Packard argues that "every group involved in the crisis exhibited some form of the new nationalism": conservatives promoted the treaty in terms of their own national interests; the left tried to negate the image of Japan as a subservient nation to the United States; the progressive intellectuals insisted that Japan should have its own democracy; and students tried to rid themselves of their inferiority complex to the United States (p. 334).

However, the Security Treaty Crisis was largely an urban phenomenon. The rural women in Nagano did not begin questioning such notions as democracy and rationalization until the early 1970s, around the time when they began to form their own groups, such as those in which I participated. The author who recounted her friend's abortion experiences waited until the 1980s to express her protest against rationalization and democracy. But the notions of democracy and rationalization had begun to be criticized in the discourse of the new nationalism in the early 1970s. In their place, an ability unique to Japan to modernize its polity, economy, and society became a powerful source of the new, post-postwar, nationalism. Does this mean that the discourse of the new nationalism coopted the narratives of the rural women similarly criticizing democracy and rationalization?

THE POST-POSTWAR NAGANO COUNTRYSIDE

"The shrinking globe," "the global village," "the expansion of a knowable world" all are phrases recently used in commercial advertisements of multinational corporations. These catchphrases give us, the consumers in a postindustrial society such as the United States or Japan, an illusion that we already know the world or can know it through the power of telecommunications. This illusion is powerful precisely because it is liberating: the shrinking globe makes us free and active individuals, and we can move as we wish.[9]

Women and men in rural Nagano, as both consumers and producers, also possess this illusion. Kelly suggests that the countryside in contemporary Japan should more appropriately be called "regions"; such regions are "peripheries of a national state and metropolitan culture" (1990b, 211). As consumers, women and men in rural Nagano can visit pricy department stores, chic boutiques, trendy coffee shops, or beauty parlors that have been built in every provincial town in Nagano since the early 1970s. Furthermore, such regions as Nagano are also peripheries of the shrinking globe. As producers, women and men in Nagano work daily in this periphery, which is a part of the space created by multinational capitalism. To demonstrate this, I will share an incident that took place in Tabata in 1984.

Dozens of farmers were growing and selling tomatoes to a food processing company located near Tabata. I was told there were approximately six thousand tomato growers in Nagano prefecture as a whole who had similar contractual agreements with six different food processing companies (see Tamanoi 1988). This particular company, which manufactured tomato sauce, paste, catsup, and juice, began its operation locally in the immediate postwar period. By the early 1980s, it was a fairly large operation, having opened several other factories in other parts of Japan. In 1988, the company decided to contract with California farmers who, according to a company official, were highly cost-effective in tomato production. Thus, despite protests from local tomato growers, the company substantially lowered the purchase price of tomatoes grown by the Nagano farmers. What interests me, however, is the force sweeping through the Nagano countryside that challenged the material force created by multinational capitalism.

Material growth in Japan no longer obeys the law of classical capitalism: the existence of national boundaries has become irrelevant. Yet there emerged the discourse of a new nationalism in the 1970s where the nation (Japan) was still imagined to be limited by its national boundaries, without its former colonies. As we will see shortly, the discourse of a new nationalism has also flourished in the Nagano countryside since then. The tension between these opposing forces is not new, nor is this a postindustrial phenomenon. Although it is always dangerous to make historical analogies, we can go back to the early twentieth century and see, in the discourses of Japanese native ethnologists and of the Nagano middling farmers, a similar tension between the expansion of the Japanese empire and the search for an authentic location for Japanese identity.

In the context of the age of multinational capitalism, Fredric Jameson suggests that we should conceptualize this period in terms of the dialectic relationship between "socioeconomic reality" and "cultural ideology" (1984, 53).[10] In the context of rural Nagano, "socioeconomic reality," on the one hand, refers to the kind of material forces that local tomato growers faced. On the other hand, "cultural ideology" is the new Japanese nationalism. What is important is that cultural ideology cannot be assigned an objective meaning independent of socioeconomic reality, for it is always created through socioeconomic reality. In what follows, I will present several ethnographic sketches. In each of these, I try to convey to the reader the tension between material and cultural forces. Let me begin with what ensued after the offensive move of the tomato processing company.

"Do You Still Feel Like Eating?"

Against the expansion of this company and other agribusiness industries into the multinational space, the local agricultural cooperatives undertook a massive campaign to protect things "Japanese," that is, "Japanese" agricultural products.

On a hot summer day, one of my neighbors, who worked for the local agricultural cooperative office, invited me to the first screening of a video movie in his office. The movie, called "Do You Still Feel Like Eating?" was made by the national headquarters of the agricultural cooperative. Japan was then (and still is) under the strong pressure of the U.S. government to ease the trade imbalance between the two countries. Consequently, the Japanese government was considering the liberalization of imports of citrus fruits and beef from the United States. The agricultural cooperatives produced this video to send the message that they opposed such liberalization. The movie began with a view of a doll, presented as a token of friendship to the port city of Yokohama in 1920 by the U.S. government, with the narrator's voice asking, "How do you [referring to the doll] see the recent Japan bashing [taking place in the United States]?" The main message of this movie was a simple one: imported food from the United States is dangerous; it will destroy not only "our," that is "Japanese," bodies, but also the bodies of our descendants. But the complex visual representations of this danger in imported food were, as one viewer put it, indeed "unbearable" (*tamaranai*).

The movie had a scene in which "American" customs officers wearing gas masks are spraying "poisonous chemicals" on citrus fruit exports bound for Japan. In another scene, we see congenitally united twins at play somewhere in Vietnam. An ominous voice states that the dioxin used by the U.S. army during the Vietnam War caused such conditions and is now used by "American" farmers for rice production. It also had a scene in which "Japanese" children suffering from hitherto unknown diseases are visiting a pediatric clinic somewhere in Japan. The next scene concerned "Japanese" farmers devoting their time and energy to organic farming. The last scene was a place called the "Monkey Center" on an island in the Seto Naikai, where many of the monkeys were born deformed because of the "imported" feed they were given. As the movie ends, we see a legless monkey gazing at the camera, a pitiful creature entreating us to save their lives.

After the movie, none of us wanted to sip the green tea served by the office secretary. My friend said to me, "Hey, are people in America really eating that stuff?" The movie did not say "American" consumers ate oranges and grapefruits sprayed with chemicals. And the movie did not say whether those chemicals were used only on fruit exports. Hence viewers tend to see the visual representations of the perils of imported food in terms of simple juxtapositions like safety versus danger and Japan versus the United States; Japanese agricultural products are safe to eat, U.S. products are poisonous. After having seen the movie, no one mentioned the multinational companies based in Tokyo that import food from the United States. Nor did we talk about the officers of the Japanese Ministry of Health who were somehow reluctant to check the safety of imported foods. Nor did we talk about the customs officers of the Port of Yokohama who further sprayed the imported foods with more chemicals, for fear of spreading unknown germs in Japan. Although all these agents are present in the movie, their faces are blurred, effectively concealing their identities. Furthermore, any agent who might question the simple dichotomy of safe Japan versus dangerous America was visually underrepresented. When such agents were seen on film, the scenes were brief and instantly superseded by the next scene.

While viewing the movie, I was aware of statistics that indicated that the amount of chemical fertilizers used on a hectare of land in Japan was three times greater than the amount used in the United States (see, for example, Redclift 1987, 23). But because I too was overwhelmed by the images of human and animal deformities, I was no longer able to believe such a figure presented by an "American" agronomist. The movie "Do You Still Feel Like Eating?" succeeded in leading its viewers (including myself) to believe that questions of food safety should be a national concern.

In negotiations between company representatives and local tomato growers, the latter expressed their concern about the quality and safety of California tomatoes. They pointed out: "Japanese" tomatoes were of better quality than "American" ones; we spend more time taking care of even each individual tomato by, say, covering it with a paper bag to protect it from insect attacks; California farmers use airplanes and helicopters to spray chemicals on tomatoes; you (referring to the company) do not know what kind of tomatoes you are using to produce tomato sauce and catsup. Company representatives then promised local farmers that they would use "Japanese" tomatoes for manufacturing tomato juice, commenting that "Japanese" consumers were particularly sensitive to the taste of juice. Thus, local farmers ended up continuing to grow tomatoes for this company, but only for the production of tomato juice.

The campaign organized by Japanese agricultural cooperatives particularly appealed to housewives. The narrator of the movie constantly speaks to housewives as the ones who carry the important mission of controlling the stomachs and therefore the health of their children and husbands. In the movie, it is mothers who take the children suffering from unknown diseases to the pediatric clinic. It is mothers who are eager to buy vegetables from "Japanese" organic farmers. In one scene, the agricultural cooperative officer point out a mountain of rotten grapefruits to a group of housewives and tells them that the "inadequate" use of chemicals caused them to rot. They then understand that the grapefruits they buy contain an amount of chemicals that is great beyond belief. There is thus a clear message that Japanese women should protect things "Japanese," more so than Japanese men.

The agricultural cooperatives, even though they campaigned for things "Japanese," have become one huge multinational corporation like any other agribusiness corporation. The Japanese agricultural cooperatives sell millions of *nōkyō*—the Japanese abbreviation for the agricultural cooperatives—brand products. They cannot always use solely "Japanese" ingredients to produce a variety of food items. On the contrary, the cooperatives must use imported raw ingredients in order to sell processed foods competitively on Japanese as well as international markets.[11]

Furusato

If the agricultural cooperatives have been integrated into multinational capitalism, so has the Japanese government. And so have the Japanese rice farmers who have relied on the government. Since the end of World War II, the government has excessively protected rice farmers, because rice is not only the staple food but also a dominant symbol and metaphor for the Japanese (see Ōhnuki-Tierney 1993). Furthermore, the government has functioned through its powerful hold on the rural vote since 1945. This is why the government has "doubly subsidized rice farmers by subsidizing both farmland and rice production" (p. 16; see also Calder 1988). Now that the demand for rice has decreased among Japanese consumers, the government "pays rice farmers not to use their land for rice." At the same time, the government exempts from reducing rice production those farmers who implement ways to increase rice production (Ōhnuki-Tierney 1993, 17).

In the summer of 1988, the rice farmers belonging to a local agricultural cooperative and local sake-brewers organized a festival, which they named in English "Jazz Concert and Sake/Rice Festival." The intention of the organizers was to promote the consumption of rice in Japan and to oppose the government's pending liberalization of the import of foreign rice. The participants, including myself, enjoyed a full-course meal of rice salad, gratin of rice cakes, and ice cream made with rice, while listening to tunes played by internationally known Japanese jazz musicians. The dinner was prepared in accordance with the Western codes of food preparation. The music was Western. Yet, the West was not celebrated. Instead, "rice" was celebrated as a metaphor for Japanese culture throughout the event. Also celebrated was the ability of the Japanese to blend Japanese and Western civilizations, creating a culture unique to Japan. And, because the organizers promoted a novel way of consuming rice, they were exempted from reducing rice production.[12]

Before presenting more of these ethnographic sketches, I will introduce the notion of *furusato*. In my view, this notion is intimately related to the cultural ideology side of multinational capitalism. *"Furusato"* commonly means "one's hometown or village" or "one's native place." Additionally, the term has a range of more historical and public meanings, such as "a place of ancient habitation," "historic ruins," or "an ancient capital" (Ivy 1995, 103). *Furusato* can apply to an individual or a collectivity of Japanese. It is the latter, that is, *furusato* of a collectivity of Japanese, that concerns me here.

I have demonstrated that the Japanese countryside has been integrated into multinational capitalism. Precisely for this reason the *furusato* for Japanese is "in danger of vanishing" (Ivy 1995, 104).[13] Since the early 1980s, Japanese politicians in the central as well as local governments and mass media advertisers and programmers have used *furusato* as the "dominant representation of 'the Japanese' past and future" (J. Robertson 1991, 14). Restated, the *furusato* is vanishing; it therefore has to be searched for or created. Kelly argues: "There are no agrarian countrysides in contemporary Japan, except in the (senti)mental imagery of *furusato* motifs (1990b, 224). Japanese countrysides, the many villages and towns where *"furusato-zukuri"* or *furusato* making took place (ibid., 4), have been valorized and have reappeared as *furusato* for all Japanese. *Furusato* motifs contradict the rationalization motifs of the immediate postwar period. Sentimentalized countrysides have to be rural, remote, non-American, nonrational, and authentically Japanese.

The post-postwar sentimentalization of Japanese countrysides may resonate with Yanagita's sentimentalization of the countryside in the early twentieth century. Yanagita's "urban-rural continuum theory" is based on his assumption that every Japanese has his or her own *furusato*. Furthermore, as there was no distinction between the city and the countryside in the Japanese past, Japan in its entirety could become a single *furusato*. There is, however, a significant difference between Yanagita's and the post-postwar sentimentalization of the Japanese countryside. The latter is a "truly national, pervasive, *mass* phenomenon" that has been fostered by media technology (Ivy 1988b, 21; emphasis in original). As a mass phenomenon, not only politicians, city planners, and mass media advertisers and programmers, but also rural women and men participate in the *furusato* making. Though they are objects of sentimentalization, the women and men living in the post-postwar Nagano countryside or region are also eager participants in the business of sentimentalizing themselves. Let me present several examples of such sentimentalization that took place in the late 1980s and early 1990s in Tabata and its vicinity. I will pay specific attention to gender, that is, how women and men participate differently in these processes of being sentimentalized and sentimentalizing themselves.

The Yanagita Boom

In the spring of 1988, the Iida government decided to build a Yanagita Museum, using his "study" (*shosai*) as its centerpiece. Hence the local government transported his study, part of his house located in Setagaya ward in Tokyo, all the way to Iida. Yanagita was the son of the Matsuoka family, but he became an adopted son of the Yanagita family through his marriage to Yanagita's daughter, Kō. Kō's father, Yanagita Naohei, was born in Iida in 1849. In the name of this connection to Yanagita and Japanese native ethnology, the Iida government claimed possession of Yanagita's study. They saw in his study the symbolic return of the founder of Japanese native ethnology to his home village: after all, Iida is his *furusato*. In the same year, they hosted a meeting called Yanagita Kunio Yukari Summit, "summit meeting of the leaders of the local administrative bodies with connections to Yanagita Kunio and his works." They invited about 150 local government officials from nine villages and towns, including fourteen from Tōno, as well as several internationally known Yanagita scholars. Discussion at this Yanagita summit meeting included the importance of "village revitalization" with *jōmin* as its main participants. Participants discussed the need to exchange information between local administrative bodies to create a cultural town or village (*bunka-teki machi zukuri*) and the importance of creating villages that would value "heart" (*kokoro*), not "materials" (*mono*).[14] Although the local organizers of the conference collaborated with several Yanagita scholars in Tokyo, they were also eager to use this opportunity to revitalize town life, by attracting more businesses and tourists.

The Yanagita summit meeting was hardly an isolated event. To the contrary, Yanagita seems to have captured the minds of many Japanese, who were weary of Japan's postwar material growth. The "Yanagita boom," a term coined by the Japanese mass media, referred not only to the movement among Japanese intellectuals to return to Yanagita's texts in the age of multinational capitalism. It was also, and still is, a national fad incorporating millions of Japanese, who buy and read Yanagita's texts and visit any place that attracted Yanagita's attention. Ivy also reports from Tōno on the "Yanagita boom." Already in the 1960s, the city of Tōno "began actively reappropriating Yanagita's narratives, turning its romanticized history of darkness and primitivity into a civic asset" (1995, 100). Her chronicle of this "Tōnopia plan" nearly parallels a series of events that took place in Iida. By the time of Ivy's field research in 1982 and 1985, Tōno became the "self-proclaimed folktale and folklore *furusato*": the whole town had transformed itself into a "museum city" (p. 105). Millions of tourists and numerous "Yanagita scholars" have visited Tōno since then. In this sense, Tōno has become a Japanese *furusato*.

Flower Wine

The term "village revitalization" (*mura okoshi*) was apparently coined by national planners, who emphasized the importance of the countryside in an age of multinational capitalism. Nurturing and serene, the countryside not only produces food and fiber, but offers solace to the Japanese (Gotō 1993, 5–6). During my field research in 1988, Tabata received state subsidies to "revitalize" the village. The residents of Tabata could have revitalized, for example, their village festival, long uncelebrated because of youth apathy. They could have increased the production of a certain agrarian product, advertised it nationally through the mass media, and accepted mail orders from urban consumers. Nothing as spectacular as the creation of the Yanagita Museum evolved in this village, except for a heated discussion among the village assemblymen, which I overheard. One assemblyman insisted that they should buy bottles of wine from Yamanashi prefecture, located just east of Nagano, put flowers from apple trees in each bottle, and sell them as "flower wine," claiming it as an authentic product of their own village. His suggestion was taken as a joke, on which another assemblyman commented: "Up north [in Japan], people can even sell 'canned air' of their village. 'Flower wine' may not be so bad." For these assemblymen, village revitalization meant bringing in businesses and money, which could help revitalize village life. In this respect, village revitalization is deeply involved with the mechanism of multinational capitalism. The rhetoric of nostalgia gently conceals the material aspect of village revitalization.[15]

Soba

In the village of Fujimi, the sentimentalization of local culture generated novel job opportunities for local women. Every weekend during the summer of 1988, Miyuki worked at a restaurant built with a national government subsidy in the woods of Mt. Yatsugatake. At the foot of this mountain, an increasing number of families from the city have been building summer homes since the 1970s. Miyuki's job was to demonstrate her age-old skill of making buckwheat noodles (soba) behind a glass window, to the marveling eyes of the city folk. Not only buckwheat noodles, but also her own skill and body (she confessed to me that she made up her face only on days she worked at the restaurant) are sentimentalized and commodified in this particular village revitalization.

Foreign Workers

Some village revitalization movements have "transnational" aspects. As part of the village revitalization, a group of small-scale factory owners in a town near Tabata gathered one day and decided to invite *nanmin* from Southeast Asian countries to work in their town. *"Nanmin"* literally means "refugees." Since the Japanese government accepts very few refugees, what they meant by this term is both legal and illegal foreign workers. Since the mid-1980s, there has been a rise of migrant workers in Japan, mainly from Southeast Asia. John Lie explains this rise in terms of the "structural inequality between Japan and its neighboring countries" (1992, 36). He also lists concrete push and pull factors that contributed to this rise: the poverty in the rural sector in Southeast Asia; the downturn in the oil industry in the early 1980s; and the decline of the two low-wage labor groups, namely, farmers and women, in Japan. Consequently, there were about two hundred thousand such migrant workers in Japan in 1990, the majority of whom worked in the sex industry (for women) or in construction jobs (for men) (pp. 37–38).

The factory owners in this town were somehow convinced that the foreign workers living in big cities could not possibly feel the kindness of their neighbors. They therefore resorted to the rhetoric of the "days of regions" (*chihō no jidai*), another term coined by national planners, claiming that it was their turn to offer these workers a place to live, work, and feel the kindness of their neighbors. In terms of socioeconomic reality, these factory owners had been suffering from a labor shortage. They attributed this labor shortage to the rural exodus and women's decision to have fewer children. They also believed that the invitation of foreign workers would revitalize the cultural life of their town, for they would bring "exotic" cultures.[16] The factory owners also hoped that those men in their thirties or forties who still had not found lifetime partners might fall in love with foreign women. In the end, however, their plan failed. When they tried to find housing for the foreign workers, many of their own neighbors objected. Nobody was willing to offer a house, apartment, or room. The factory owners, facing the sentiments of local residents, eventually scrapped what they had thought to be a well-thought-out plan. This case well illustrates that when foreign workers are seen as real people instead of labor, the people who must live with them are less than hospitable.

Bride Famine I

It is not clear to me who coined the term *"yome kikin,"* or "bride famine." It refers to a phenomenon in rural Japan where an increasing number of men, often in their thirties and forties, are unable to find brides. Indeed, one of my neighbor's sons, who was well over forty, was a bachelor. "Mrs. A is seriously looking for a bride for her son," "Do you know someone appropriate for Mrs. B's son?" or "My neighbor's forty-five-year-old son is finally getting married" were phrases I frequently heard at women's group meetings. *Yome kikin* became such a serious problem by the late 1980s that the local government decided to give a more solemn name to it, *"kōkeisha taisaku."* This term means "how to take measures to retain heirs to the agricultural way of life."

My neighbor who worked for the agricultural cooperatives invited me to his office whenever the office held its "marriage consultation day." It was held regularly on the tenth of every month. To my surprise, it was almost always the parents of the bachelor sons who came. This does not mean that their sons were not desperate, but perhaps they felt ashamed to disclose their own problems. In one town, the members of a young men's association invited single women from Tokyo, Osaka, and Nagoya to experience the farming way of life, using the state's subsidy for village revitalization. They named this event "travel to flowers, greenery, and romantic encounters" (*hana to midori to deai no tabi*).

Another village near Iida invited five young women who were third-generation Japanese-Brazilian. Their visit was arranged by a former resident of this village who had migrated to Brazil, but had been deeply concerned with the plights of young men in his home village in Japan. He therefore created this opportunity for the single men of his *furusato* to meet Japanese-Brazilian women of marriageable age. The mayor of this village inadvertently disclosed his own thoughts when interviewed by a journalist from the local newspaper. He said: "This is my personal opinion, but I do not necessarily exclude the idea that the second and third generations of Japanese-Brazilian women are preferable to, say, Filipino women, because they have Japanese blood."[17] The men in his village were searching for brides beyond the national boundaries, yet the mayor wanted to preserve the Japaneseness of his village population.[18]

Bride Famine II

An increasing number of marriage brokers in the area were trying to bring women directly from the Philippines or other Southeast Asian countries. Some of my neighbors argued that the local government, not these private marriage brokers, should be directly involved in the arrangement of international marriages, so that Japanese farmers did not have to pay a large sum of money to the private brokers. In Nagano, the local governments had not yet taken this measure as of the early 1990s, so that the private marriage brokers had free rein in advertising their "commodities," the women from Southeast Asia.[19] One marriage broker advertised Sri Lankan women as "persevering, subservient to their husbands and parents, Buddhists, and virgins before marriage." The subliminal messages was the following: young Japanese women today are none of these; they are too independent; they have become very choosy about men; and farmers are the last category of men they would marry.[20]

The national debate over international marriages between Japanese farmers and Southeast Asian women is quite complex. Women's organizations in the Tokyo area have deplored such arranged international marriages as a "violation of human rights of Asian [here excluding Japanese] women." Indeed, such organizations as HELP in Tokyo have provided shelter for Asian (including Japanese) women (Babior 1993). According to numerous articles published in these organizations' newsletters, an increasing number of Southeast Asian women had come to Japan responding to various advertisements, such as ads for computer programmers, only to find themselves trapped in an Asian-brides-for-sale racket. Expecting to come to the glittering city that had so often flashed across their television sets, some felt tricked at being brought to the remote countryside. Others fled from abusive husbands or parents-in-law in the Japanese countryside. One Filipina woman sued her marriage broker, while another sued her Japanese husband, and so forth and so on. These are only a few examples out of many newsletter articles.[21]

Back in Nagano, a group of women in the town of Nagano called a public meeting in 1988 to discuss the "lack of brides" in rural Japan. Most of the male participants, farmers themselves, lamented that it was they who were truly suffering, unable to find lifetime partners. The men argued that today's young Japanese women were to blame, because they did not want to marry farmers. They also bitterly criticized the Japanese government for ignoring the fate of agriculture in the age of multinational capitalism. Neither the men nor the women present at this discussion session asked the following questions: why would these Southeast Asian women want to come to Japan?; and how could Japanese farmers pay such an exorbitant fee to marriage brokers? A man seeking help from a private marriage broker would pay a fee as high as $25,000, although fees vary according to the cost of airplane tickets, the length of time spent in the prospective wife's country, and the cost of the marriage ceremony and honeymoon.

What do all these material and cultural forces sweeping throughout the post-postwar Nagano countryside tell us about gender? Reporting from the village of Kurokawa on Shōnai Plain in the northeast region of Japan, Kelly does not fail to mention the presence of women in its village revitalization movement, the Noh festival. It is a "tradition" that has recently been revitalized and become the central focus of attention of "professional Noh actors, university scholars, media people, amateur photographers and festival freaks, casual tourists and curious relatives"(1990a, 73). After each performance, at about five o'clock in the morning, the women must clean and fold robes thrown off by the actors, the village men. This "tradition" depends on the labor of rural women, just as "tradition" depended on their labor in the early twentieth century. Do these women also sentimentalize and nostalgize the Kurokawa Noh festival to the same extent as Noh actors, scholars, media people, photographers, and tourists? Indeed, some village revitalization movements in Nagano are similar to the Kurokawa Noh festival, specifically asking women to engage in hard physical labor. Miyuki, herself "sentimentalized" while kneading soba dough and making noodles, often complains about the extra labor she has added to her life. Of course, she is making money for her "revitalized" performance. Complaining about her stiff shoulders and back pain, however, she often wonders aloud whether it is worthwhile for her to continue work at this restaurant.

In many other village revitalization movements in Nagano, women are more likely to constitute the audience. In the movie "Do You Still Feel Like Eating?" the agricultural cooperative office invites a group of housewives to visit the port of Yokohama. I saw more women/housewives among the audience at the Sake/Rice festival than men, while its organizers were all men. The Yanagita museum was built largely by the efforts of village officials and scholars, most of whom were men, but it has been visited largely by women, children, and the old. Sadako remembered that, as a child, she had participated in the "dance of the deer" (*shika odori*), a festival where children wearing deer masks pray for rain and an abundance of crops.

"It was a small local affair and our village and our neighboring village alternated to host it," said Sadako. The "dance of the deer" was one of the events revitalized in her village in the late 1980s by her village assemblymen, all of whom were men.[22] But these assemblymen rarely attend the "dance of the deer." It is women and children who do.

Such a revitalized festival or ritual is called *"ivento"*—"event" transliterated into the Japanese *kana* syllabary. Field argues that *"ivento"* refers to the festivals of capitalism—which have incorporated the once traditional festivals marking nodes of agricultural time— and that the planning of *ivento* has recently become a much-heralded growth industry in Japan (1991c, 9). *"Ivento"* is thus a ritual conducted "under modern regimes of knowledge" in late capitalist Japan (Ivy 1995, 139). This term often appears with another term in the Japanese mass media, *"shikakenin,"* a planner of *ivento* who makes the occasion into a profit-making opportunity. As we have seen, *shikakenin* are almost always men, while the audiences of *ivento* are largely women. Women's presence, then, gently hides the socioeconomic reality of multinational capitalism. Although the "dance of the deer" is no longer a rite to pray for rain and an abundance of crops, Sadako urges her grandchildren to participate in it because, in her own words, "it is educational." She and her daughter-in-law accompany them every year to the school playground to see this revitalized festival.

Yet village revitalization movements organized by factory owners or marriage brokers castigate rural women for their lack of interest in the farming way of life. We have seen that urban women were removed from the discourse of nationalism in the early twentieth century. In the late 1980s, Japanese rural women, once regarded as "truly modern" women, were removed from the discourse of nationalism because of their alleged unwillingness to marry farmers. Yanagita once bitterly criticized Japanese women who tried to change Japanese culture, but he never promoted non-Japanese Asian women over Japanese women. The discourse of these village revitalization movements, however, finds the authentic locus of Japanese culture in non-Japanese Asian women. Still, a mayor preferred Japanese-Brazilians as bridal candidates for his village youth. In the town where factory owners tried to invite foreign workers, their plan eventually failed when they could not find anyone who was willing to rent apartments to them. Here, the figure of the non-Japanese Asian woman plays the role of a scapegoat. After all, marriage brokers, local factory owners, local government officials, and the local people themselves do not want non-Japanese foreign women actually to come. They merely use such figures to remind Japanese rural women of what they think the women have lost. Furthermore, the mass media's discourse about women from Southeast Asia is ambivalent: while some newspaper and magazine articles praise them for their diligent work in a strange environment, others criticize them for their lack of education and knowledge about Japan. The media often focuses on women who had been tricked into an Asian-brides-for-sale racket but then escaped from abusive husbands. Although the media coverage of these women is mostly sympathetic, it also castigates them for their lack of patience in adjusting to a different culture.

Local women, old and young, are not allies of the Southeast Asian women either. In 1988, a group of housewives, who were also members of a women's group, criticized a Filipina woman behind her back for squandering money on phone calls back home. This woman had moved to Nagano as the wife of a farmer in his late forties. I was told that her mother-in-law had received an exorbitant telephone bill. Yet they admired a baby with round black eyes who was the son of another couple consisting of a Filipina wife and a Japanese husband. Thus, as in the past, since the 1970s, the rural women in Nagano have been implicated in sustaining the cultural ideology of a new Japanese nationalism. Yet, as they have done in the past, they have also disturbed the same cultural ideology. This is because, in the past as in the post-postwar period, nationalist discourse has always spoken for Japanese rural women, without letting them speak.

Let me conclude by returning to these women's narratives of memories of their pasts, in which they worked as nursemaids, factory women, and farming women during and after the wartime period. Let me compare their narratives with the narratives of History, which has incorporated much of the discourse of a new Japanese nationalism. The latter is linear: Japan opened itself to the West; it modernized itself to such an extent that Japan now enjoys the postmodern information era much more so than the West; this is not only because of the Japanese people's industriousness and ability to learn from the West, but because of the "special quality of Japan's culture"; there was, however, a dark moment in modern Japanese History, but the Japanese people themselves did not produce it; rather, they became the victims of a few individuals who produced it, namely, the military leaders; and the atrocities the Japanese committed on the peoples of Asia are incomparable to the suffering the Japanese themselves incurred during the war.[23] In this respect, History constitutes the institution for the social regulation of memory (see Schwarcz 1994, 50; Connerton 1989, 1).

History with a capital H has also incorporated the "tradition" of the Japanese countryside and "rural women" as its embodiment. History has made them into the surrogate mothers who knew the scientific methods of child rearing, good wives and wise mothers of silkworms and silk thread, *jōmin* women embodying an authentic Japanese tradition, truly modern and truly cultural women, farming women in the "kitchen" of Japan, vanguards of democracy, and women who must relearn an authentic Japanese tradition in the postindustrial and postmodern era.

However, History is "neither the whole nor even all that remains of the past. In addition to written history, there is a living history that perpetuates and renews itself through time (Halbwachs 1980, 64).[24] The women who come to the group meetings in Nagano have their living histories. Yet, inevitably, they must chart their living histories in relation to History. Those moments I find most valuable are the ones in which they realize they cannot do so. They then "realize their identities, not simply *within* the framework of nationalist discourse and official procedures, but—at least as much—*against* it" (Herzfeld 1991, xiv; emphasis in original). I do not think that these women came to have a collective memory: their memories are fragmented, diffuse, and multilayered. Even the books and booklets they have published themselves remain largely unauthored. However, their memories attract me precisely because they disturb History.

Epilogue:
A Short Critique of
the Notion of Identity

While England was still at war, Virginia Woolf tried to understand British nationalism and patriotism from the vantage point of the "daughters of educated men" in England, for whom the army, the navy, the stock exchange, the diplomatic service, the church, the press, the civil service, and the bar were still largely closed. In *Three Guineas*, which first appeared in 1938, Woolf provided answers to three separate requests she received for a guinea— one from the treasurer of a women's college, one from the society for obtaining employment for professional women, and the third from the society to prevent war. Addressing the third request, she states her position as an outsider, for she, as a woman, cannot share the glory provided by fighting with the sons of educated men. "As a woman, I have no country. As a woman I want no country. As a woman my country is the whole world," she declares (1938, 197). She thus refuses to sign the manifesto pledging herself to "protect culture and intellectual liberty" in England. Instead, she proposes a Society of Outsiders to serve the cause of peace through the concerted "inaction" of women.

The rural women in Nagano did not and could not act like Woolf. Politics was closed for them, except for supporting the state, an act not regarded as "political." And most, unlike Woolf, accepted the status of national subject. To the contrary, the action (or rather inaction) taken by Woolf is indeed an act of resistance: she asserted her identity as a woman against the British national identity that was simply given to her. I cannot, however, apply this generalized conception of identity to the Nagano rural women, because their histories cannot be written in terms of a single or several identities. Perhaps they have had many identities or none at all; "identity" is just not the way they talk about their living histories. The identity of a "rural woman" was simply created in the discourse of Japanese nationalism; I also use it to interrogate a variety of nationalist discourses. But the lives of all these women have nothing to do with the so called identity politics "so pervasive in current scholarship" (J. Kelly 1995, 485).[1]

In this book, I have tried to present the rural women in Nagano as complex human beings, much more complex than the term "national subject" implies. To this end, I have placed their living histories in a long time frame, from the mid–nineteenth century to the present. Their narratives often contradict what they actually did, but they seem always to have tried to make their lives (in the past and in the present) meaningful for them. "In times of uncertainty, when there is no sure vision of the future against which to tell the story of the past . . . national history tends to become more nationalistic, a trend that is apparent in Japan and around the world in the early 1990" (Gluck 1993, 94). This observation of historian Carol Gluck still holds today. I hope that the narratives of these rural women in Nagano, in which they have woven their politics and their poetics, can provide us with a vision of the future not only in Japan but around the world.

Notes

CHAPTER 1: INTRODUCTION

1. I agree with Veena Das, who argues: "The anthropologist must appear not in the role of an observer but that of a hearer, and the subject must correspondingly appear in the role of a speaker." Replacing "vision" or "gaze," a "voice" is "expected to be more open to the fragmented and multiple character of social experience" (1995, 18).

2. Mikiso Hane writes: "The number of silk filatures increased rapidly [in the late nineteenth century] and, before long, the region around Suwa Lake in Nagano prefecture became a flourishing center of silk production. By 1891, Nagano prefecture was producing 19 percent of the nation's raw silk, and, by 1911, 27 percent" (1982, 173). Okaya is located right on the west edge of Suwa Lake.

3. Nagano is not exceptional for the presence of these women's groups. In his *Fujin, josei, onna: Josei-shi no toi* (Women: Questions of women's history), Kanō Masanao introduces us to a variety of women's groups whose members study the women's histories of their own localities (1989, 176–209). Matsubara Nao's chapter "Josei-shi o manabō nettowaaku" (The network to study women's histories) is a more practical guide for those who are interested in joining the group activities throughout Japan (1987, 198–213).

4. Vicente Rafael uses "textual strategy" in the context of the early colonial history of the Philippines. He has explored the possibility of reading missionary texts that were written by the Spaniards in Tagalog against the grain of their ostensible meaning, that is, "in terms of how they might have been received by the Tagalogs who heard them" (1992, 71). I paraphrase his explication of this "textual strategy" for my own purpose.

5. I conducted field research at several different times between 1984 and 1991. The length of each field research period varied. In 1984, I stayed in Tabata in the southern part of Nagano prefecture for three months. From 1988 to 1989, I lived in the same community for approximately a year. In addition to these two relatively long-term stays, I visited and stayed in the same general area during the summers of 1985, 1986, 1987, 1990, and 1991, for about one month. Place names appearing in this book are the actual names of towns and villages within Nagano prefecture. As the name of the prefectural capital is also called Nagano, I use the "town of Nagano" for the capital and "Nagano" for the entire prefecture.

6. In truth, Tabata is now a hamlet that is a part of the administrative unit of Minami-minowa village. Its residents, however, still refer to Tabata as their "village." Hence I will retain this term throughout this book.

7. This argument reminds me of the argument proposed a long time ago by

Yoshimoto Takaaki, one of the postwar scholars of Japanese nationalism. Yoshimoto asserts that the experiences of the Japanese masses during the wartime period and the memories of those experiences that they later write or speak are different in nature and that memories cannot recuperate the past experiences. He suggests that we should rely on "popular songs" *(taishū kakyoku)*, which can potentially reveal everyday, but unconscious, experiences during the wartime period (1964).

8. In modern Japanese history, there was another moment when a group of distinguished intellectuals, academics, and critics proclaimed the "overcoming of the modern." It was 1942, only months after the outbreak of the Pacific War. "The modern," then, largely meant the West which they thought had afflicted the "traditional" way of Japanese life. Hence they conceptualized World War II as the "agent capable of finally conquering the modern" (Harootunian 1989, 69; see also Takeuchi 1983; Sakai 1989).

9. In *The Texture of Memory: Holocaust, Memories, and Meaning*, James E. Young argues for the need to break down the notion of "collective memory." Instead, he prefers to examine "collected memories," an aggregate collection of people's many, often competing memories (1993, xi). While I agree with him, I also emphasize the need to see the emergence of a "collective memory" whenever we can identify such a process.

10. Ortner's paper "Resistance: Some Theoretical Problems in Anthropological History and Historical Anthropology" was first published in 1992 for the Program in the Comparative Study of Social Transformations (CSST) at the University of Michigan. She later revised and published it in *Comparative Study of Society and History* with the title of

"Resistance and the Problem of Ethnographic Refusal" (1995). In both pieces, Ortner attends to a range of problems of resistance studies, including (1) resistance studies do not, ironically, adequately address political issues by dealing with the subordinate as a coherent body of population ("sanitizing politics"); (2) they tend to neglect the cultural richness of the subordinate ("thinning culture"); and (3) they tend to neglect the complexity of consciousness, subjectivity, intentionality, and identity of each subject among the subordinate ("dissolving subjects/actors").

11. Renan's lecture "Qu'est-ce qu'une nation?" was originally published in French in *Oeuvres complètes* (Paris, 1947–1961), vol. 1, pp. 887–907. Here, I use a version translated and annotated by Martin Thom that was published in *Nation and Narration* (1990), edited by Homi Bhabha.

12. Duara criticizes the idea that a nation is a uniquely modern form of community (1995, 51–54). In his criticism of Benedict Anderson and Ernest Gellner, whose works have become dominant in the study of nationalism, Duara argues that there is nothing modern in the consciousness of belonging to a community. We must distinguish, however, between the imagining of a community that transcends a face-to-face interaction (which is old) and the imagining of a community in which members are conationals (which is new).

13. In his *Nationalist Thought and the Colonial World: A Derivative Discourse*, Chatterjee treats the history of nationalism as a political idea in a much more extensive way than my summary here suggests. He refers to the works by John Plamenatz (1976), Hans Kohn (1944, 1955, 1962), Karl W. Deutsch (1966), Anthony D. Smith (1971), John Breuilly (1982), Ernest Gellner (1964), Elie

Kedourie (1970), Horace B. Davis (1978), and Benedict Anderson (1983). I cite these works in my bibliography.

14. Although Chatterjee admits his debt to Benedict Anderson, he disagrees with Anderson's thesis on the New World origins of nationalism. In the preface to the second edition of his *Imagined Communities* (1991), Anderson argues: "European scholars, accustomed to the conceit that everything important in the modern world originated in Europe, too easily took 'second generation' ethnolinguistic nationalisms (Hungarian, Czech, Greek, Polish, etc.) as the starting point in their modeling, no matter whether they were 'for' or 'against' nationalism" (p. xiii). In order to criticize such "Eurocentric provincialism," he retitled chapter 4, formerly "Old Empires, New Nations," "Creole Pioneers."

15. It is Hugh Seton-Watson who coined the term "official nationalisms" in the context of the history of Eastern Europe (1977). Anderson argues that "official nationalism," i.e., the "willed merger of nation and dynastic empire," always "developed *after,* and *in reaction to,* the popular national movements proliferating in Europe since the 1820s" (1983, 83; emphasis in original). In other words, they are responses by power groups "threatened with exclusion from, or marginalization in, popular imagined communities" (p. 102). This definition of "official nationalism" should be reconsidered in the context of modern Japan.

16. See Maruyama Masao, "Nihon ni okeru nashonarizumu" (Nationalism in Japan), in *Gendai seiji no shisō to kōzō,* vol. 1 (1956, 158). Volumes 1 and 2 have both been translated into English and published as *Thought and Behavior in Modern Japanese Politics* (1969).

17. While some *Nihonjinron* is serious academic discourse, the great bulk of it is

"discoursed in popular genre—in newspapers, television, radio, magazines and popular books" (Manabe and Befu 1992, 89; see also Yoshino 1992).

18. William Kelly argues that the anthropology of Japan has been shaped by a "broad range of competing national characterizations that reify Japan in contrast to equally totalizing images of the West" (1991, 396). Dorrine Kondo correctly points out that such collective identities as "Japanese self" or "Japanese management style" are not fixed essences but "assertions" (1990, 10).

19. In this respect, George Santayana once commented: "Our nationality is like our relations to women: too implicated in our moral nature to be changed honourably, and too accidental to be worth changing" (quoted in Gellner 1983). This quote suggests that, for him, a nation is gendered as a male, excluding "women," who are placed only in relation to "men," who embody the nation.

20. *Jogaku zasshi,* vol. 57, p. 123.

21. *Den'en fujin,* January 25, 1906.

22. In his criticism of Anderson's "official nationalism," Ranajit Guha argues: "And in so far as Indian nationhood had a large peasant component in it, it would make little sense to characterize it simply as a 'cultural artefact,' as if the peasant's striving towards a nationalist consciousness had nothing to do with the striving of a peasant economy towards a national market" (1985, 105).

23. This quote is from Takahashi Kōhachiro's "La place de la révolution de Meiji dans l'histoire agraire du Japon," which was published in *Revue historique,* vol. 210, no. 2, in 1953.

24. While my focus is on "rural women," I also point to numerous examples of nationalist discourses that depict a nongender category of "farmers" as national subjects. For example, Yokota

Hideo, an ideologue of agrarianism, wrote in his *Nōson kyūsairon* (On rescuing the farm villages), published in 1914: "Isn't it true that the brilliance of our national essence, which all lands should envy, is that it is maintained by the farmers? . . . The most important thing our farm villages produce are *the silent apostles of nationalism*. . . . Our two-thousand-year-long history is the history of one great family, with the imperial throne at the center. Thus the farmers are truly the creators of this brilliant history" (quoted in Havens 1974, 123; emphasis added).

25. The quotation cited by Bhabha is from Edward Said's *The World, the Text, and the Critic* (1983, 171).

26. In Singapore today, Heng and Devan argue, the nation's mothers, incipient and actual, are being accused of "imperiling the country's future by willfully distorting patterns of biological reproduction"; they thus provide the raw material for "narratives of national crisis" (1992, 343–344).

27. In this book, I use pseudonyms for most of the women I met in Nagano. Complete names consisting of family names and personal names, when used, are real names of women who have authored books, booklets, or articles that have already been published.

CHAPTER 2: FIELDWORK

1. For a detailed history of the use of the Tenryū River as a water route during the Tokugawa and Meiji periods, see Kären Wigen, *The Making of a Japanese Periphery, 1750–1920* (1995).

2. This document was issued by the Nagano prefectural government. Here, I quote from *Minami-minowa-mura sonshi* (Minami-minowa-mura Sonshi Kankō Iinkai 1985, 664). Owing to the amalgamation of the villages in the beginning of the Meiji period, this document refers not to Tabata alone, but to a newly amalgamated unit of which Tabata was a part.

3. This population increase is a natural one, caused by the combination of a higher birth rate and a lower infant mortality rate in the area (ibid., 847).

4. Hiroko was married to a second son whose parents lived in a nearby town. Hiroko's own mother, who had lived in Tabata, died a few years before my first stint of field research. Her father lived in the same village with his oldest son's family. Thus, Hiroko's family was a nuclear one, composed of Hiroko, her husband, and their three children.

5. In his article, titled "How to *Jibunshi*: Making and Marketing Self-histories of Shōwa among the Masses in Postwar Japan," Gerald Figal translates "*jibunshi*" as "self-histories" for several reasons. First, *jibunshi* are "self made" history. Second, many *jibunshi* writers mention the "discovery, making, or exercising of one's self through such writing." Third, *jibunshi* is distinct from *jiden* or "autobiography," and yet has something in common with the modern genre of *watakushi-shosetsu* or "I-novel" (1996, 903). He then outlines a genealogy of *jibunshi* from popular writing movements in the first half of the Shōwa period (1926–1989) to present-day activity caught in the mechanisms and media for mass marketing *jibunshi*. His focus, however, is *jibunshi* writing as an individual project, which "becomes standardized and marketed to fit and sell an ideal narrative pattern" of History (p. 906). *Jibunshi* writing among Nagano rural women is based on their collective endeavor of remembering and is quite different from the mass marketed version. For this reason, I will translate "*jibunshi*" as the "representation of one's own pastness."

6. It may be dangerous to use the Western (auto)biography as a reference model here, for the Western (auto)biography is not uniform in its style and content. However, its general description may be helpful to understand "one's own pastness." The Western idea of (auto)biography is often "life-historical" with a tendency toward closure; it has a linear framework with a beginning, a middle, and an ending, anticipating the future. Furthermore, it has been suggested that Western biographers often structure their subjects based on early childhood experiences. In this sense, biographers do emphasize the development of a subject's inner self and refer to the historical process or context that influences the subject's identity formation. Western biographers do so based on their solitary investigations in libraries or wherever pertinent documents are housed (see Basso 1989; Anderson 1990, chap. 7).

7. Other groups incorporated into Wa include the association of women consumers, the association to review children's books, the women's club of the agricultural cooperative, and so forth.

8. Avon Cultural Center for Women has developed a variety of programs since its establishment in Tokyo in 1979. One of these programs is "Avon Group Support," which provides financial support to various women's groups in Japan. These 242 groups were the ones that applied to this particular program in 1986 and 1987.

9. I learned of this important article by Philip Abrams in Michael Taussig's article "Maleficium: State Fetishism" (1992a, 113–114).

10. Radcliffe-Brown here uses "the State" with a capital S, since "state," according to him, means a territorial group within a larger political system, in which its relations with other such "states" are defined by war, treaties, or international law.

11. For the implication of anthropology in colonial enterprises, see Talal Asad, "Introduction" to his edited volume, *Anthropology and the Colonial Encounter* (1973). See also Jack Stauder, "The 'Relevance' of Anthropology to Colonialism and Imperialism" (1974).

12. See Karl Marx, "Critique of Hegel's Doctrine of the State" (1843) and "On the Jewish Question" (1843). I used *Karl Marx: Early Writings* (1975), edited by Quintin Hoare and introduced by Lucio Colleti. I am grateful to Norma Field and Miriam Silverberg, who urged me to go back to Marx's early writings on the question of the state.

13. Hosokawa Junjirō's article "Kokuryoku to josei kyōiku to no kankei" (The relationship between the nation's military power and women's education) was published in 1895 in the journal *Dai-Nippon kyōiku-kai zasshi* (The journal of the Greater Japan Association for Education) (quoted in Fukaya 1990, 138–139).

14. *Shinano mainichi shinbun*, February 10 and April 30, 1887.

15. Not only women's associations but the Nagano Educational Committee asserted that it was necessary for women to learn from Western civilization, because the two imported religions (from China), Confucianism and Buddhism, had created an environment in Japan that despised women (Shinano Kyōiku-kai 1898, 11).

16. *Shinano mainichi shinbun*, October 26, 1888.

17. This passage is in the prospectus of Nagano Fujin Kyōkai (Nagano-town Women's Association), founded in 1888 (Nagano-ken-shi Kankō-kai 1987, 949).

18. *Shinano mainichi shinbun*, April 20, 1899.

19. On this issue of enlightenment scholars' refusal to endorse *danjo dōken*, see the following three articles translated into the English language: "Abuses of Equal Rights for Men and Women," by Katō Hiroyuki (1875, in Braisted 1976, 376–377); "Abuses of Equal Rights for Men and Women, Part II," by the same author (1875, in Braisted 1976, 377–379); and "Distinguishing the Equal Rights of Husbands and Wives," by Tsuda Mamichi (1875, in Braisted 1976, 435–436).

20. Despite this historical truism, few books and articles, particularly in English, have been published about rural women in modern Japan. Both Gail Lee Bernstein (1983, 1988) and Patricia E. Tsurumi (1984b, 1990) lament that rural women have been neglected in the American mainstream scholarship on Japanese history. However, the increasing number of feminist scholars have begun to shed new light on the culture and history of rural women in modern Japan. In addition to the works by Bernstein and Tsurumi, the following studies touch on the relationship of rural women and the development of Japanese capitalism: G. R. Saxonhouse, "Country Girls and Communication among Competitors in the Japanese Cotton-Spinning Industry" (1976, 97–125); Yasue Aoki Kidd, *Women Workers in the Japanese Cotton Mills, 1880–1920* (1978); Mikiso Hane, *Peasants, Rebels, and Outcasts: The Underside of Modern Japan* (1982); Joyce Lebra, "Women in an All-Male Industry: The Case of Sake Brewer Tatsu'uma Kiyo" (1991, 131–148); Kathleen Uno, "Women and Changes in the Household Division of Labor" (1991, 17–41); and Anne Walthall, "The Life Cycle of Farm Women in Tokugawa Japan" (1991, 42–70). I may be unaware of many of the increasing number of publications on rural women in modern Japan in Japanese-language sources, although I cite some of them in this book.

21. Cole and Tominaga argue that Japanese society was still basically agrarian up until 1920 and that "agriculture was perceived in terms of a livelihood (*nariwai*), that is, as life itself, rather than as an occupation in the modern sense with functionally specific roles containing a differentiated set of duties" (1976, 56). This is a rather nostalgic view of rural Japan in the early twentieth century. On the contrary, it was well integrated into the national economy, and its women constituted the major labor force for the textile industry.

22. The term "*ryōsai kenbo*" was coined by another enlightenment scholar, Nakamura Masanao. Despite the popular belief in the West as well as in Japan that the "good wife and wise mother" ideology is a reflection of premodern Confucianism, it is an amalgam of Confucianism and the nineteenth-century Western "cult of domesticity" (see Cherry 1987; Koyama 1986; Mackie 1988; Roberts 1994; Sievers 1983; R. Smith 1983).

23. *Shinano mainichi shinbun*, January 20, 1903.

24. *Shinano mainishi shinbun*, October 9, 1894.

25. Most of the documents, i.e., the prospectuses and the minutes of regular meetings, of various local groups of the Japan Women's Patriotic Association in Nagano have been compiled and published in *Nagano-ken-shi* (Nagano-ken-shi Kankō-kai 1987, 811–874).

26. For biographical information on Okumura Ioko, see Sievers (1983, 217, chap. 6, n. 1). Sievers describes her as a "Meiji period leader in women's social work . . . whose earliest political interests stemmed from her family's close connections to the *son'nō jōi* (revere the Emperor, throw out the barbarians) fac-

tion in late Tokugawa. Married and widowed, Ioko remarried in 1872 and then was divorced in 1887. At that point she began to devote much of her energy to Japan's interests in Korea and China. When Japanese troops were sent to North China during the Boxer Rebellion, she recognized that the wounded would need proper care and their families would require assistance, and with the backing of Konoe Atsumaro, president of the Upper House of the Diet, founded the Aikoku Fujinkai."

27. An editorial in a Nagano local newspaper, however, criticized the way members were recruited into the Patriotic Association, commenting that illiterate local women were forced to become members. See *Nanshin nichinichi shinbun*, October 13, 1907.

28. *Fujo shinbun*, March 11, 1901.

29. Even by the time of the Manchurian Incident in 1931, the Nagano branch of the Japan Women's Patriotic Association had slightly fewer than fifty thousand members (Aoki 1987, 253). The stagnation in the association's membership could later be contrasted with the swift increase in the membership of another patriotic organization, Dai-Nippon Kokubō Fujin-kai (Great Japan National Defense Women's Association). While its Nagano chapter had only 2,684 members at the time of its founding, the membership had grown to 260,935 by 1941. In the same year, the Nagano branch of the Japan Women's Patriotic Association had only 111,056 members (p. 266).

30. This means that the nature of the boundaries of the Japanese nation-state was also altered. In fact, even before the acquisition of Taiwan, Japan's boundaries as a nation-state were unclear. A case in point is the geographical location and the cultural position of

Okinawa. Though unified under a strong monarchy in the fifteenth century, the kingdom was controlled by the Shimazu clan during the Tokugawa period. Only nine years later, after the Meiji Restoration, was it incorporated into Japan as a prefecture. After Japan's surrender in World War II in 1945, Okinawa was ceded to the U.S. forces for indefinite occupation. It was finally reincorporated into Japan as Okinawa prefecture in 1972. Throughout modern Japanese history, however, its unique culture has made its position vis-à-vis *Yamaton-chu*—those who live on the main four islands of Japan—ambivalent (see Field 1991b, 33–104). See also Yoshimi Yoshiaki's (1987) chapter "Minzoku joretsu" or the "Order of Races," in which he argues that both Okinawans and Ainu were placed at the bottom of the racial hierarchy within Japan.

31. *Shinano mainichi shinbun*, January 31, 1942.

32. This letter was sent by the head of the section on internal affairs of the Nagano prefectural government to all the mayors and school principals in Nagano on January 24, 1946 (quoted in Tsujimura 1966, 78).

CHAPTER 3: *KOMORI*

1. For the culture and history of European (mainly English) nursemaids and nannies, see, for example, Gathorne-Hardy (1972); McBride (1976, 1978); Branca (1975); Robertson (1975); Gillis (1979); Higgs (1986); and Davidoff and Hall (1986).

2. For example, Fujin Eisei-kai, the Hygienic Organization for Women, which was founded in 1888 in Tokyo, organized a series of lectures by a prominent medical doctor about how to find "good" wet nurses for upper-class

women, who often had to attend social gatherings, leaving their children at home (Miyamoto 1888, 1889). Elite families often hired wet nurses during the Tokugawa period. Uno (1987) mentions Tokugawa child-rearing tracts that include sections on criteria for selecting wet nurses of good character.

3. Merchants' households in the city were exceptions. They needed the help of *komori*, many of whom were recruited from the countryside. Wakita Haruko, a scholar of Japanese medieval history, told me of her childhood memory of growing up as one of eight siblings in a wealthy merchant's household near Kōbe. Each of her siblings, including herself, had her or his own *komori* (Wakita, personal communication).

4. Akamatsu Keisuke argues that *komori* disappeared much earlier than 1945, in and around the 1910s and 1920s. He attributes their disappearance to the fact that those who could hire indentured *komori* were no longer able to do so in the wave of economic recessions, having become impoverished tenants by the early twentieth century (1993, 87). The increasing number of community day-care facilities (see Chapter 6) also explains the *komori's* decline. But my fieldnotes suggest that there were still a significant number of *komori* in the Nagano countryside in the 1930s and 1940s. Both Sumiko and Sayo, who will appear later in this chapter, worked as indentured *komori* in the 1930s, while others like Chieko were *komori* for their own siblings or neighbors' children.

5. Také, whose complete name is Koshino Také, also appears in the two photographs published in the English version of *Tsugaru* that were taken at the time of the unveiling of the Dazai Memorial in Aomori in 1965 (Westerhoven 1987).

6. Such decrees were issued several times in Nagano, beginning in 1870 (Nagano-ken-shi Kankō-kai 1987, 400, 404). Although similar decrees were issued during the Tokugawa period, they were largely designed to check the excessive independence of rural young men from the Bakufu authorities (see Varner 1977) and hence different from the Meiji decrees.

7. *Onna no rekishi to minzoku* (The history and folklore of women; 1993) was originally published in 1950 with a different title, *Kekkon to ren'ai no rekishi* (The history of marriage and love). I am grateful to Professor Ueno Chizuko of Tōkyō University, who alerted me to this important publication.

8. My interview with Takayama Sumiko was conducted in the summer of 1991 at her home. She published a book in 1987 of her memories as the wife of a peasant settler in Manchuria during the 1930s, titled *Nono-san ni narundayo* (You will become a little buddha). I interviewed her to explore Japanese colonialism in China and particularly in Manchuria, but she also provided me with this precious information about her days as a *komori*.

9. *Komori kyōiku kenkyū kiroku* (Reports on the study of *komori's* education) of Takashima Elementary School mentions "fourteen more *komori* students who came to school for the first time" on February 15, 1899, among whom three were boys. On March 9 of the same year, ten *komori* students graduated from the third grade, among whom three were boys. This is the last record I found that contains evidence of the presence of male *komori* (Nagano-ken Kyōiku-shi Kankō-kai 1976, 619–621; see also Uno 1987, 31).

10. For the notion of "manliness" in the early Meiji period, see Donald

Roden, *Schooldays in Imperial Japan* (1980), and Earl Kinmonth, *The Self-made Man in Meiji Japanese Thought* (1981). According to Roden, the notion of "manliness" in early Meiji was represented by the "values of masculine domination: asceticism, achievement, and public service" (1990, 39). Note that such a notion of "manliness" is possible only if it is complemented by a notion of "womanliness" that signifies the domesticity of women.

11. Most of the households in the Nagano countryside were not able to afford the type of arrangement mentioned by Wakita Haruko (see n. 3). Consequently, either one *komori* took care of all the siblings, or older siblings acted as the *komori* for the younger ones.

12. Itō Chōhichi, a teacher of a class for *komori* at the Takashima Elementary School in Suwa County, also wrote: "An increasing number of four- and five-year-old toddlers came to school with *komori*. The total number is indeed one hundred ten" (Nagano-ken Kyōiku-shi Kankō-kai 1976, 619–621). Itō recorded the number of *komori* who attended the class as sixty. This means that the number of toddlers who came with them was as large as fifty.

13 . *Tan* is used to measure the length of cloth for making kimono. One *tan* is about eight meters long and thirty centimeters wide.

14. *Katei hōmon roku: Komori Ji-ai no kumi* (1907). This particular *komori*'s teacher visited his students' employers and parents once a year at their homes.

15. *Jogaku zasshi* 57 (1887): 121–123. The author of the editorial is not given, although one might speculate that the author is Iwamoto Yoshiharu, the founder of *Jogaku zasshi*.

16. *Katei hōmon roku: Komori Ji-ai no kumi* (1907).

17. Ibid.

18. Several scholars of nativism (*kokugaku*) had advocated these ideas, the quantitative and qualitative control of the population, already in the early nineteenth century to save villages devastated by natural calamities and the peasants living in them. See, for example, Tachibana Yoshio's "song admonishing peasants not to desert their children" (*sutego kyōkai no uta*) (1861) cited by Mitsuda (1985, 104).

19. *Gekkei shinshi*, January 13, 1879.

20. *Shinpi shinbun*, 1873, no. 3.

21. This "fine episode" was publised in *Kankoku kōgiroku*, an enormous record of eight thousand "filial," "chaste," "faithful," and "laudable" women and men found among the commoners. It was compiled by Matsudaira Sadanobu in 1787.

22. *Shinano mainichi shinbun*, March 17, 1883.

23. *Saku shinpō*, October 7, 1898.

24. *Shinano mainichi shinbun*, July 20, 1901.

25. *Shinano mainichi shinbun*, June 6, 1901.

26. *Shinano mainichi shinbun*, July 3, 1901.

27. Many of my informants, however, told me that there were "quite a few" girls who brought their siblings and charges to school in the 1930s and 1940s. This means that *komori* also attended schools with regular school children, particularly if local schools did not offer them special programs. The Shimo Mizu'uchi county government, for example, issued a decree in 1917 to prohibit *komori* from attending regular schools (Nagano-ken Kyōiku-shi Kankō-kai 1976, 212–213).

28. *Shinano mainichi shinbun*, March 5, 1893.

29. The structure of a counting song relies on the progression of the numbers from one to ten through the first ten stanzas. At the same time, the sound of each number forms part of the opening word for each line.

30. As *komori* is a generic term, so is *komori uta*: it could mean any lullaby. Here, I use this term specifically for the songs created and sung by the young girls who worked as *komori* in the early modern history of Japan.

31. In fact, they could recall this song only partially, so I have supplemented it here with the same song (with slight differences in wording) recorded by Watanabe Tomio and Matsuzawa Shunsuke among elderly women in Niigata prefecture (1979). A large number of women in Niigata were sent to Nagano as indentured *komori* in the late nineteenth and early twentieth centuries.

32. *Kae-uta* could be translated as either "changed songs" or "changing songs." In the sense that *komori*'s songs were constantly being changed, I use the latter translation. Miriam Silverberg also uses this translation, referring to the songs of factory women in the silk and cotton industries in modern Japan. See her *Changing Song: The Marxist Manifestos of Nakano Shigeharu* (1990). I will introduce some of these factory women's songs in the following chapter.

33. Watanabe and Matsuzawa also recorded this song but with somewhat different verses: "Listen my mistress (*anesa*) and you too. If you treat *komori* badly, we can have an evil influence on your children" (1979, 32).

34. For an excellent critique of the use of dichotomies in the study of resistance, see Timothy Mitchell, "Everyday Metaphors of Power" (1990). Mitchell criticizes the use of dichotomies as a misleadingly narrow approach to understanding modern methods of domination and argues that such methods of domination themselves work through constructing a dualistic world.

CHAPTER 4: FACTORY WOMEN

1. Yokota (Wada) Ei learned the modern method of silk spinning at Tomioka Mill in 1873 and 1874. She described the everyday life of factory women at this mill, from recollections of her youth, when she was about fifty years old. *Tomioka nikki* (Tomioka diary) was published posthumously in 1976.

2. Eguchi Zenji and Hidaka Yasohichi of the Nagano branch of the Greater Japan Silk Spinning Association edited three volumes of the set of books titled *Shinano sanshi-gyō-shi* (The history of silk spinning in Nagano) in 1937. In chapter 9 of the third volume, *The Japanese Imperial Household and the Silk Spinning Industry in Nagano*, they emphasized the important relationship between the silk spinning industry in Nagano and the Japanese imperial household by explaining that the peasants in Nagano had presented silk to the emperor Yūryaku in 1122 (1937, 1350–1365).

3. McDougall argues: "Modernization in one branch of an industry could cause expansion in more traditional branches of the same industry." For example, "as cotton spinning became a factory occupation and thread output rose in early nineteenth-century England, the number of cotton hand-loom weavers increased" (1977, 259). As I will demonstrate shortly, the coexistence of the factory and the family workshop in the early phase of the industrial revolution is also observed in the silk industry in Japan.

4. For various explanations of the motives of rural women to move elsewhere for work in industry in the United

States and Europe, see, for example, Thomas Dublin, *Women at Work: The Transformation of Work and Community in Lowell, Massachusetts, 1826–1860* (1981); Philip S. Foner, *The Factory Girls* (1977); Tamara Hareven and Randolph Langenbach, *Amoskerg: Life and Work in an American Factory City* (1978). I learned of these works from Molony's article "Activism among Women in the Taishō Cotton Textile Industry" (1991).

5. Teresa McBride argues that nineteenth-century Europe "discovered" the woman worker as an "object of pity, and the Victorian social conscience was aroused as never before by the plight of working women and children" (1977, 282). Japanese social reformers shared this Victorian social conscience with their European counterparts.

6 . Miwada Masako (1843–1927) was a specialist on women's education in the Meiji period. After her husband, Miwada Mototsuna, died in 1879, she founded several schools for women in Matsuyama and Tokyo. She also helped in founding Nippon Joshi Daigaku (Japanese Women's College) and became part of its faculty in 1919. She authored numerous books in order to teach Japanese women the ideology of the "good wife and wise mother."

7. *Shinano mainichi shinbun*, May 18, 1901.

8. *Shinano mainichi shinbun*, June 1, 1901.

9. *Shinano mainichi shinbun*, January 26, 1893.

10. *Shinano mainichi shinbun*, July 17, 1914.

11. Discourses emphasizing the promiscuous nature of factory women were found not only locally but also in the metropolis. For example, *Kokumin shinbun* reported, specifically commenting on the factory women who came

from Nagano to work in Gunma prefecture: "The behavior of factory women is unmentionable. . . . Those who are only seventeen or eighteen years old earn seven or eight yen in wages every month, but send it to their parents only until they are twenty-seven or twenty-eight years old. After that, they keep moving from one factory to another and eventually become (1) the wives of day laborers, (2) the wives or concubines of gamblers, (3) the concubines of ruffians, or (4) prostitutes" (quoted in *Jogaku zasshi*, vol. 355 [October 14, 1893], pp. 406–407).

12. *Shinano nippō*, July 30, 1924 (quoted in Hosokawa 1982, 28).

13. *Shinano nippō*, May 2, 1926 (quoted in Hosokawa 1982, 28).

14. These two employers were Higuchi Ainosuke of the village of Shimosuwa and Takei Kunikichi of the village of Hirano. They presented their recommendation to the representative of the Nagano prefectural governor.

15. *Gekkei shinshi*, March 10, 1879.

16. This curriculum was also proudly made public in an article published in the local newspaper *Shinano mainichi shinbun* (August 26, 1901).

17. Data on the number of factories believed to have offered some sort of education to their employees vary greatly and are hence quite unreliable. In 1915, for example, a Nagano educational committee reported that fifty-one out of approximately six hundred silk industry factories in Nagano offered such education, while Nagano prefectural government reported that as many as 106 factories did (see Kōzu 1974, 458).

18. *Shinano mainichi shinbun*, July 8, 1915.

19. Similarly, Yamazaki Nobukichi, an ideologue of popular agrarianism, commented in 1906: "Sericulture is the most

appropriate work for women. We find only in women the ability to pay attention to the details and to feel the deep compassion [for silkworms]." See *Den'en fujin*, vol. 6 (May 1, 1906).

20. My explication of the ideology of *kokutai* here derives from my reading of *Kokutai no hongi* (The principles of kokutai) published in 1937, and *Shinmin no michi* (The way of subjects) published in 1941 by the Japanese Ministry of Education (Monbushō 1941). For *Kokutai no hongi*, I have relied on its English translation by Tsunoda, de Bary, and Keene (1965, 278–288).

21. See, for example, articles published in *Shinano mainichi shinbun*, November 8, 1885; October 30, 1889; and March 22, 1913, which reported on the award ceremonies for "excellent factory women" (*yūtō kōjo*).

22. The lyrics of this particular song are "Put all your strength into your work. It's for yourself, it's for your family, it's for the country of Japan" (Tsurumi 1990, 93).

23. "Eisei-gaku jō yori mitaru jokō no genkyō" was originally published in *Kokka igaku-kai zasshi*, vol. 322, in 1913. A year later, the National Association of Medicine published this article together with his lecture as a booklet. I used the version compiled by Kagoyama Takashi, titled *Jokō to kekkaku* (1970), and refer to the article (Ishihara 1970a) and lecture (Ishihara 1970b) separately.

24. Ishihara, however, particularly emphasized the degraded working conditions of night shifts for factory women in the cotton spinning industry. He argued: "Although it depends on how one sees this issue, I think the night shift is a long-term process that can draw the breath out of human beings" (1970b, 180).

25. In 1881, the Ministry of Agriculture and Commerce became independent from the Home Ministry.

26. Yokoyama Gennosuke was one of the temporary employees in the factory survey office. Prior to the publication of *Shokkō jijō*, to which he contributed greatly, Yokoyama published *Nihon no kasō shakai*, in which he meticulously described the working conditions of the lower working class, including the spinners and weavers in the silk and cotton industries.

27. For example, Kōtoku Shūsui is "generally known as a socialist and anarchist who participated in the plot against the life of the Meiji emperor in 1910 and was executed for the crime of 'high treason' the following year" (Notehelfer 1971, 31). But Fred Notehelfer argues that socialism for Kōtoku was a "means of preserving the mission idea of the radical and popular nationalism which he had accepted as the essence of the early Meiji experience" (p. 37). For an excellent analysis of socialism and Marxism, which, as an offspring of the universalist ideas of the Enlightenment (of which nationalism is also one), has not sufficiently challenged nationalism, see Shlomo Avineri, "Marxism and Nationalism" (1991).

28. Hirasawa's article, "Jokō-san no seikatsu" (The everyday lives of factory women), was originally published in 1916 in *Yūai fujin*. Hirasawa was a socialist journalist who became a chief editor for *Rōdō shūhō* (Labor weekly). One of the ten victims of the so-called Kameido Incident, he was brutally murdered by the police for his "dangerous thought" in the aftermath of the Great Kanto Earthquake in 1923 (see Gordon 1991, 177–181). Brief biographical information on Hirasawa in English can be found in Andrew Gordon's book *Labor*

and Imperial Democracy in Prewar Japan (p. 345).

29. Although written by a businessman (in the cotton industry), *Jokō no shitsuke-kata to kyōiku* (How to discipline and educate factory women), published in 1921, has striking similarities with *Jokō aishi*. Ishigami Kinji published this book for administrators in the textile industry. The book is composed of the following nineteen chapters: (1) Introduction; (2) First, You Should Train Yourself; (3) Recognizing the Personality of Factory Women; (4) Dissecting the Psychology of Factory Women; (5) Necessary Conditions for Training Factory Women; (6) How to Implement Good Habits; (7) How to Discipline Factory Women; (8) Some Criticism of Disciplining Factory Women; (9) How to Give Instructions to Factory Women; (10) To What Extent You Should Scold Factory Women; (11) How to Discipline Stubborn Factory Women; (12) How to Discipline Factory Women Who Lie; (13) How to Discipline Oversensitive Factory Women; (14) How to Discipline Lazy Factory Women; (15) Factory Women's Education and Facilities; (16) Factory Women's Education and Factory Slogans; (17) Factory Women's Education and Factory Hygiene; (18) How to Manage Factory Women's Physiology; and (19) You Should Utilize Model Factory Women. Although Ishigami did not have the slightest vision of socialist revolution, he also aimed at making "factory women" into "women" (*fujin*), not only for the company but for the nation (1984).

30. Hasegawa Kōichi, "Honpō ni okeru fujin rōdō no sūsei to sono kentō" (The trend of women's labor in Japan and its investigations), published in 1931 in *Shakai seisaku jihō*, vol. 135.

31. Tsurumi also quotes this passage.

Here, I use her translation (1984b, 4). Molony points out, quite correctly, that these labor organizers and historians ignored "social constraints" on factory women, such as "restrictions by management on the economic independence of female workers" or the "workers' own views of what was appropriate behavior for women" (1991, 218).

32. Kōfu is the prefectural capital of Yamanashi prefecture, which is located adjacent to Nagano prefecture.

33. Another notable Marxist intellectual in the early twentieth century is Morito Tatsuo, a professor of economics at Tokyo Imperial University, and a member of the Ōhara Social Problems Institute. He was jailed in 1920 for his communist and socialist ideas. His article "Nihon ni okeru joshi shokugyō mondai" (The labor problems among women in Japan), was originally published in *Shakai seisaku gakkai ronsō: Fujin rōdō mondai* in 1919 (see Akamatsu 1977, 515–554).

34. For the history of prostitution and the antiprostitution movement in Japan, see Fujime 1994; Garon 1993. Unlike the history of the antiprostitution movement in England (see, for example, Walkowitz 1980, 1983), the movement in Japan is extremely interesting in its relation to nationalism. That is, by the 1920s, the antiprostitution movement began to honor prostitutes as national subjects as long as they were licensed prostitutes. They were believed to uphold the "country's tradition of filial piety" (Garon 1993, 123). For a similar movement in Nazi Germany, see Mosse 1985, 167.

35. For the details of the motherhood protection debates and the discussion of other women activists who engaged in these debates, see Sievers (1983,

chap. 8), Nishikawa (1985), Tsurumi (1985), Ueno (1990), and Rodd (1991). I learned of these important books and articles from my reading of Barbara Molony, "Equality Versus Difference: The Japanese Debate over 'Motherhood Protection,' 1915–50" (1993), and Patricia E. Tsurumi, "Visions of Women and the New Society in Conflict: Yamakawa Kikue Versus Takamure Itsue" (1995).

36. Yamada Waka published "Kongo no fujin mondai o teishō su" (A discourse on women's problems from now on; undated) and "Bosei hogo mondai" (The motherhood protection question) in the September 1918 issue of *Taiyō* (The sun). Yamakawa's article "Fujin o uragiru fujin ron" (Women's opinion that stabs women in the back) was published in the August 1918 issue of *Shin Nihon* (New Japan). Patricia Tsurumi correctly points out that "exchanges in print regarding motherhood protection had been going on since 1915, but the argument was hot and heavy" by the time Yamada and Yamakawa jumped into the debate in 1918 (1995, 3–4).

37. Yamada Waka, one of the early participants in these debates, is somewhat different from all the others in terms of her upbringing and career. Born in a small fishing village near Yokohama, she was beckoned to come to America by a man who exaggerated tales of riches in the United States. When she landed, "he compelled her to become a prostitute in a Seattle brothel under the nickname Oyae of Arabia." Even though she fled once, she was forced once again into prostitution in a Chinatown brothel in San Francisco. After that, she finally managed to escape and "through eventual self-education became a writer-critic upon her return to Japan" (Ichioka 1977, 8).

38. Hiratsuka Raichō is the pen name of Hiratsuka Haruko. In Japan, as a

writer comes to be accepted into the "great tradition," he or she is known by his or her first name. Hiratsuka Haruko is thus known as Raichō.

39. This passage appears in "Bosei no shuchō ni tsuite Yosano Akiko ni atau" (To Yosano Akiko: About advocating motherhood), which was published in *Bunshō sekai* in May 1916.

40. Most state officials and the business community opposed implementation of the Factory Law. Consequently, the law was not enforced until 1926, and one of its most important articles, which prohibited the labor of women and children between ten o'clock in the evening and four o'clock in the morning, was shelved until 1929.

41. In his criticism of the same law, Hane points out that government officials supported the law in order to prevent socialistic movements from gaining support among factory workers (1982, 194; see also Garon 1988, 18–29, and Marshall 1967).

42. This statement was originally published in 1939 in *Kiryū orimono-shi* (The history of weaving in Kiryū), which was edited by Kiryū Orimono-shi Hensan-kai. Referring to the weavers' workshop in the Japanese countryside in a much later period of the early twentieth century, Akamatsu reports on the "song battles" (*uta-genka*): upon beginning their work, one weaver begins to sing, followed by another; the one who knows the most songs apparently wins. Akamatsu also reports that the content of the ballads seems to have been judged by other weavers to decide who was the winner (Akamatsu 1991, 226–227).

43. This song was first recorded and published in *Shūkan chokugen* (Weekly opinions), vol. 2, no. 7 (1905).

44. *Ah, Nomugi touge* was originally published in 1968. I use here the Kadokawa Bunko version of the book,

which was published in 1977. Hane also cites this particular narrative in his *Peasants, Rebels, and Outcasts: The Underside of Modern Japan* (1982, 182). I have used his translation but modified certain words.

45. In this respect, following E. P. Thompson, Jean Comaroff argues: "The impersonal clock is the fundamental instrument for internalizing the organization of work essential to industrial capitalist production. . . . During the process of proletarianization, the impartial clock prizes labor free from its embeddedness in undifferentiated social practice, setting apart 'work' from 'leisure,' and masking the unrequired surplus value transferred from the wage earner to his employer" (1985, 142; see Thompson 1967; see also T. Smith 1988, 200).

46. For detailed information about textile factory women's wages, see Hane 1982, 176–179.

47. Nakanishi's article "Kōjo to den'en no fujin rōdō" (Women's labor at factories and in the fields) was originally published in *Kaihō*, vol. 6, no. 11, in 1927.

48. Rural women in Nagano called (and still call) silkworms "honorary silkworms" in their everyday parlance. The honorific prefix (*o*) and suffix (*sama*), which are normally reserved only for persons, suggest that they honored silkworms for the economic benefits they brought not only to their families but to Japan.

49. When a company recruited a woman, it usually paid a considerable sum of money as an advance payment to her parents. This meant that a factory woman, at the time she began her work, had already incurred a considerable debt to her company. In addition, she incurred other company expenses for room and board. (One woman at the group meeting said: "If you bought snacks at the company store, the company would deduct the cost from your wages.") She was thus paid her earnings only after the company deducted all the above expenses, normally before a seasonal leave.

50. To maintain the consistency of my own translation, I have changed "factory girls" in Tsurumi's translation to "factory women."

51. In the translation of this ballad, I have again changed "factory girls" to "factory women."

52. Hosoi reports that, when 452 factory women at a cotton mill in Tokyo were asked to respond to questionnaires regarding their everyday lives, almost all of them chose to compose songs instead of writing their answers in prose (*futsū no bunshō*). According to him, they composed songs about "success, religion, food, sex, broken marriages, pride, filial piety, self-debasement, contempt of factory men, militarism, bodily pain, homesickness, resistance, love, praise of capitalism, and other matters" (Hosoi 1954, 325–326; see also Silverberg 1990, 107, n. 15).

53. Bon festival was held in midsummer, when the spirits of the ancestors of each household were supposed to return home. As factory women could not go home in the midst of their summer shift, they apparently celebrated it at their factories and dormitories.

54. Local historians and folklorists recorded many different versions of the "Prison Lament" in Nagano. Tsurumi also introduces a slightly different version of this song (1990, 98–99). My translation here is based on hers, but I have changed certain words, deleted some phrases, and added new ones, to be consistent with my fieldnotes.

55. Denier is a unit of weight by which the fineness of silk, rayon, or nylon yarn is estimated.

56. We see this in the increasing number of magazines, pamphlets, and newspapers for working women published by women labor activists themselves. The examples include *Yūai fujin* (Friendship for working women; 1916), *Rōdō fujin* (Working women; 1927), and *Musan fujin e* (To working women; 1925) (see Akamatsu 1977, 235, 401, 402, 449, 450, 451, 453). For autobiographies of some of these women activists, see Yamanouchi Mina, *Yamanouchi Mina jiden* (The autobiography of Yamanouchi Mina; 1975) and Takai Toshio, *Watashi no "Jokō aishi"* (My "Jokō aishi"; 1980). Takai is Hosoi Wakizo's wife. Molony interviewed two of these activists, Kumagai Kikuko and Umezu Hagiko (1991, 226, 228).

57. One other category of songs of factory women are songs of longing "not for the country or the company but for their homes and parents" (Tsurumi 1990, 101). Confined to factories and dormitories day and night, they sang, for example: "On rainy days and at night, I think of home. The factory closes and I return to the dormitory to think of home where frogs croak at night" (Yamamoto 1977, 368, translated in Tsurumi 1990, 101).

CHAPTER 5: THE COUNTRYSIDE AND THE CITY 1

1. In order to avoid confusion with the nation-state, I will use the term "countryside" for the country except where its meaning is clear, as in "the country and the city."

2. I follow Harry Harootunian's and Marilyn Ivy's translation of *minzoku-gaku*, "native ethnology," in addition to the usual "folklore studies" (Harootunian 1988, epilogue; Ivy 1988a, chap. 3; 1995, chap. 3, especially 66, n. 1). It can be also

translated "ethnographic folklorism" or "popular tradition."

3. Gluck also cites this text by Raymond Williams in discussing what she has called the "agrarian myth" (1985, 178). She argues: "Confronted with a modernity that threatened to shake the social foundations of the nation, the ideologues turned to the verities of the past—the village and the family, social harmony and communal custom—to cure civilization of its fevers so that society as they envisioned it might yet survive" (pp. 177–178).

4. Williams argues that the other times in the history of England when the reflections of the country and the city carried specific meaning are the late sixteenth and early seventeenth centuries, and the late eighteenth and early nineteenth centuries (1973, 291).

5. I hasten to add that other intellectuals had published essays or articles bearing the title of "The Countryside and the City" before 1929. They are, for example, Tokutomi Ichirō (Sohō), Sawayanagi Masatarō, and Yokoi Tokiyoshi (Gluck 1985, chap. 6). I single out Yanagita primarily because of his status as the founder of Japanese folklore studies and the number of publications by him on the cleavage between the city and the countryside.

6. In Ueda and its vicinity, the ratio of mulberry fields (for silkworms) to total agricultural land was 50.3 percent in 1925. The ratio of income from sericulture to total income in the same year was 67.0 percent (Kanō 1973, 102).

7. *Shinano mainichi shinbun*, November 20, 1930.

8. *Shinano mainichi shinbun*, December 19, 1929.

9. *Shinano mainichi shinbun*, October 18, 1930.

10. *Shinano mainichi shinbun,* May 14, 1931.

11. The term "middling" signifies the economic status of a farmer and, by extension, his style of agricultural production. He is a self-cultivating farmer who relies solely on his family's labor. Thus, "middling" is not synonymous with the middle class.

12. Indeed, already during the 1880s and 1890s, agriculture based on the system of family farming had begun to decline. Large landholdings grew larger and absentee ownership gradually increased. By 1908, tenancy had reached 45.5 percent of cultivated land, the level it maintained until the end of World War II (Gluck 1985, 33). By the late 1920s, more than two million of approximately 5.6 million agricultural households in Japan were tilling less than half a hectare each (Asada 1993, 83).

13. It is believed that Yokoi Tokiyoshi, himself an advocate of agrarianism, coined this term in 1897 (see Gluck 1985, 180, 362 n. 106).

14. Halliday argues that "agrarianism was never powerful enough *materially* to alter the chosen orientation of business either at home or abroad" (1975, 139; emphasis mine). Indeed, it was big business that played the major role in Japanese economic and political expansion after the depression era (see also B. Moore 1966, chap. 5). Yet, both Halliday and Barrington Moore admit that "agrarianism *as an ideological element* had great potency" in modern Japanese history (Halliday 1975, 139; emphasis mine).

15. His argument, however, is not new. In 1959, British anthropologist Melville J. Herskovits expressed his admiration for those struggling for the independence of an African nation, stressing their ability to use the "field of folklore . . . to exalt national character and a

national destiny" (1959, 219). But the apparent continuity of the topic of folklore studies and nationalism obscures a rift that separates Linke from Herskovits. Herskovits was interested in the "good" nationalisms of African nations' struggles for independence by nationalists. But before these nationalist movements, the field of folklore in Africa had been one of the "invented traditions" undertaken by colonials as a part of their "colonializing" project (Ranger 1983; see also Duara 1995, 23). Linke is more broadly interested in the field of folklore as a form of power and knowledge.

16. Hannjost Lixfeld (1994) also explores the thesis of folklore as a logical extension of "nation building" in Germany. He argues that, in Germany, scholarly folklore associations were born with the Third Reich, and folklore fell prey to Nazi politicians and ideologues, regardless of how folklorists felt about it. Lixfeld's study is significant in that it has broken the myth of "two folklores," which has been entertained in postwar Germany, one that served the Third Reich and the other that did not. Lixfeld argues that the so-called bourgeois national folklorists might not have been actively involved in Nazi politics, but their texts were vigorously appropriated in Nazi discourse during the Third Reich.

17. One notable exception is the work by the late historian Murakami Nobuhiko *Takamure Itsue to Yanagita Kunio: Konsei no mondai o chūshin ni* (Takamure Itsue and Yanagita Kunio: With emphasis on the question of the marriage system; 1977). I will refer to this text in my own discussion of Yanagita's "power of women."

18. Fukuda Ajio states that Yanagita used *"jōmin"* only twenty times in his texts published between 1906 and 1930

but forty-eight times in those published between 1931 and 1960 (1984, 210–212). Furthermore, according to Fukuda, Yanagita's use of "*jōmin*" is concentrated in the wartime texts of 1931 to 1945, where it appears thirty-eight times.

19. Although the accepted translation of *Tōno monogatari* is *The Legends of Tōno*, I here follow the translation by Harootunian (1988) and Ivy (1988a; 1995). Ivy argues: "'Tales' preserves the broad meaning of *monogatari* as 'narrative.' 'Legends' has a more precise, limited meaning in folklore. Most of what is recorded in *Tōno monogatari* are not legends at all; bits of geography, historical information, gossip, and memories are interspersed with legendary accounts" (1988a, 88, n. 1; 1995, 66, n. 1).

20. Yanagita, however, completely refashioned the prose of the texts and negated the dialect of the storyteller. See Ivy, "Ghastly Insufficiencies: *Tōno Monogatari* and the Origins of Nativist Ethnology," an excellent critical commentary not only on *Tōno monogatari* but on the question of "orality" in Japanese native ethnology (1995, chap. 3).

21. For an English translation of *Tōno monogatari*, I have relied on Ronald A. Morse's translation, *The Legends of Tōno* (1975), but I have changed the translations of certain words. I also referred to the original *Tōno monogatari* in Japanese, published in *Teihon*, vol. 4 (Yanagita 1963e, 1–54).

22. *Yamabito-kō* was originally delivered as a lecture at a meeting of the Japanese Association of History and Geography in 1917.

23. Akasaka Norio argues, based on his close reading of Yanagita's early texts, that Yanagita in fact created two distinct concepts of *yamabito*, mountain people, and *sanmin*, mountain folk. The former refers to the true natives of Japan, while the latter refers to a portion of the "foreign" tribe who arrived at the archipelagoes of Japan and opted to live in the mountains instead of in the lowlands. While the mountain people were wanderers, the mountain folk enjoyed a sedentary pattern of life (Akasaka 1991). Although Akasaka's text sheds much light on Yanagita's thought regarding the origin of the Japanese people, my one reservation is that Akasaka occasionally develops his argument as Yanagita did, identifying not *jōmin* but "mountain folk" as a metonym for all Japanese (see, for example, 1991, 230–235).

24. Among the tales in which lowland men fall victim to mountain women is the tale of a peasant who sees a mountain woman and becomes ill from the "fright of that moment [of encounter]" and eventually dies (Yanagita 1963e, 12; 1975, 13–14). In another tale, several laborers at a matchstick factory in a village are taken captive by a mountain woman, and "after returning they do not remember anything for two or three days" (1963e, 32; 1975, 52–53). However, in another tale, a lowland man kills a mountain woman, who thus becomes his victim (1963e, 12; 1975, 13).

25. These two quotes from *Yama no jinsei* indicate that, as far as women are concerned, Yanagita tends to go beyond the framework of one nation, Japan, to extend his argument to other cultures. This tendency seems to work against the role of folklore in nation building. This contradiction involves a question of larger significance, which should be another topic for study in and of itself.

26. That later scholars of Yanagita specifically focus on "*jōmin*" among these terms is probably because it was coined by Yanagita himself, while most of the others are generic terms, and thus represents a higher level of abstraction in his thought. In this chapter, I rely mainly

on the following texts by later scholars for Yanagita's notion of *jōmin*: Kamishima Jirō, "Minzoku-gaku no hōhōron-teki kiso: Ninshiki taishō no mondai" (The methodological foundation of native ethnology: the problems of the identification of its objects; 1975); Gotō Sōichirō, "Yanagita-gaku no shisō to gakumon" (The thought and scholarship of Yanagita's native ethnology; 1972); Itō Mikiharu, "Yanagita Kunio to bunmei hihyō no ronri" (Yanagita Kunio and the logic of his critique of civilization; 1972); Aruga Kizaemon, "Nihon jōmin seikatsu shiryō sōsho sōjo" (General introduction to the collection of documents on the everyday lives of Japanese peasants; 1971); Nakai Nobuhiko, "Rekishi-gaku to shiteno Yanagita minzoku-gaku: jōmin gainen o chūshin ni" (Yanagita's native ethnology as historiography: with special reference to the notion of *jōmin*; 1974); and Sugimoto Jin, "Yanagita-gaku ni okeru 'jōmin' gainen no isō" (Various aspects of the notion of *jōmin* in Yanagita's native ethnology; 1975).

27. Historian Irokawa Daikichi (1978) has also criticized Yanagita's abandonment of marginalized people, including mountain people, nonsedentary populations, and *burakumin* or the untouchables whom Yanagita occasionally identified with mountain people or mountain folk.

28. Yanagita argued that parents did not spend a penny on their children in the past but left them simply to grow, hence the high rate of infant mortality. Yanagita observed that parents now bought milk for children and paid tuition for their schooling (1964b, 10).

29. This, however, is an excruciating task, as Yanagita himself uses "*jōmin*" in a slightly different way each time he employs it. This tendency has made later scholars say, for example, "Yanagita has

never refined or clearly theorized the notion of *jōmin*" (Irokawa 1978, 37), or "Yanagita himself has never given any clear-cut explanation of "*jōmin*" (Fukuda 1984, 203).

30. Those "really simple peasants" were forbidden to have family names before the Meiji period.

31. This whole explication of the notion of *jōmin*, however, has been deleted in *Kyōdo seikatsu no kenkyū-hō*, which was published in volume 25 of *Teihon* (1964c). In the epilogue to volume 25 of *Teihon*, the compilers offer the reason that the "chapters after the "Classification of Ethnographic Data" [of the original version] are Yanagita's lectures that were later edited [for the purpose of publication]" (p. 562). *Kyōdo seikatsu no kenkyū-ho* went through three printings after its first publication in 1935 (1940, 1964c, 1967). Except for the *Teihon* version, the versions are identical to the original.

The version I used (1967) has a somewhat different title, *Kyōdo seikatsu no kenkyū*, with "*hō*" in the original title deleted. This is presumably because the earlier *Teihon* version, though different from the original, retains the original title of *Kyōdo seikatsu no kenkyū-hō*.

32. "Kafu to nōgyō" is a chapter in his *Momen izen no koto* (On matters before cotton affected our lives; 1964f), originally published in 1929.

33. This passage was published in *Kyōdo-shi ron* (Theory on the Ethnography of the Countryside; 1964d), originally published in 1923.

34. Similar to the case with *Kyōdo seikatsu no kenkyū-hō*, this passage has been deleted in *Minkan denshō-ron* as published in volume 25 of *Teihon* (1964e). According to the compilers of *Teihon*, only the first chapter is Yanagita's own writing, the rest consisting of the lecture notes of his student. However,

the name of the author on the original version is Yanagita Kunio. I have used the original version here.

35. I must mention here that Yanagita became secretary of the imperial household in 1908 at the age of thirty-four. For Yanagita's detailed biography, see Yanagita Kunio Kenkyū-kai, *Yanagita Kunio-den* (The biography of Yanagita Kunio; 1988).

36. Regarding this last group, we must see how Yanagita defined the discipline of native ethnology. He defined it as the study of the folklorists' own people and race, including folklorists themselves (Yanagita 1964k). In other words, in Japanese native ethnology, knowing subjects, i.e. the folklorists, shared the life and customs of the objects of their studies, i.e., *jōmin* (see Harootunian 1990, 101).

37. "Saishū techō" was later published in *Nihon minzoku-gaku nyūmon* (Guide for Japanese native ethnology) (Yanagita and Seki 1948).

38. In his critique of Yanagita and Japanese native ethnology, Akamatsu identifies himself with "those below *jōmin*" whom he named "*hi-jōmin.*" *Hi-jōmin* include landless peasants, nonsedentary people such as peddlers, blacksmiths, coopers, and beggars, *komori*, factory women, prostitutes, those who migrated to the city out of rural poverty and lived in urban ghettos, those who worked at urban cafes, inns, and restaurants, and Koreans and Chinese who were brought to Japan by the Japanese imperial army to work in mines and construction sites. It is interesting to note that the mountain people and mountain folk formulated by Yanagita can be included in this very category of *hi-jōmin* (1986, 1991).

39. Biographies of Yanagita written by later scholars suggest that he saw this *jōmin* woman figure in his own mother,

who "was equipped with the superb power of remembering and of storytelling, even though completely illiterate" (Irokawa 1978, 66).

40. In 1950, Yanagita wrote a preface to *Ama-ki* (The ethnography of women divers), which was written by one of his few female disciples, Segawa Kiyoko. In it, he argues: "As for the facts of everyday life of the past, there are many men, particularly among the old, who remember well what was written and thus recorded. However, since they grew up in the busy early days of Meiji, they could not afford the leisure of remembering things that were not written. Naturally, they left this task for women, especially smart women" (Segawa 1950a, 1).

41. This article was originally published in *Shin jo-en* in 1945.

42. Based on the same ethnographic records collected by Yanagita and his students, historian Murakami Nobuhiko argued against Yanagita by emphasizing the oppression of young village women by men (1970, 1977). In addition, Tomio Kentarō questions whether the control exercised by young men's groups over the sexuality of village women can be viewed as more "liberated" than the parental control that became the norm by the time of Yanagita's fieldwork (Tomio 1986).

43. *Meiji Taishō-shi sesō-hen* (Yanagita 1963b) was originally published as a series of articles in the national newspaper *Asahi Shinbun* in 1930.

44. This title, *Thoughts on the Matrilocal Marriage*, is somewhat misleading, as Yanagita attempted to deny the presence of matrilocal marriage in the history of the Japanese marriage system.

45. According to Murakami, Takamure presented her *Bokei-sei no kenkyū* (Study on the matrilineal system), published in 1938, to Yanagita. He in turn sent a letter of thanks to Takamure, in which

he wrote: "I will read your book prompt-ly. I will also make sure that my student, Mr. Omachi, who studies the Japanese family system, reads it through" (quoted in Murakami 1977, 14). Yanagita, how-ever, never referred to Takamure's works in his texts.

46. The Japanese state did not permit the publication of *The Japanese Bride*, written originally in English. Murakami Nobuhiko criticized Yanagita (and the state, which coopted folklore study in exercising its own power) for ignoring "history" in favor of "folklore study," which, in Yanagita's own words, "started with a sense of nostalgia for things swift-ly disappearing" (Murakami 1977, 103–104; see also Mulhern 1985).

47. Unlike Yanagita, who suppressed the actual voices of rural women, Segawa Kiyoko presents them without much editing. Murakami, however, points out—correctly, I believe—that, when Segawa interprets the narratives of women, she comes to almost identical conclusions about *jōmin* as does Yanagita. For example, after having described the almost slavelike labor of farming women under the patriarchal family system, she concludes: "I do not necessarily approve of the feudal system, but there are many different patterns of communal life. I have discovered that people in those days simply enjoyed living along the lines of those patterns without questioning them" (quoted in Murakami 1977, 162).

In addition to *Ama-ki*, Segawa Kiyoko published numerous ethnogra-phies, for example, *Hanjo* (Women sell-ers; 1950b), *Shikitari no naka no onna* (Women in traditions; 1961), *Okinawa no kon'in* (The Marriages in Okinawa; 1969), *Mura no onna-tachi* (Women in the village; 1970), and *Wakamono to musume o meguru minzoku* (Folklore con-cerning young men and women; 1972).

48. I here cite only a passage from a Yanagita's text about Japan's colonial expansion. He wrote in 1942: "It is pos-sible to argue that the 2,600 years of Japanese history is a history of continu-ous migration and settlement. Every his-torical document reveals that, even before we finally reached Hokkaido, Karafuto, Taiwan, and Korea, we had sent out our fellow countrymen to every corner of virgin land and made efforts to create new villages. If we had not been able to welcome our *kami* [each village's tutelary gods or goddesses] to the [new] shrine we dedicated to *kami*, life would have been quite lonely. Such thoughts still survive in our plans to create a Korean shrine or a North Manchurian shrine" (1962b, 204).

I discovered the involvement of Japanese native ethnology and of Yanagita in particular in Japanese colo-nialism from the recent thought-pro-voking works of Murai Osamu. See his *Nantō ideologii no hassei: Yanagita Kunio to shokuminchi-shugi* (The genesis of Nantō ideology: Yanagita Kunio and colonial-ism; 1995); "Nihon minzoku-gaku to fashizumu" (Japanese native ethnology and fascism; 1993a); "Shin-kokugaku to shokuminchi-shugi" (New nativism and colonialism; 1993c); and "Origuchi Shinobu to Yanagita Kunio: Okinawa e no manazashi" (Origuchi Shinobu and Yanagita Kunio: perspectives toward Okinawa; 1993b). See also Iwamoto Yoshiteru, "Shokuminchi seisaku to Yanagita Kunio: Chōsen, Taiwan" (Colonial policies and Yanagita Kunio: Korea and Taiwan; 1993).

CHAPTER 6: THE COUNTRYSIDE AND THE CITY 2

1. There are two excellent secondary sources regarding these village newspa-pers. One is *Taishō democrashii no teiryū*:

Dozoku-teki seishin e no kaiki (Taishō democracy: Return to the secular spirits), by Kanō Masanao (1973). Its chapter 2, "Seinendan undō no shisō" (The thought in the youth movements) is especially useful (see also Kanō 1976). The other is "Keizai kosei undō to nōson tōgō: Nagano-ken Chiisagata-gun Urazato-mura no baai" (Economic regeneration in Chiisagata county), by Nakamura Masanori, published in the book *Fashizumuki no kokka to shakai*, vol. 1, *Shōwa kyōkō* (The state and society during the fascist period, vol. 1, Shōwa depression), edited by Tōkyō Daigaku Shakai Kagaku Kenkyū-sho (1978, 197–262).

2. Because of the limited period of my field research, I read only several village newspapers: *Urazato sonpō*, *Ebōshi no hana* (later called *Motohara jihō*), *Kamishina jihō*, *Shiojiri jihō*, and *Kangawa jihō*. In the present chapter, I focus on *Urazato sonpō* and refer to other village newspapers when necessary.

3. Some village newspapers, notably *Urazato sonpō*, became *kōhō* between 1940 and 1942, and printed only the central government's notifications for the local residents. *Kōhō* were thus no longer village newspapers, but the central government's newspapers.

4. *Urazato sonpō*, March 15, 1922.

5. Local youth groups in most of these thirty villages resumed the publication of their village newspapers after the end of World War II. The village newspapers had disappeared by the early 1960s. For the past ten years or so, groups of local historians in the Ueda region have been attempting to publish *fukkokuban*, reprints of ceased titles of village newspapers.

6. Those measures included (1) the Tenancy Conciliation Law of 1924, (2) the Regulations for the Establishment of Owner-Cultivators of 1926, and (3)

the revision of the Industrial Cooperative Law of 1900 (see Waswo 1988, 588).

7. *Urazato sonpō*, August 15, 1922.

8. *Urazato sonpō*, February 15, 1923.

9. *Urazato sonpō*, May 10, 1926.

10. *Urazato sonpō*, February 1, 1922.

11. *Ebōshi no hana*, May 1, 1919. The name of this *sonpō* means "flowers of Ebōshi," the mountain located in the village of Motohara.

12. *Urazato sonpō*, May 15, 1922.

13. *Urazato sonpō*, May 1, 1932.

14. *Urazato sonpō*, March 15, 1923.

15. *Ebōshi no hana*, March 5, 1921.

16. *Urazato sonpō*, October 25, 1933.

17. *Ie no hikari* was first published in 1925 by the national headquarters of the agricultural cooperatives (Sangyō Kumiai Chūōkai) and has been distributed to its subscribers from then on through the local branches of agricultural cooperatives (see Chap. 7).

18. *Ie no hikari*, October 1928, p. 144.

19. For an excellent discussion of the Modern Girl and the Modern Boy, see Roden 1990 and Silverberg 1991. For a discussion of the relationship between the rise of the Modern Girl in mass media and the change in the household structure of urban Japan, see Ueno 1987.

Both Roden and Silverberg argue that the "New Woman" (and to a lesser extent the "New Man") also contributed to the erosion of gender roles in urban Japan. Her difference from the Modern Girl, however, is significant. The New Woman is a woman of a "firm self-confidence and an emotional independence from the patriarchal family" (Roden 1990, 43). And yet, the New Woman remains a wife and mother, and does not offer a new economic model for everyday life (Silverberg 1991, 247–248). The Modern Girl exhibits similar resistance to patriarchal authorities. However, she resists a single definition: she may be a decadent and passive consumer, an apolitical woman, a promiscuous woman, a wage worker, or a fervent revolutionary. Thus, what distinguishes the Modern Girl from the New Woman is her economic self-sufficiency and autonomy.

20. Several urban critics of popular culture also made distinctions between the Modern Girl and the truly Modern Girl, but they did so in order to eliminate certain interpretations of the urban Modern Girl. For example, Kiyosawa Kiyoshi wrote in the 1920s that the "real Modern Girl lived outside Japan, whereas the Japanese Modern Girl was a colorful but apolitical and anti-intellectual migration" (quoted in Silverberg 1991, 249). In other words, Kiyosawa does not acknowledge the existence of the real Modern Girl among Japanese. Another critic, Ōya Sōichi, wrote in 1929 that "one hundred percent moga" was the "daughter of heroic activists who had been imprisoned countless times; she thus had no sense of family other than the police, the jails, and the streets" (quoted in ibid.). Or, according to the woman activist Hiratsuka Raichō, the "Modern Girl As She Should Be" would have a social conscience, unlike the seemingly liberated woman in a brightly colored ensemble of Western clothing with matching hat (quoted in ibid.). For these critics, the real Modern Girl is an autonomous, political, intellectual, and even revolutionary woman, not a passive and decadent consumer. However, they do not take into account the rural space in presenting their visions.

21. The quotation marks around "culture" (and "civilization") are meant to indicate the historical specificities of the discursive constructions of these terms. However, I will not continue to use quotation marks around these terms in the rest of this chapter.

22. The way these scholars compare and contrast the Meiji and Taishō eras does not mean that there is a clear rupture between these two periods in terms of people's lives in Japan. Rather, the Taishō era, which roughly corresponds to the interwar period, can serve as a marker indicating a new societal trend, namely, the popularization of the so-called culture industries that altered people's lives significantly. I therefore follow their practice here.

23. *Urazato sonpō*, March 15, 1924.

24. *Urazato sonpō*, February 15, 1923.

25. *Urazato sonpō*, May 15, 1922.

26. *Urazato sonpō*, April 15, 1922.

27. Using the results of *Shokugyō fujin ni kansuru chōsa* (Research on working women), published by the Tokyo Social Affairs Bureau in 1924, historian Margit Nagy maintains that, of the 3.5 million women in the labor force in the mid-Taishō era, "nearly three-quarters of these employed women (2.6 million) were classified as manual workers, while the remaining one-fourth engaged in intellectual or mental work" (1991, 202). The image of the Modern Girl emphasizes her identity not only as a consumer but as a middle-class professional. Both Silverberg (1991) and Nagy, however, emphasize her identity as a producer, who often worked in poor conditions and thus could be politically active in the labor movement.

28. *Ebōshi no hana*, November 10, 1922.

29. *Ebōshi no hana*, April 5, 1924.

30. See, for example, *Urazato sonpō*, November 15, 1923.

31. *Urazato sonpō*, March 15, 1924.

32. *Urazato sonpō*, December 15, 1924.

33. *Urazato sonpō*, February 15, 1924.

34. *Urazato sonpō*, June 15, 1922.

35. *Urazato sonpō*, May 15, 1923.

36. A reader of *Ie no hikari* sent the journal a song he composed to promote the movement to improve the quality of everyday life. It is a changing song of the popular children's song "The Tortoise and the Hare," in which he replaces the tortoise with "the savings." Like the tortoise who is slow at the beginning of the race but eventually defeats the hare, the savings, in his song, is first "thin" but gradually becomes fatter. *Ie no hikari*, November 1928, p. 144.

37. *Motohara jihō*, June 15, 1925.

38. *Urazato sonpō*, April 15, 1922; December 15, 1924.

39. *Urazato sonpō*, September 15, 1922; June 15, 1924.

40. For a variety of laws, regulations, and guidelines regarding the movement to improve the quality of everyday life, which developed not only in Nagano but in other predominantly agricultural prefectures, see Kusumoto and Takeda 1985.

41. *Kamishina jihō*, January 15, 1925.

42. *Ie no hikari*, September 1927, quoted in Adachi 1960, 67. Many readers of *Ie no hikari* protested to its editorial board for its having published a full-page color illustration of a woman in the journal's first issue. The reason, according to them, was that she resembled the popular actress Mizutani Yaeko and that the actress was necessarily the product of decadent urban civilization (Ie no Hikari Kyōkai 1986, 18).

43. *Urazato sonpō*, May 15, 1923. As a rebuttal to this article, a letter sent by an anonymous woman was published in *Urazato sonpō* a month later. She laments the weakness of this male author who could not see "women" but only "snakes." She then argues: "We women have respected you men. Indeed, your physical strength, knowledge, and will are all far superior to ours. You men are always 'senior' to women. The flower of culture is the product of the efforts of both men and women, but I believe it is largely men who constructed it. . . . Please, you should be stronger and wiser. While you see us as snakes, your soul remains impure. Even if we women are snakes, do not be afraid of us like frogs. You should be generous enough to teach us women."

44. *Kamishina jihō*, January 15, 1925.

45. *Ebōshi no hana*, March 20, 1922.

46. *Motohara jihō*, June 15, 1924.

47. *Shiojiri jihō*, September 11, 1919.

48. *Kangawa jihō*, May 1, 1925.

49. *Ebōshi no hana*, February 15, 1923. In 1925, a young unmarried women's association of the village of Urazato was reported to have traveled to Karuizawa, where they visited a Western-style hotel and were invited by the hotel staff for hot chocolate. "True modernity" thus had significant Western elements in it (*Urazato sonpō*, October 10, 1925).

50. *Kamishina jihō*, June 15, 1926.

51. *Ebōshi no hana*, February 15, 1924.

52. *Urazato sonpō*, November 10, 1925.

53. Mainstream historians, such as Maruyama Masao (1969, chap. 2) or Barrington Moore, Jr. (1966, chap. 5), make a distinction between the 1910s and early 1920s and the late 1920s and 1930s (see Waswo 1988, 555–559). The former is a "revolutionary" period whereas the latter is a "conservative" period in terms of farmers' political behavior and ideology. Some Japanese historians call the transition from the first to the second period *nōson no fashizumuka*, "the fascismization of the countryside" (see Nakamura 1978). "Fascismization" refers not only to the taming of militant farmers by physical forces but also to the process by which

farmers themselves accepted and participated in the consolidation of the Japanese state and the expansion of the Japanese empire.

Indeed, the National Tenants Union (Nihon Nōmin Kumiai), founded in 1922, increased the number of its local branch offices in Nagano throughout the 1920s. The number of tenant disputes began to increase in 1920 and peaked at 264 in 1934 in Nagano (Morosawa 1969b, 197; see also Yasuda 1979; Aoki Keiichirō 1964; Nishida 1978; and Aoki Takaju 1987).

But revisionist scholars such as Waswo and Vlastos try to see the coexistence of both "revolutionary" and "conservative" voices, while affirming the trend among farmers toward less militancy in the late 1930s. In my reading of village newspapers, I also see the coexistence of both types of discourses among the articles as well as within single articles throughout the entire period of their publication.

54. Farmers were also highly valued in the Tokugawa period. Yet Vlastos points out that they were valued "only as producers, and their beliefs, values, and communities were disparaged and viewed with suspicion" (1994, 41).

55. *Kangawa jihō*, July 1, 1927.

56. One can characterize Yanagita as a powerful ideologue of agrarianism who emphasized the importance of an agrarian community composed of self-farming households. See his two essays "Chūnō yōsei-saku" (Policies to nurture middling farmers), originally published in *Chūō nōji-hō* in 1904 (1964a, 409–423), and "Sangyō kumiai no dōtoku-teki bunshi" (Moral elements in the agricultural cooperatives), originally published in *Sangyō kumiai* in 1910 (1964j, 430–435).

57. This system of grading seems to have been used often in the 1930s with the sense of caricature toward the objects to be classified. Tenants in the village of Goka in Nagano who fought over the reduction of farm rent together with Nakamura Hiroshi also classified their landlords in the manner of grading Sumo wrestlers. The "grand champion" (*yokozuna*) was the most exploitative landlord (Aoki 1964, 343).

CHAPTER 7: THE WARTIME PERIOD

1. In the 1980s, many of my neighbors subscribed to *Ie no hikari* or to *Kodomo: Ie no hikari* (*The Light of Home* for children), which is now published separately.

2. *Ie no hikari*, March 3, 1933.

3. There are four different terms currently in use in Japan for referring to the wartime period: *dai niji sekai taisen* (World War II), *taiheiyō sensō* (the Pacific War), *dai tōa sensō* (the Great East Asia War), and *jūgonen sensō* (the Fifteen-Year War), each with its distinct ideological connotation (see Ienaga 1978; Field 1991a; Gluck 1993). For the purpose of my argument, the Fifteen-Year War, which refers to the fifteen years between 1931 and 1945, may be most appropriate, yet I must emphasize that wartime for the Nagano rural women was longer than fifteen years.

4. *Shinano mainichi shinbun*, November 9, 1943.

5. *Shinano mainichi shinbun*, November 10, 1943.

6. Ibid.

7. *Ie no hikari* printed the narratives of numerous "Imai Umes" in the 1930s and 1940s. For example, in a June issue published in 1933, a farming woman in Shimane prefecture was reported to have said: "We will do anything we can in order to reconstruct the economy of our families and village." A women's associ-

ation in rural Ishikawa prefecture created a slogan: "Our kitchens will lead the
nation" (*daidokoro wa kokka ni tsūzu*).
Each one of the 430 women in a village
in Nagano decided to save ten *sen* every
month so that the elderly and children of
their village could enjoy the New Year
celebration.

8. This passage can be found in *Jinkō
seisaku kakuritsu yōkō* (Guidelines for the
establishment of population policies),
issued by the cabinet in 1941 (Mori
1976, 316).

9. Kawakami's *Nihon son-nō-ron*
(Revering Japanese farmers) was originally published in 1904. As a future
Marxist, Kawakami differs from the other
ideologues of agrarianism in several
respects. He believed that Japanese agriculture could still be upheld on economic grounds and asserted that it should be
stimulated equally to the manufacturing
industry. Furthermore, he did not idealize
local autonomy or village communalism,
but "took a distinctly forward-looking
view of farm growth" (Havens 1974, 119;
see also Bernstein 1976).

10. The figures Kawakami presents,
however, are quite questionable. Citing
national census data, Maruoka reported
that the 1930 infant mortality rates in
Aomori and Iwate, the two predominantly agricultural prefectures, were 18.1 (per
100 mothers) and 14.8 respectively, while
the rate in Tokyo was 9.7 (1948, 132).

11. *Shinano mainichi shinbun*, March 11,
1941. See also the March 12, March 13,
March 14, and March 15 issues of the
same year.

12. *Shinano mainichi shinbun*, August 23,
1942.

13. Manchukuo is a Japanese invention,
a "separate state under Chinese leaders
who took their orders from Japanese
officers and civilian officials" (Duus
1989, xxviii). For this reason, scholars of
Japanese colonialism call Manchuria an

informal, as opposed to a formal, colony
of Japan.

14. Since Japan took control over the
Russian leasehold and concession in
southern Manchuria right after the
Russo-Japanese War, Japanese migration
to Manchuria began much earlier than
the 1930s. These earlier migrants were
mostly employees of the South
Manchurian Railway Company and their
families. Unlike these earlier settlers,
peasants were settled in the north, near
the border with the Soviet Union.

15. The number of settlers from
Nagano was 32,637. This represents
about 12 percent of the total number of
settlers from Japan (Nagano-ken
Kaitaku Jikyō-kai Manshū Kaitaku
Kankō-kai 1984).

16. *Kamishina jihō*, June 15, 1938. This
quote is from a *tsutatsu*, an ordinance
issued by the central and prefectural
governments.

17. *Kamishina jihō*, October 15, 1938.

18. The history of Japanese peasant settlers in Manchuria deserves an entire
book of its own. It is the topic of my
current research. Here, I have presented
it only briefly.

19. In "Kinrō bosei hogo" (The protection of working motherhood), published in 1943, Maki Ken'ichi concurs
with Tōjō when he argues: "Working
women shoulder the mission of soldiers
of production, but they have another,
more important, mission of multiplying
and strengthening the Japanese race"
(quoted in Akamatsu 1977, 488). This is
a chapter of the book *Joshi kinrō kanri
zensho*, published by Tōyō Shokan.

20. Havens states that the female
Japanese labor force rose less than 10
percent between 1940 and 1944, while
more than six million American women
took jobs during the war, raising the
total number of working women by 50

percent. He also demonstrates that the percentage of women in the wartime Japanese industrial work force actually declined, while the proportion rose from 25.2 percent in 1939 to 35.6 percent in 1944 in Germany (1975, 918).

21. *Shinano mainichi shinbun,* February 3, 1944.

22. I have already mentioned *Shinmin no michi* (The way of subjects), published in 1941 (see Chap. 4, n. 20). While *Shinmin no michi* dealt with the issue of how an individual Japanese should behave as an imperial subject, *Ie no michi* dealt with the same issue at the level of the household.

23. We should note that such an analytic distinction cannot be applied even in the West, for "domestic relationships are part and parcel of the political structure of a society" (Yanagisako 1979, 191).

24. Although primogeniture was and still is the general rule of inheritance and succession in this area, there were and are many exceptions to it.

25. It is interesting that, in the same village, a total of 189 households left for Manchuria (Takahashi 1976, 371).

26. Koreans and Chinese began to migrate to Japan immediately after Korea and Taiwan became Japan's colonies, but these earlier immigrants seem to have been concentrated in the city in the early twentieth century.

We now know that more than six thousand Koreans and hundreds of Chinese living in Japan were massacred right after the Great Kanto Earthquake of 1923. Rumors of insurrectionary Korean riots were reported in the newspaper, and the Japanese state immediately reacted to such rumors by declaring martial law. See, for example, Kang Touk-sang, *Kantō daishinsai* (The Great Kanto Earthquake; 1975); and Imai Seiichi and Inumaru Yoshikazu, *Kantō daishinsai to Chōsen-jin gyakusatsu*

(The Great Kanto Earthquake and the massacre of the Koreans; 1975).

Furthermore, Kim Ch'an-jong argues that each cotton mill in the Osaka metropolitan area recruited two or three hundred women in Korea annually and brought them to Japan in the 1920s and 1930s (1982, 9). Kim further argues that Japanese academia completely ignored their presence in the factory work force until the late 1960s. In this respect, the discourse of labor history in Japan is parallel to the discourse of Yanagita and his students and Nagano middling farmers.

27. Anthony Brandt's article "A Short Natural History of Nostalgia" was published in *Atlantic Monthly* 242 (December 1978): 58–63.

CHAPTER 8: THE POSTWAR "DEMOCRACY" AND THE POST-POSTWAR NATIONALISM

1. Herbert Passin, a young officer during the Occupation period, recalls square dancing as the "magic key to transforming Japan into a democratic society" (1990, 119).

2. The quotation marks around "democracy" are meant to indicate the historical specificity of the time when the notion was introduced. I will, however, generally not use quotation marks around this term in the rest of this chapter.

3. McCormack and Sugimoto argue that "democracy" in Japanese society has not been studied much among scholars of Japan: "In the non-European world, no nation has made greater strides than Japan to achieve the transformation of its productive economy by the adoption of the institutions of capitalism. . . . But *democracy? Japanese democracy?* Not a single monograph has been published on the subject in English" (1986, 9; emphasis in original). Since 1986, however, several books have been published

on this topic, including Masao Miyoshi and Harry D. Harootunian, eds., *Postmodernism in Japan* (1989); Andrew Gordon, ed., *Postwar Japan as History* (1993); and Masao Miyoshi and Harry D. Harootunian, eds., *Japan in the World* (1993).

4. The final two-part report of the committee was published in two separate volumes of *Shinano kyōiku* in 1941 (1941a, 1941b). The committee also recommended the establishment of an association for young brides (during the first two years after their marriages), who would be the "imperial subjects who nurture the foundation of their families, village, and nation" (Nōson Josei Kyōiku Kenkyū Iinkai 1941b, 79).

5. In "America's Japan/Japan's Japan," Harootunian describes the same continuity as a "new stage of [American] imperialism and colonialism without territorialization [of Japan]" (1993, 200).

6. The well bucket (*tsurube*), a bucket to which a long rope is attached, is a more primitive technology than a pump for getting well water. In winter, however, pumps easily froze, while one simply had to break the ice on the well's surface to get water with a bucket.

7. Hōzuki is the name of a plant believed to have been used by women to induce abortion.

8. My argument on the relationship between the Security Treaty Crisis of 1960 and Japanese nationalism owes much to Wesley Sasaki-Uemura's Ph.D. dissertation, "Citizen and Community in the 1960 Anpo Protests" (1993).

9. An illusion is a concept that presupposes the existence of social reality, for an illusion is supposed to mask the latter. However, Slavoj Žižek argues, in postindustrial societies, a (unconscious) fantasy structures social reality itself: what is real cannot be separated from what is fantasized (1989).

10. Jean-François Lyotard (1984) analyzes the postmodern period in a similar manner, that is, in terms of the relationship between the postindustrial (which corresponds to Jameson's "socioeconomic reality") and the postmodern (which corresponds to Jameson's "cultural ideology"). Lyotard also analyzes the postindustrial/postmodern age in terms of the interdependence of scientific and narrative knowledge. Scientific knowledge is composed of denotative statements, which may be declared true or false. Knowledge, according to Lyotard, is not scientific knowledge alone. It also includes "notions of 'know-how,' 'knowing how to live,' 'how to listen,' etc.," which "conform to the relevant criteria (of justice, beauty, truth, and efficiency respectively) accepted in the social circle of the 'knower's' interlocutors" (pp. 18–19). This "customary" or "traditional" knowledge is knowledge legitimized within the pragmatics of oral discourse. Hence its quintessential form is narration (p. 19). Lyotard then argues that this narrative knowledge has not been superseded by scientific knowledge but that, in the postindustrial age, people need narrative knowledge to legitimize scientific knowledge.

11. This campaign by the Japanese agricultural cooperatives reminds me of the novel by Siegfried Lenz *The Training Ground* (1991). In this novel, the Zellers, who have lost everything in divided Germany, leave the East on a boat and move to the plains of Schleswig in northern West Germany. After finally being accepted by their neighbors, Herr Zeller receives an order from the authorities: "All trees must come from German seed, otherwise they were not to be sold" (p. 382). Facing an influx of people of many nationalities, the authorities needed to ensure the "unity" of the nation. By then, the Zellers owned more than a hundred thousand young oak

trees. When Herr Zeller found out that the seeds had actually come from Romania, he had to pull them all up and burn them: "German seed, German trees: it's all so wonderfully reminiscent of the Nazi race laws-they'll soon be talking of incest between trees" (p. 383). The campaign by the Japanese agricultural cooperatives is also reminiscent of the wartime ideology that found "purity" only in the Japanese race. I learned of this novel in reading Stanley Tambiah's article "Ethnonationalism: Politics and Culture" (1993).

12. Ōhnuki-Tierney, however, reports that the Japanese government imports Korean rice precisely in order to establish leverage over the agricultural cooperatives (1993, 16–17).

13. I must hastily add here that *furusato* is *always* "in danger of vanishing" in modern Japanese history. Recall the discourses of Japanese native ethnology and agrarianism, in which the disappearing countryside is always mourned.

14. This was the second such summit meeting. The first was held in Tōno in 1987. Two short articles published in the local newspaper *Shinano mainichi shinbun* (May 28 and 29, 1988) and another in the national newspaper *Asahi shinbun* (May 28, 1988) covered this second Yanagita summit meeting held in Iida May 17–28.

15. Gotō Junko (1993) reports on another village revitalization movement in the town of Asuke in Aichi prefecture, where local residents have been suffering, rather than profiting, from the consequences of revitalization (in this case, the revitalization of tourism, which has brought more people, cars, vans, chartered buses, and garbage). She argues that their village revitalization still remains as public planning and propaganda without the active participation of the local residents themselves.

16. By the same token, a local newspaper reported the story of a young college professor who invited the foreign students at his university in Tokyo to the village in Nagano where he had built his summer house. He organized a speech contest in which all these foreign students participated, which has become an annual summer event in this particular village. See *Shinano mainichi shinbun,* July 28, 1988.

17. *Shinano mainichi shinbun,* May 21, 1988.

18. Although the Japanese government has maintained the "principle" of not accepting "unskilled laborers," the new Immigration Law of 1990 softened restrictions against foreign people of Japanese descent *(nikkei)* in light of the acute labor shortage in the Japanese economy. The majority of *nikkeis* come from Brazil.

19. Nakamura Hisashi, an economic historian in Japan, estimates that there are more than seven hundred marriage brokers importing Asian women to Japan. He can only estimate, because there is no organization that oversees their activities. One source indicates that the number of foreigners marrying Japanese men soared to 17,800 in 1989, from 4,386 in 1980, and just 2,108 in 1970. Another source indicates that 14,237 women from Southeast Asia married Japanese men in 1986 but that the figure tripled in 1989. I obtained these data from the article "In the Want Ads: Forced Weddings," published in *The New York Times* on April 12, 1991, and another article, "Japan's Balky Brides," in *The Chicago Tribune,* June 4, 1989.

20. *The Chicago Tribune* published an interesting article about Mr. Iizuka, a farmer who married a Sri Lankan woman through a marriage broker. He is reported to have said: "I think women from Sri Lanka are the best. . . . They

are the way Japanese women were during the Meiji Era. They respect their mother-in-law, they are cheerful, which makes the whole house a happy place; they are strong inside, they work hard and they always respect their husbands" (June 4, 1989).

21. I am grateful to Professor Hara Hiroko and the staff of Josei Shiryō Bunka Kenkyūjo (The Institute for the Study of Women and Culture) of Ochanomizu Women's College in Tokyo, who allowed me to read the newsletters of various grass-roots women's organization in the Tokyo area in 1984.

22. Ivy also reports that Tōno has a revitalized version of the "dance of the deer" (1995, 131).

23. Some may argue that, now that the 1990s are coming to an end, this "Japanese amnesia" (of past conduct in Asia) is no longer pervasive; those in power in the present government are contriving to come to terms with the past through a partial acknowledgment of their nation's wrongdoing in Asia (Yoneyama 1995, 504). And yet, Lisa Yoneyama argues, this is largely because the "primary nationalist agenda in the present government is to secure Japan's status in the post Cold War global economy" (p. 501), and the conservative elites would like simply to turn the page and, "if possible, wipe the nation's past wrongdoing from memory" (Adorno 1986, 115; quoted also in Yoneyama 1995, 505).

24. I learned of Halbwachs' work in my reading of Watson, who cites the same quotation (1994a, 71).

EPILOGUE

1. Criticizing such identity politics, anthropologist John Kelly states: "Three problems that arise from scholarly fetishism of identity are particularly relevant here: blurring of sameness imposed on others with sameness 'imagined,' as we now like to reiterate, as morally crucial parts of an active self (Christian or post-Christian, still confessing or witnessing); underestimating the importance of specificities of the discourse of race, especially regarding imputations about moral inferiority and capacity; and, sanitizing the role of the will, both individual and collective, in actual political history" (1995, 485).

References

Abrams, Philip. 1988. "Notes on the Difficulty of Studying the State." *Journal of Historical Sociology* 1 (1): 58–89.

Adachi Seiko. 1960. "Ie no hikari no rekishi" (The history of *Ie no hikari*). *Shisō no kagaku* 18:59–76.

Adorno, Theodor W. 1986. "What Does Coming to Terms with the Past Mean?" In Geoffrey H. Hartman, ed., *Bitburg in Moral and Political Perspective*, 114–29. Bloomington: Indiana University Press.

Akamatsu Keisuke. 1986. *Hi-jōmin no minzoku bunka* (Folklore among non-*jōmin*). Tokyo: Akashi Shoten.

———. 1991. *Hi-jōmin no sei minzoku* (Folklore and sexuality among non-*jōmin*). Tokyo: Akashi Shoten.

———. 1993. *Onna no rekishi to minzoku* (The history and folklore of women). Tokyo: Akashi Shoten.

Akamatsu Ryōko, ed. 1977. *Nihon fujin mondai shiryō shūsei*, vol. 3, *rōdō* (The compilation of Japanese women's problems, vol. 3, Labor]. Tokyo: Domesu Shuppan.

Akasaka Norio. 1991. *Yama no seishin-shi: Yanagita Kunio no hassei* (The spiritual history of the mountains: The genesis of the thought of Yanagita Kunio). Tokyo: Shōgakukan.

Allison, Anne. 1996. *Permitted and Prohibited Desires: Mothers, Comics, and Censorship in Japan*. Boulder: Westview Press.

Anderson, Benedict. 1983, 1991. *Imagined Communities: Reflections on the Origins and Spread of Nationalism*. London: Verso.

———. 1990. *Language and Power: Exploring Political Cultures in Indonesia*. Ithaca: Cornell University Press.

Aoki Keiichirō. 1964. *Nagano-ken shakai undō-shi* (The history of social movements in Nagano prefecture]. Tokyo: Gannan-dō.

Aoki Takaju. 1987. *Shinshū onna no Shōwa-shi: Senzen-hen* (The Shōwa history of women in Nagano: Prewar period]. Nagano: Shinano Mainichi Shinbun-sha.

Aoki Kidd, Yasue. 1978. *Women Workers in the Japanese Cotton Mills, 1880–1920*. Ithaca: Cornell University, East Asia Papers 20.

Arendt, Hannah. 1973. *The Origins of Totalitarianism*. San Diego: Harcourt Brace Jovanovich, A Harvest/HBJ Book.

Ariès, Philippe. 1962. *Centuries of Childhood: A Social History of Family Life*. New York: Vintage Books.

Arndt, H. W. 1987. *Economic Development: The History of an Idea.* Chicago: University of Chicago Press.

Aruga Kizaemon. 1971. "Nihon jōmin seikatsu shiryō sōsho sōjo" (General introduction to the collection of documents on the everyday lives of Japanese *jōmin*). In Nihon Jōmin Bunka Kenkyū-sho, ed., *Nihon Jōmin seikatsu shiryō sōsho,* 1:1–42. Tokyo: San'ichi Shobō.

Asad, Talal. 1973. "Introduction." In T. Asad, ed., *Anthropology and the Colonial Encounter,* 9-19. Atlantic Highlands: Humanities Press.

Asada Kyōji. 1993. "Manshū nōgyō imin to nōgyō tochi mondai" (Peasant settlers in Manchuria and agrarian land problems]. In Ōe Shinobu et al., eds., *Iwanami kōza: kindai Nihon to shokuminchi,* vol. 3, *Shokuminchi-ka to sangyō-ka,* 77–102. Tokyo: Iwanami.

Avineri, Shlomo. 1991. "Marxism and Nationalism." *Journal of Contemporary History* 26:637–657.

Avon Josei Bunka Sentā (Avon Cultural Center for Women). 1988. *Kusanone gurūpu katsudō no jittai to riidā no ishiki chōsa* (Survey of the activities of the grass-roots groups for women and the consciousness of their leaders). Tokyo: Avon Josei Bunka Sentā.

Babior, Sharman Lark. 1993. "Women of a Tokyo Shelter: Domestic Violence and Sexual Exploitation in Japan." Ph.D. thesis, Department of Anthropology, University of California, Los Angeles.

Balibar, Etienne. 1991. "The Nation Form: History and Ideology." In Etienne Balibar and Immanuel Wallerstein, eds., *Race, Nation, Class: Ambiguous Identities,* 86–106. London: Verso.

Basso, Ellen. 1989. "Kalapalo Biography: Psychology and Language in a South American Oral History." *American Anthropologist* 91 (3): 551–569.

Benjamin, Walter. 1968. *Illuminations.* Trans. Harry Zohn. Ed. Hannah Arendt. New York: Schocken Books.

Bernstein, Gail Lee. 1976. *Japanese Marxist: A Portrait of Kawakami Hajime, 1879–1946.* Cambridge, Mass.: Harvard University Press.

———. 1983. *Haruko's World: A Japanese Farm Woman and Her Community.* Stanford: Stanford University Press.

———. 1988. "Women in the Silk-reeling Industry in Nineteenth-century Japan." In G. L. Bernstein and H. Fukui, eds., *Japan and the World: Essays on Japanese History and Politics in Honour of Ishida Takeshi,* 54–77. New York: St. Martin's Press.

Bhabha, Homi. 1990. "Introduction: Narrating the Nation." In H. Bhabha, ed., *Nation and Narration,* 1–7. London: Routledge.

Boyarin, Jonathan. 1994. "Space, Time, and the Politics of Memory." In J. Boyarin, ed., *Remapping Memory: The Politics of Time and Space,* 1–37. Minneapolis: University of Minnesota Press.

Braisted, William R. 1976. *Meiroku Zasshi: Journal of the Japanese Enlightenment.* Cambridge: Harvard University Press.

Branca, Patricia. 1975. *Silent Sisterhood: Middle-class Women in the Victorian Home*. London: Croom Helm.

Breuilly, John. 1982. *Nationalism and the State*. Manchester: Manchester University Press.

Calder, Kent. 1988. *Crisis and Compensation: Public Policy and Political Stability in Japan, 1949–86*. Princeton: Princeton University Press.

Certeau, Michel de. 1980. "On the Oppositional Practices of Everyday Life." *Social Text* 3:3–43.

Challaye, Felicien. 1915. *Le Japon illustré*. Paris: Librarie Larousse.

Chamberlain, Basil Hall. 1904. *Things Japanese*. London: J. Murray.

Chatterjee, Partha. 1989. "Colonialism, Nationalism, and Colonized Women: The Contest in India." *American Ethnologist* 16 (4): 622–633.

———. 1993a. *Nationalist Thought and the Colonial World: A Derivative Discourse*. Minneapolis: University of Minnesota Press.

———. 1993b. *The Nation and Its Fragments: Colonial and Postcolonial Histories*. Princeton: Princeton University Press.

Cherry, Kittredge. 1987. *Womansword: What Japanese Words Say about Women*. Tokyo: Kōdansha International.

Chodorow, Nancy J. 1978. *The Reproduction of Mothering: Psychoanalysis and the Sociology of Gender*. Berkeley, Los Angeles, and London: University of California Press.

Cole, Robert E., and Ken'ichi Tominaga. 1976. "Japan's Changing Occupational Structure and Its Significance." In H. Patrick, ed., *Japanese Industrialization and Its Social Consequences*, 53–95. Berkeley, Los Angeles, and London: University of California Press.

Comaroff, Jean. 1985. *Body of Power, Spirit of Resistance: The Culture and History of a South African People*. Chicago: University of Chicago Press.

Connerton, Paul. 1989. *How Societies Remember*. New York: Cambridge University Press.

Dartnell, Colette. 1996. "Reality and Representation: The Roles of Women." In Kendall B. Brown, ed., *Light in Darkness: Women in Japanese Prints of Early Showa (1926–1945)*, 80–87. Los Angeles: Fisher Gallery, University of Southern California.

Das, Veena. 1995. *Critical Events: An Anthropological Perspective on Contemporary India*. Delhi: Oxford University Press.

Davidoff, Leonore, and Catherine Hall. 1986. *Family Fortunes: Men and Women of the English Middle Class, 1780–1850*. Chicago: University of Chicago Press.

Davis, Horace B. 1978. *Toward a Marxist Theory of Nationalism*. New York: Monthly Review Press.

Dazai Osamu. 1987. *Return to Tsugaru*. Trans. James Westerhoven. Tokyo: Kōdansha International.

Deutsch, Karl W. 1966. *Nationalism and Social Communication*. Cambridge: MIT Press.

Dirks, Nicholas B. 1990. "History as a Sign of the Modern." *Public Culture* 2 (2): 25–32.

Dorson, Richard M. 1975. "Foreword." In Yanagita Kunio, *The Legends of Tōno*, trans. R. A. Morse, ix–xiii. Tokyo: The Japan Foundation.

Dower, John W. 1979. *Empire and Aftermath: Yoshida Shigeru and the Japanese Experience, 1878–1954.* Harvard East Asian Monographs 84. Cambridge, Mass.: Harvard University Press.

———. 1986. *War without Mercy: Race and Power in the Pacific War.* New York: Pantheon.

Duara, Prasenjit. 1995. *Rescuing History from the Nation: Questioning Narratives of Modern China.* Chicago: University of Chicago Press.

Dublin, Thomas. 1981. *Women at Work: The Transformation of Work and Community in Lowell, Massachusetts, 1826–1860.* New York: Columbia University Press.

Duus, Peter. 1989. "Introduction: Japan's Informal Empire in China, 1895–1937: Overview." In P. Duus, R. H. Myers, and M. R. Peattie, eds., *The Japanese Informal Empire in China, 1895–1937*, xi–xxix. Princeton: Princeton University Press.

Eguchi Zenji and Hidaka Yasohichi. 1937. *Shinano sanshi-gyō-shi* (The history of the silk spinning industry in Nagano), vol. 3. Nagano: Dai Nippon Sanshi-kai Shinano Shikai.

Field, Norma. 1991a. "Beyond Pearl Harbor." *The Nation*, December, 817–821.

———. 1991b. *In the Realm of a Dying Emperor: A Portrait of Japan at Century's End.* New York: Pantheon.

———. 1991c. *Resident Korean Literature and Japanese Postmodernity.* Paper presented at the Annual Meeting of the Association for Asian Studies, April, New Orleans.

Fields, Barbara Jeanne. 1990. "Slavery, Race and Ideology in the United States of America." *New Left Review* 181:95–118.

Figal, Gerald. 1996. "How to *Jibunshi*: Making and Marketing Self-histories of Shōwa among the Masses in Postwar Japan." *Journal of Asian Studies* 55 (4): 902–933.

Foner, Philip S. 1977. *The Factory Girls.* Urbana: University of Illinois Press.

Foucault, Michel. 1980. *The History of Sexuality*, vol. 1, *An Introduction.* New York: Vintage Books.

Fujime Yuki. 1994. *"Kin-gendai Nihon no sei to seishoku tōsei to shakai undō"* (Sex, sexual control, and social movements in modern Japan). Ph.D. thesis, Department of History, Kyoto University.

Fukaya Masashi. 1990. *Ryōsai kenbo-shugi no kyōiku* (Education based on the "good wife and wise mother" ideology). Nagoya: Reimei Shobō.

Fukuda Ajio. 1983. "Nihon minzoku kenkyūshi nenpō" (A chronological chart of Japanese native ethnology). *Kokuritsu rekishi minzoku hakubutsukan hōkoku* 2: 41–81.

———. 1984. *Nihon minzoku-gaku hōhō josetsu: Yanagita Kunio to minzoku-gaku* (General introduction to the methodologies of Japanese native ethnology: Yanagita Kunio and folklore studies). Tokyo: Kōbundō.

Garon, Sheldon. 1987. *State and Labor in Modern Japan.* Berkeley, Los Angeles, and London: University of California Press.

———. 1993. "The World's Oldest Debate? Prostitution and the State in Imperial Japan, 1900–45." *The American Historical Review,* 98 (3): 710–732.

Gathorne-Hardy, Jonathan. 1972. *The Rise and Fall of the Victorian Nanny.* London: Weidenfeld and Nicolson.

Gellner, Ernest. 1964. *Thought and Change.* London: Weidenfeld and Nicolson.

———. 1983. *Nations and Nationalism.* Ithaca: Cornell University Press.

Gillis, John R. 1979. "Servants, Sexual Relations and the Risks of Illegitimacy in London, 1801–1900." *Feminist Studies* 5 (1): 142–173.

Gluck, Carol. 1985. *Japan's Modern Myths: Ideology in the Late Meiji Period.* Princeton: Princeton University Press.

———. 1993. "The Past in the Present." In Andrew Gordon, ed. *Postwar Japan as History,* 64–95. Berkeley, Los Angeles, and London: University of California Press.

Gordon, Andrew. 1991. *Labor and Imperial Democracy in Prewar Japan.* Berkeley, Los Angeles, and London: University of California Press.

———. ed. 1993. *Postwar Japan as History.* Berkeley, Los Angeles, and London: University of California Press.

Gotō, Junko. 1993. "Rural Revitalization (*Chiiki Okoshi*) in Japan: A Case Study of Asuke Township." Ph.D. thesis, University of California, Los Angeles.

Gotō Sōichirō. 1972. "Yanagita-gaku no shisō to gakumon" (The thought and scholarship of Yanagita's native ethnology). In Gotō Sōichirō, *Yanagita Kunio-ron josetsu,* 3–155. Tokyo: Dentō do Gendai-sha.

———. 1976. "Taishō-ki minshū no nashonarizumu" (Mass nationalism during the Taishō Period). *Dentō to gendai* 1 (37): 124–135.

Guha, Ranajit. 1985. "Nationalism Reduced to 'Official Nationalism': Review of Benedict Anderson, Imagined Communities." *Asian Studies Association of Australia Review* 9 (1): 103–108.

Gupta, Akhil, and James Ferguson. 1992. "Beyond 'Culture': Space, Identity, and the Politics of Difference." *Cultural Anthropology* 7 (1): 6–23.

Halbwachs, Maurice. 1980 (orig. 1950). *The Collective Memory.* Trans. Francis Ditter and Vida Y. Ditter. New York: Harper and Row.

Halliday, Jon. 1975. *A Political History of Japanese Capitalism.* New York: Monthly Review Press.

Hane, Mikiso. 1982. *Peasants, Rebels, and Outcasts: The Underside of Modern Japan.* New York: Pantheon.

———. 1986. *Modern Japan: A Historical Survey.* Boulder: Westview Press.

———. 1988. *Reflections on the Way to the Gallows: Rebel Women in Prewar Japan.* Berkeley, Los Angeles, and London: University of California Press.

Hareven, Tamara, and Randolph Langenbach. 1978. *Amoskeag: Life and Work in an American Factory City.* New York: Pantheon Books.

Harootunian, Harry D. 1974a. "Between Politics and Culture: Authority and the Ambiguities of Intellectual Choice in Imperial Japan." In Bernard Silberman and H. D. Harootunian, eds., *Japan in Crisis: Essays on Taishō Democracy*, 110–55. Princeton: Princeton University Press.

―――. 1974b. "Introduction: A Sense of an Ending and the Problem of Taishō." In Bernard Silberman and H. D. Harootunian, eds., *Japan in Crisis: Essays on Taishō Democracy*, 3–28. Princeton: Princeton University Press.

―――. 1988. *Things Seen and Unseen: Discourse and Ideology in Tokugawa Nativism*. Chicago: University of Chicago Press.

―――. 1989. "Visible Discourses/Invisible Ideologies." In M. Miyoshi and H. D. Harootunian, eds., *Postmodernism and Japan*, 63–92. Durham: Duke University Press.

―――. 1990. "Disciplinizing Native Knowledge and Producing Place: Yanagita Kunio, Origuchi Shinobu, Tanaka Yasuma." In J. T. Rimer, ed., *Culture and Identity: Japanese Intellectuals during the Interwar Years*, 99–127. Princeton: Princeton University Press.

―――. 1993. "America's Japan/Japan's Japan." In M. Miyoshi and H. D. Harootunian, eds., *Japan in the World*, 196–221. Durham: Duke University Press.

Harootunian, Harry D., and Najita, Tetsuo. 1988. "Japanese Revolt against the West: Political and Cultural Criticism in the Twentieth Century." In P. Duus, ed., *The Cambridge History of Japan*, vol. 6, *The Twentieth Century*, 711–774. Cambridge: Cambridge University Press.

Hartman, Geoffrey H. 1986. "Introduction, 1985." In G. H. Hartman, ed., *Bitburg in Moral and Political Perspective*, 1–12. Bloomington: University of Indiana Press.

Hartsock, Nancy C. M. 1985. *Money, Sex, and Power: Towards a Feminist Historical Materialism*. Boston: Northeastern University Press.

Harvey, David. 1989. *The Condition of Postmodernity: An Enquiry into the Origins of Cultural Change*. Oxford: Basil Blackwell.

Havens, Thomas R. H. 1974. *Farm and Nation in Modern Japan: Agrarian Nationalism, 1870–1940*. Princeton: Princeton University Press.

―――. 1975. "Women and War in Japan, 1937–1945." *American Historical Review* 80 (4): 913–934.

Heidegger, Martin. 1959. *An Introduction to Metaphysics*. Trans. Ralph Manheim. New Haven: Yale University Press.

Heng, Geraldine, and Janadas Devan. 1992. "State Fatherhood: The Politics of Nationalism, Sexuality and Race in Singapore." In Andrew Parker, Mary Russo, Doris Sommer, and Patricia Yaeger, eds., *Nationalisms and Sexualities*, 343–364. New York: Routledge.

Herskovits, Melville J. 1959. "Prepared Comments." *Journal of American Folklore* 72: 216–220.

Herzfeld, Michael. 1991. *A Place in History: Social and Monumental Time in a Cretan Town*. Princeton: Princeton University Press.

Higgs, Edward. 1986. *Domestic Servants and Households in Rochdale, 1851–1871.* New York: Garland.

Hobsbawm, Eric J. 1990. *Nations and Nationalism since 1780.* Cambridge: Cambridge University Press.

Hosoi Wakizō. 1954 (orig. 1925). *Jokō aishi* (The pitiful history of factory women). Tokyo: Iwanami.

Hosokawa Osamu. 1982. *Kōjo no michi: Nomugi touge* (The path for factory women: Nomugi path). Nagano: Ginga Shobō.

Ichioka, Yuji. 1977. "Ame-yuki-san: Japanese Prostitutes in Nineteenth-Century America." *Amerasia Journal* 4 (1): 1–21.

Ienaga, Saburo. 1978. *The Pacific War, 1931–45.* New York: Pantheon.

Ie no Hikari Kyōkai, ed. 1986. *Ie no hikari kyōkai rokujū-nen shi* (Sixty years of history of *Ie no hikari*). Tokyo: Ie no Hikari Kyōkai.

Imai Seiichi and Inumaru Yoshikazu. 1975. *Kantō daishinsai to Chōsen-jin gyakusatsu* (The Great Kanto Earthquake and the massacre of the Koreans). Tokyo: Tokuma Shoten.

Inada Masatane. 1917. *Fujin nōgyō mondai* (Problems of farming women). Tokyo: Maruyama-sha.

Irokawa Daikichi. 1978. *Nihon minzoku bunka taikei*, vol. 1, *Yanagita Kunio* (A general overview of Japanese native ethnology, vol. 1, Yanagita Kunio). Tokyo: Kōdansha.

Ishigami Kinji. 1984 (orig. 1921). *Jokō no shitsuke-kata to kyōiku* (How to discipline and educate factory women). Tokyo: Nihon Tosho Center.

Ishihara Osamu. 1970a (orig. 1913). "Eisei-gaku jō yori mitaru jokō no genkyō" (The current conditions of factory women seen from the perspective of hygienics). In T. Kagoyama, ed., *Seikatsu koten shōso*, vol. 5, *Jokō to kekkaku*, 77–171. Tokyo: Kōsei-kan.

———. 1970b (orig. 1913). "Jokō to kekkaku" (Factory women and tuberculosis). In T. Kagoyama, ed., *Seikatsu koten shōso*, vol. 5, *Jokō to kekkaku*, 173–234. Tokyo: Kōsei-kan.

Itagaki Kuniko. 1978. "*Ie no hikari* ni miru nōson fujin" (Rural women described in *Ie no hikari*). In Kindai Josei-shi Kenkyū-kai, ed., *Onna-tachi no kindai*, 309–336. Tokyo: Kashiwa Shobō.

———. 1992. *Shōwa senzen senchū-ki no nōson seikatsu* (Everyday life in the agrarian countryside before and during the wartime period in Shōwa). Tokyo: Sanrei Shobō.

Itō Mikiharu. 1972. "Yanagita Kunio to bunmei hihyō no ronri" (Yanagita Kunio and the logic of his critique of civilization). *Gendai no Esupuri* 57:5–22.

Ivy, Marilyn. 1988a. "Discourses of the Vanishing in Contemporary Japan." Ph.D. thesis, Cornell University.

———. 1988b. "Tradition and Difference in the Japanese Mass Media." *Public Culture* 1 (1): 21–29.

———. 1995. *Discourses of the Vanishing: Modernity, Phantasm, Japan.* Chicago: University of Chicago Press.

Iwamoto Yoshiteru. 1993. "Shokuminchi seisaku to Yanagita Kunio: Chōsen, Taiwan" (Colonial policies and Yanagita Kunio: Korea, Taiwan). *Kokubungaku* 38 (8): 46–54.

Jameson, Fredric. 1984. "Postmodernism, or the Cultural Logic of Late Capitalism." *New Left Review* 146:53–92.

Kagoyama Takashi. 1970. "Kaisetsu: Jokō to kekkaku" (Commentary: Factory women and tuberculosis). In T. Kagoyama, ed. *Seikatsu koten sōsho*, vol. 5, *Jokō to kekkaku*, 1–46. Tokyo: Kōsei-kan.

Kaibara, Ekken. 1906. "Women and Wisdom of Japan." In L. Cranmer-Byng and S. A. Kapadia, eds., *Women and Wisdom of Japan*, 31–64. New York: E. P. Dutton and Company.

Kamishima Jirō. 1975. "Minzoku-gaku no hōhōron-teki kiso: Ninshiki taishō no mondai" (The methodological foundation of native ethnology: The problems of the identification of its objects). In T. Noguchi, N. Miyata, and A. Fukuda, eds., *Gendai Nihon minzoku-gaku* 2:17–33. Tokyo: San'ichi Shobō.

Kaneko Heiichi. 1932. "Nōson fujin no mezamubeki shoten" (On several issues to which rural women should awaken). *Nōson fujin* 1 (6): 18–19.

Kang Touk-sang. 1975. *Kantō daishinsai* (The Great Kanto Earthquake). Tokyo: Chūō Kōron-sha.

Kanō Masanao. 1973. *Taishō democrashii no teiryū: Dozoku-teki seishin e no kaiki* (Taishō democracy: Return to the secular spirits). Tokyo: NHK Books.

———. 1976. *Nihon no rekishi*, vol. 27, *Taishō democrashii* (Japanese history, vol. 27, Taishō democracy). Tokyo: Shōgaku-kan.

———. 1989. *Fujin, josei, onna: Josei-shi no toi* (Women: Questions of women's history). Tokyo: Iwanami.

Katari-tsugu Ina no Onna Henshu Iinkai. 1984. *Katari-tsugu Ina no onna* (The women in the Ina Valley who impart their memories to subsequent generations). Iida: Shimo Ina-gun Rengō Fujin-kai.

Katō, Shūichi. 1974. "Taishō Democracy as the Pre-Stage for Japanese Militarism." In B. S. Silberman and H. D. Harootunian, eds., *Japan in Crisis: Essays on Taishō Democracy*, 217–236. Princeton: Princeton University Press.

Katō Sōichi. 1955. "Seishi kouta to sono rekishi" (The ballad of silk factory workers and its history). *Rekishi hyōron* 65:24–43.

Kawaji Fujin-kai. 1977. *Ishoku ni matsuwaru haha-tachi no sensō taiken* (The Wartime experiences of our mothers: Concerning clothes and food). Iida: Kawaji Kōminkan.

Kawakami Hajime. 1977 (orig. 1904). Nihon son-nō-ron (Respecting Japanese farmers). In Y. Kondō, ed., *Meiji Taishō nōsei keizai meicho-shū*, vol. 6, *Kawakami Hajime*, 35–137. Tokyo: Nōsan Gyoson Bunka Kyōkai.

Kedourie, Elie, ed. 1970. *Nationalism in Asia and Africa*. London: Weidenfeld and Nicolson.

Keizai Kikaku-chō. 1976 (orig. 1956). *Keizai hakusho* (White paper on the Japanese economy). Tokyo: Nihon Keizai Hyōron-sha.

Kelly, John D. 1995. "Diaspora and World War, Blood and Nation in Fiji and Hawai'i." *Public Culture* 7 (3): 475–497.

Kelly, William. 1982. *Irrigation Management in Japan: A Critical Review of Japanese Social Science Literature*. East Asia Papers Series 30. Ithaca: Cornell University China-Japan Program.

———. 1986. "Rationalization and Nostalgia: Cultural Dynamics of New Middle Class Japan." *American Ethnologist* 13 (4): 603–618.

———. 1990a. "Japanese No-Noh: The Crosstalk of Public Culture in a Rural Festivity." *Public Culture* 2 (2): 65–81.

———. 1990b. "Regional Japan: The Price of Prosperity and the Benefits of Dependency." *Daedalus* 119 (3): 209–227.

———. 1991. "Directions in the Anthropology of Contemporary Japan." *Annual Review of Anthropology* 20:395–431.

Kern, Stephen. 1983. *The Culture of Time and Space, 1880–1918*. Cambridge: Harvard University Press.

Kim Ch'an-jong. 1982. *Chōsen-jin jokō no uta* (The ballad of Korean factory women). Tokyo: Iwanami.

Kinmonth, Earl. 1981. *The Self-made Man in Meiji Japanese Thought*. Berkeley, Los Angeles, and London: University of California Press.

Kobayashi Kōji. 1977. *Manshū imin no mura: Shinshū Yasuoka-mura no Shōwa-shi* (A village of peasant settlers of Manchuria: The case of Yasuoka-mura in Nagano). Tokyo: Chikuma.

Kobayashi Tomojirō. 1906. "Kōtō shogakkō san yon gakunen joshi ni yōsan-ka o kuwauru no kibō" (My hope for adding instruction in sericulture to the third and fourth grade girls curriculum at the higher elementary school). *Shinano kyōiku* 241:13–16.

Kōgen ni Ikiru Onna Henshū Iinkai, ed. 1984. *Kōgen ni ikiru onna* (The women who live in the highlands). Nagano: Fujimi-chō Fujin-kai.

———. 1995. *Fujimino ni ikite* (Having lived in Fujimino). Nagano: Okaya Tōyōban.

Kohn, Hans. 1944. *The Idea of Nationalism*. New York: Macmillan.

———. 1955. *Nationalism, Its Meaning and History*. Princeton: Van Nostrand.

———. 1962. *The Age of Nationalism*. New York: Harper.

Kondo, Dorinne K. 1990. *Crafting Selves: Power, Gender, and Discourses of Identity in a Japanese Workplace*. Chicago: University of Chicago Press.

Koonz, Claudia. 1987. *Mothers in the Fatherland: Women, the Family and Nazi Politics*. New York: St. Martin's Press.

Kosai Yutaka. 1986. *The Era of High-Speed Growth: Notes on the Postwar Japanese Economy*. Trans. Jacqueline Kaminski. Tokyo: University of Tokyo Press.

Koschmann, J. Victor. 1985. "Folklore Studies and the Conservative Anti-Establishment in Modern Japan." In J. V. Koschmann, Ōiwa Keibo, and Yamashita Shinji, eds., *International Perspectives on Yanagita Kunio and Japanese Folklore Studies*, 131–64. Ithaca: Cornell University East Asia Papers 37.

Koyama Shizuko. 1986. "Ryōsai kenbo shugi no reimei" (The dawn of the "good wife and wise mother" ideology). *Joseigaku nenpō* 11 (7): 11–20.

Kōzu Zenzaburō. 1974. *Kyōiku aishi* (The pitiful history of education). Nagano: Ginga Shobō.

Kusumoto Masahiro and Takeda Tsutomu, eds. 1985. *Nō-san-gyo-son keizai kōsei undō shiryō shūsei* (Compiled documents on the movement to improve the quality of everyday life in farming, mountain, and fishing villages), 7 vols. Tokyo: Kashiwa Shobō.

Lebra, Joyce C. 1991. "Women in an All-Male Industry: The Case of Sake Brewer Tatsu'uma Kiyo." In G. L. Bernstein, ed., *Recreating Japanese Women, 1600–1945*, 131–48. Berkeley, Los Angeles, and London: University of California Press.

Lenz, Siegfried. 1991. *The Training Ground*. Trans. Geoffrey Skelton. New York: N. Holt.

Lewis, Michael. 1990. *Rioters and Citizens: Mass Protest in Imperial Japan*. Berkeley, Los Angeles, and London: University of California Press.

Lie, John. 1992. "Foreign Workers in Japan." *Monthly Review* 44 (1): 35–42.

Linke, Uli. 1990. "Folklore, Anthropology, and the Government of Social Life." *Comparative Studies in Society and History* 32 (1): 117–148.

Liu, Lydia. 1994. "The Female Body and Nationalist Discourse: Manchuria in Xiao Hong's Field of Life and Death." In Angela Zito and Tani E. Barlow, eds., *Body, Subject, and Power in China*, 157–177. Chicago: University of Chicago Press.

Lixfeld, Hannjost. 1994. *Folklore and Fascism: The Reich Institute for German Volkskunde*. Trans. James R. Dow. Bloomington: Indiana University Press.

Lyotard, Jean-François. 1984. *The Postmodern Condition: A Report on Knowledge*. Minneapolis: University of Minnesota Press.

Machida Shōzō. 1953. "Meiji nenkan ni okeru Shinshū seishi-gyō ni tsuite no oboegaki" (Notes on the silk industry in Nagano during the Meiji Period). *Shinano* 5 (10): 1–16.

Mackie, Vera. 1988. Feminist Politics in Japan. *New Left Review* 167:53–76.

Maki Yoshitarō. 1893. "Yashiro jinjō shōgakkō komori gakkō setsuritsu-shui kisoku" (Prospectus of a class for *komori* at Yashiro Primary School). *Shinano kyōiku-kai zasshi* 77 (2): 30–35.

———. 1898. "Yashiro komori kyōiku jōkyō torishirabe" (Conditions of education for *komori* at Yashiro). *Shinano kyōiku* 136 (1): 16–19.

———. 1899. "Komori kyōiku ni tsuite" (About the education of *komori*). *Shinano kyōiku* 155 (8): 25–26.

Makino Fumio. 1980. "1930 nendai no rōdō idō" (Movements of the labor force during the 1930s). *Hitotsubashi daigaku keizai kenkyū* 31 (4): 362–367.

Malkki, Liisa H. 1992. "National Geographic: The Rooting of Peoples and the Territorialization of National Identity among Scholars and Refugees." *Cultural Anthropology* 7 (1): 24–44.

———. 1995. "Refugees and Exile: From 'Refugee Studies' to the National Order of Things." *Annual Review of Anthropology* 24:495–523.

Manabe, Katsufumi and Harumi Befu. 1992. "Japanese Cultural Identity: An Empirical Investigation of Nihonjinron." *Japanstudien* 4:89–102.

Marshall, Byron K. 1967. *Capitalism and Nationalism in Prewar Japan: The Ideology of the Business Elite, 1868–1941*. Stanford: Stanford University Press.

Maruoka Hideko. 1948 (orig. 1937). *Nihon nōson fujin mondai: atarashiki shuppatsu* (Issues of rural women in Japan: A new start). Tokyo: Yakumo Shoten.

Maruyama Masao. 1956. "Nihon ni okeru nashonarizumu" (Nationalism in Japan). In *Gendai seiji no shisō to kōzō* 1:149–166. Tokyo: Miraisha.

———. 1969. *Thought and Behavior in Modern Japanese Politics*. Ed. Ivan Morris. Expanded edition. London: Oxford University Press.

Marx, Karl. 1975a (orig. 1843). "Critique of Hegel's Doctrine of the State." In Quintin Hoare, ed., *Karl Marx: Early Writings*, 57–198. New York: Vintage Books.

———. 1975b (orig. 1843). "On the Jewish Question." In Q. Hoare, ed., *Karl Marx: Early Writings*, 211–241. New York: Vintage Books.

———. 1977. *Capital: A Critique of Political Economy*, vol. 1. New York: Vintage.

Masuda Sayo. 1959. "Geisha." In Usui Yoshimi, ed., *Gendai kyōyō zenshū*, 138–219. Tokyo: Chikuma Shobō.

Matsubara Nao. 1987. "Josei-shi o manabō nettowāku" (The network to study women's histories). In Hisada Megumi, ed., *Onna no nettowākingu*, 197–213. Tokyo: Gakuyō Shobō.

Matsunaga Goichi. 1964. *Nippon no komori-uta* (*Komori*'s songs in Japan). Tokyo: Kinokuniya.

McBride, Theresa M. 1976. *The Domestic Revolution: The Modernization of Household Service in England and France, 1820–1920*. New York: Holmes and Meiner.

———. 1977. "The Long Road Home: Women's Work and Industrialization." In Renate Bridenthal and Claudia Koonz, eds., *Becoming Visible: Women in European History*, 280–295. Boston: Houghton Mifflin Co.

———. 1978. "'As the Twig is Bent': The Victorian Nanny." In A. S. Wohl, ed., *The Victorian Family: Structure and Stresses*, 44–58. New York: St. Martin's Press.

McClintock, Anne. 1991. "'No Longer in a Future Heaven': Women and Nationalism in South Africa." *Transition* 51:104–123.

McCormack, Gavan, and Yoshio Sugimoto. 1986. "Introduction: Democracy and Japan." In G. McCormack and Y. Sugimoto, eds., *Democracy in Contemporary Japan*, 9–17. New York: M. E. Sharpe.

McDougall, Mary Lynn. 1977. "Working-Class Women during the Industrial Revolution, 1780–1914." In R. Bridenthal and C. Koonz, eds., *Becoming Visible: Women in European History*, 253–279. Boston: Houghton Mifflin Co.

Minami Hiroshi, ed. 1965. *Taishō bunka* (Taishō culture). Tokyo: Keisō Shobō.

Minami-minowa-mura Sonshi Kankō Iinkai, ed. 1985. *Minami-minowa-mura sonshi* (The history of the village of Minami-minowa), vol. 2. Nagano: Minami-minowa Sonshi Kankō Iinkai.

Minear, Richard H. 1980. "Orientalism and the Study of Japan." *Journal of Asian Studies* 39 (3): 507–517.

Mitchell, Timothy. 1990. "Everyday Metaphors of Power." *Theory and Society* 19 (5): 545–77.

Mitsuda Kyōko. 1985. "Kindai-teki bosei-kan no juyō to hensen" (The acceptance and transformation of the modern notion of motherhood). In H. Wakita, ed., *Bosei o tou: rekishi-teki hensen* 2:100–129. Tokyo: Jinbun Shoin.

Miwata Masako. 1898. "Jokō kyōiku" (Education of factory women). *Jokan* 149:5–9.

Miyake, Yoshiko. 1991. "Doubling Expectations: Motherhood and Women's Factory Work under State Management in Japan in the 1930s and 1940s." In G. L. Bernstein, ed., *Recreating Japanese Women, 1600–1945*, 267–295. Berkeley, Los Angeles, and London: University of California Press.

Miyamoto Chū. 1888. "Uba o yatou-beki ba'ai oyobi yatoinushi to uba tono kokoroekata, I" [When wet nurses should be hired and what employers should remember about them, I). *Fujin eisei-kai zasshi* 5: 21-28.

———. 1889. "Uba o yatou-beki ba'ai oyobi yatoinushi to uba tono kokoroekata, II." *Fujin eisei-kai zasshi* 6:4–13.

Miyamoto Tsuneichi. 1969. *Miyamoto Tsuneichi chosaku-shū* (Collections of works by Miyamoto Tsuneichi), vol. 8. Tokyo: Miraisha.

———. 1984. "Tosa Genji" (Genji in Tosa). In Miyamoto Tsuneichi, *Wasurerareta Nippon-jin*, 131–58. Tokyo: Iwanami.

Miyata Noboru. 1983. *Onna no reiryoku to ie no kami* (Women's spiritual power and the Goddess of Ie). Tokyo: Jinbun Shoin.

———. 1987. *Hime no minzokugaku* (Native ethnology of women). Tokyo: Seido-sha.

Miyoshi, Masao, and Harry D. Harootunian, eds. 1989. *Postmodernism in Japan*. Durham: Duke University Press.

———. eds. 1993. *Japan in the World*. Durham: Duke University Press.

Molony, Barbara. 1991. "Activism among Women in the Taishō Cotton Textile Industry." In Gail L. Bernstein, ed., *Recreating Japanese Women, 1600–1945*, 217–238. Berkeley, Los Angeles, and London: University of California Press.

———. 1993. "Equality Versus Difference: The Japanese Debate over 'Motherhood Protection', 1915–1950." In Janet Hunter, ed., *Japanese Working Women*, 122–148. London: Routledge.

Monbushō, ed. 1941. *Shinmin no michi* (The way of subjects). Tokyo: Asahi Shinbun-sha.

Monbushō Kyōiku-shi Hensan-kai, ed. 1938. *Meiji-ikō kyōiku seido hattatsu-shi* (History of the development of the educational system since Meiji). Tokyo: Kyōiku Shiryō Chōsa-kai.

Moore, Barrington, Jr. 1966. *Social Origins of Dictatorship and Democracy: Lord and Peasant in the Making of the Modern World*. Boston: Beacon Press.

Moore, Henrietta L. 1988. *Feminism and Anthropology*. Minneapolis: University of Minnesota Press.

Mori Takemaro. 1976. "Senji-ka nōson no kōzō henka" (The structural changes of agricultural villages during the war). In *Iwanami kōza: Nihon rekishi, 20, kindai, 7*, 315–365. Tokyo: Iwanami.

Morosawa Yōko. 1969a. *Shinano no onna*, vol. 1 (The women in Nagano, vol. 1). Tokyo: Mirai-sha.

———. 1969b. *Shinano no onna*, vol. 2. Tokyo: Mirai-sha.

Morris-Suzuki, Tessa. 1986. "Sources of Conflict in the 'Information Society.'" In G. McCormack and Y. Sugimoto, eds., *Democracy in Contemporary Japan*, 76–89. New York: M. E. Sharpe.

Mosse, George L. 1985. *Nationalism and Sexuality: Respectability and Abnormal Sexuality in Modern Europe*. New York: Howard Fertiz.

Mulhern, Chieko I. 1985. "Book Review of 'Facing Two Ways,' by S. Ishimoto." *Journal of Asian Studies* 45 (1): 146–148.

Murai Osamu. 1993a. "Nihon minzoku-gaku to fashizumu" (Japanese native ethnology and fascism). *Fuji joshi daigaku kokubun-gaku zasshi* 50:26–34.

———. 1993b. "Origuchi Shinobu to Yanagita Kunio: Okinawa e no manazashi" (Origuchi Shinobu and Yanagita Kunio: Perspectives toward Okinawa). *Kokubungaku* 38 (8): 78–85.

———. 1993c. "Shin-kokugaku to shokuminchi-shugi" (New nativism and colonialism). *Nihon bungaku* 42:23–31.

———. 1995. *Nantō ideologii no hassei: Yanagita Kunio to shokuminchi-shugi* (The genesis of Nantō ideology: Yanagita Kunio and colonialism). Tokyo: Ōta Shuppan.

Murakami Nobuhiko. 1970. *Meiji josei-shi* (History of Meiji women), vol. 2a. Tokyo: Riron-sha.

———. 1977. *Takamure Itsue to Yanagita Kunio* (Takamure Itsue and Yanagita Kunio). Tokyo: Yamato Shobō.

Nagai, Michio. 1976. "Westernization and Japanization: The Early Meiji Transformation of Education." In D. H. Shively, ed., *Tradition and Modernization in Japanese Culture*, 35–76. Princeton: Princeton University Press.

Nagano-ken Kaitaku Jikyō-kai Manshū Kaitaku Kankō-kai, ed. 1984. *Nagano-ken manshū kaitaku-shi* (The history of agricultural settlement in Manchuria by Nagano farmers). Nagano: Nagano-ken Kaitaku Jikyō-kai Manshū Kaitaku Kankō-kai.

Nagano-ken Kyōiku-shi Kankō-kai. 1976. *Nagano-ken kyōiku-shi* (Educational history of Nagano prefecture), vol. 11. Nagano: Nagano-ken Kyōiku-shi Kankō-kai.

Nagano-ken-shi Kankō-kai, ed. 1987. *Nagano-ken-shi, kindai shiryō-hen* (History of Nagano prefecture, historical documents of the modern period), vol. 8. Nagano: Nagano-ken-shi Kankō-kai.

Nagano-shi Jinjō Kōtō Shōgakkō. 1920. *Komori no kokoroe* (Things to remember for *komori*). Nagano: Nagano-shi Jinjō Kōtō Shōgakkō.

Nagy, Margit. 1991. "Middle-Class Working Women during the Interwar Years." In G. L. Bernstein, ed., *Recreating Japanese Women, 1600–1945*, 199–216. Berkeley, Los Angeles, and London: University of California Press.

Nakai Nobuhiko. 1974. "Rekishi-gaku to shiteno Yanagita minzoku-gaku: Jōmin gainen o chūshin ni" (Yanagita's native ethnology as a historiography: With special reference to the notion of *jōmin*). *Dentō to gendai* 28:65–72.

Nakamura Akira. 1974. *Yanagita Kunio no shisō* (The thought of Yanagita Kunio). Tokyo: Hōsei Daigaku Shuppan-kai.

Nakamura Masanori. 1976. *Rōdōsha to nōmin* (Industrial workers and farmers). Tokyo: Shōgakukan.

————. 1978. "Keizai kōsei undō to nōson tōgō: Nagano-ken Chiisagata-gun Urazato-mura no ba'ai" (Rural integration and the movement for economic regeneration: The case of Urazato village in Chiisagata county). In Tōkyō Daigaku Shakai Kagaku Kenkyū-sho, ed., *Fashizumu-ki no kokka to shakai*, vol. 1, *Shōwa kyōkō*, 197–262. Tokyo: University of Tokyo Press.

Nakamura Tajū. 1900. "Komori kyōiku" (The education of *komori*). *Shinano kyōiku* 168 (9): 18–21.

————. 1903. "Komori kyōiku no yūgi ni tsuite" (About play in the education of *komori*). *Shinano kyōiku* 207 (12): 20–29.

————. 1906. "Komori no kyōiku"(The education of *komori*). *Shinano kyōiku* 239 (8): 10–11.

Nakano, Ako. 1990. "Death and History: An Emperor's Funeral." *Public Culture* 2 (2): 33–40.

Niimura Izuru, ed. 1976. *Kōjien* (Japanese vocabularly dictionary). Tokyo: Iwanami.

Nishida Yoshiaki. 1978. *Shōwa kyōkō-ka no nōson shakai undō: Yōsanchi ni okeru tenkai to kiketsu* (Rural social movements under the Shōwa depression: Their development and consequences in the area of sericulture). Tokyo: Ochanomizu Shobō.

Nishikawa Yuko. 1985. "Hitosu no keifu: Hiratsuka Raicho, Takamure Itsue, Ishimure Michiko" (An unbroken lineage: Hiratsuka Raicho, Takamure Itsue, Ishimure Michiko). In Wakita Haruko, ed., *Bosei o tou: rekishi-teki hensen* 2:158–191. Kyoto: Jinbun Shoin.

Nitobe, Inazō. 1905. *Bushidō: The Soul of Japan*. New York: G. P. Putnam's Sons.

Nolte, Sharon H. 1983. *Women, the State, and Repression in Imperial Japan*. East Lansing: Michigan State University, Working Papers on Women in International Development 33.

Nolte, Sharon H., and Sally Ann Hastings. 1991. "The Meiji State's Policy toward Women, 1890–1910." In G. L. Bernstein, ed., *Recreating Japanese Women, 1600–1945*, 151–174. Berkeley, Los Angeles, and London: University of California Press.

Nōson Josei Kyōiku Kenkyū Iinkai. 1941a. "Nōson joshi kyōiku, 1" (The education of rural women, 1). *Shinano kyōiku* 660:43–57.

————. 1941b. "Noson joshi kyōiku, 2" (The education of rural women, 2). *Shinano kyōiku* 661:74–96.

Notehelfer, Fred G. 1971. "Kōtoku Shūsui and Nationalism." *Journal of Asian Studies* 31 (1): 31–39.

O'Brien, Mary. 1981. *The Politics of Reproduction*. London: Routledge.

————. 1989. *Reproducing the World*. Boulder: Westview.

Ōhnuki-Tierney, Emiko. 1993. *Rice as Self: Japanese Identities through Time*. Princeton: Princeton University Press.

Oki Kiyoshige. 1893. *Komori kyōiku-sho kiji* (Everyday affairs in the class for *komori*).

Ōkouchi Kazuo. 1952. *Reimei-ki no Nihon rōdō undō* (The dawn of Japanese labor movements). Tokyo: Iwanami.

———. 1958. *Labour in Modern Japan.* Tokyo: The Science Council of Japan.

———. 1971. *Seikatsu koten sōsho,* vol. 4, *Shokkō jijo* (Classic works on people's livelihoods, vol. 4, Factory workers' conditions). Tokyo: Kōseikan.

Ōkouchi Kazuo, and Sumiya Mikio. 1955. *Nihon no rōdōsha kaikyū* (The working class in Japan). Tokyo: Tōyō Keizai Shinpō-sha.

Onna no Rekishi o Kataru Kai, ed. 1984. *Hitamuki ni ikinuite* (Having tried to survive). Nagano: Kanae-machi Kōminkan.

Ortner, Sherry. 1992. "Resistance: Some Theoretical Problems in Anthropological History and Historical Anthropology." Paper for the Program in the Comparative Study of Social Transformations (CSST), University of Michigan, Ann Arbor.

———. 1995. "Resistance and the Problem of Ethnographic Refusal." *Comparative Studies in Society and History* 37 (1): 173–193.

Ōshima Eiko. 1982. "Ryō-taisen-kan no josei rōdō" (Women's labor during the interwar period). In Josei-shi Sōgō Kenkyū-kai, ed., *Nihon josei-shi* 5:1–38. Tokyo: University of Tokyo Press.

Packard, George R., III. 1966. *Protest in Tokyo: The Security Treaty Crisis of 1960.* Westport: Greenwood Press.

Parker, A., M. Russo, and D. Sommer. 1992. "Introduction." In A. Parker, M. Russo, and D. Sommer, eds., *Nationalisms and Sexualities,* 1–18. New York: Routledge.

Passin, Herbert. 1990. "The Occupation—Some Reflections." *Daedalus* 119 (3): 107–29.

Peiss, Kathy. 1983. "'Charity Girls' and City Pleasures: Historical Notes on Working-Class Sexuality, 1880–1920." In Ann Snitow, Christine Stansell, and Sharon Thompson, eds., *Powers of Desire: Politics of Sexuality,* 74–87. New York: Monthly Review Press.

———. 1986. *Cheap Amusements: Working Women and Leisure in Turn-of-the-Century New York.* Philadelphia: Temple University Press.

Plamenatz, John. 1976. "Two Types of Nationalism." In Eugene Kamenka, ed., *Nationalism: The Nature and Evolution of an Idea,* 23–36. London: Edward Arnold.

Radcliffe-Brown, A. R. 1940. "Preface." In M. Fortes and E. E. Evans-Pritchard, eds., *African Political Systems,* xi–xxiii. Oxford: Oxford University Press.

Rafael, Vicente L. 1990. "Nationalism, Imagery, and the Filipino Intelligentsia in the Nineteenth Century." *Critical Inquiry* 16:591–611.

———. 1992. "Confession, Conversion, and Reciprocity in Early Tagalog Colonial Society." In N. Dirks, ed., *Culture and Colonialism,* 65–88. Ann Arbor: University of Michigan Press.

Ranger, Terrence. 1983. "The Invention of Tradition in Colonial Africa." In Eric Hobsbawm and Terence Ranger, eds., *The Invention of Tradition,* 211–262. Cambridge: Cambridge University Press.

Redclift, Michael. 1987. *Sustainable Development: Exploring the Contradictions.* London: Methuen.

Reischauer, Edwin O. 1978. *The Japanese.* Cambridge: Harvard University Press.

Renan, Ernest. 1990. "What Is a Nation?" In Homi K. Bhabha, ed., *Nation and Narration,* 8–22. New York: Routledge.

Riley, Denise. 1988. *"Am I That Name?": Feminism and the Category of "Women" in History.* Minneapolis: University of Minnesota Press.

Roberts, Glenda S. 1994. *Staying on the Line: Blue-Collar Women in Contemporary Japan.* Honolulu: University of Hawai'i Press.

Robertson, Jennifer. 1991. *Native and Newcomer: Making and Remaking a Japanese City.* Berkeley, Los Angeles, and London: University of California Press.

Robertson, Priscilla. 1975. "Home as a Nest: Middle-Class Childhood in Nineteenth-Century France." In L. Demause, ed., *The History of Childhood,* 407–31. New York: Harper and Row.

Rodd, Laurel R. 1991. "Yosano Akiko and the Taishō Debate over the 'New Woman.'" In G. L. Bernstein, ed., *Recreating Japanese Women, 1600–1945,* 175–98. Berkeley, Los Angeles, and London: University of California Press.

Roden, Donald. 1980. *Schooldays in Imperial Japan.* Berkeley, Los Angeles, and London: University of California Press.

———. 1990. "Taishō Culture and the Problem of Gender Ambivalence." In J. T. Rimer, ed., *Culture and Identity: Japanese Intellectuals during the Interwar Years,* 37–55. Princeton: Princeton University Press.

Rosaldo, Michelle Zimbalist. 1980. "The Uses and Abuses of Anthropology: Reflections in Feminism and Cross-Cultural Understanding." *Signs* 5 (3): 389–417.

Said, Edward E. 1979. *Orientalism.* New York: Vintage Books.

———. 1983. *The World, the Text and the Critic.* Cambridge, Mass.: Harvard University Press.

Sakai, Naoki. 1989. "Modernity and Its Critique: The Problem of Universalism and Particularlism." In M. Miyoshi and H. D. Harootunian, eds., *Postmodernism and Japan,* 93–122. Durham: Duke University Press.

———. 1991. *Voices of the Past: The Status of Language in Eighteenth-Century Japanese Discourse.* Ithaca: Cornell University Press.

Sakura Takuji. 1981 (orig. 1927). *Seishi jokō gyakutai-shi* (The history of exploited factory women of the silk industry). Nagano: Shinano Mainichi Shinbun-sha.

Sangari, Kumkum, and Sudesh Vaid. 1989. "Recasting Women: An Introduction." In K. Sangari and S. Vaid, eds., *Recasting Women: Essays in Colonial History,* 1–26. New Delhi: Kali for Women.

Sasaki-Uemura, Wesley. 1993. "Citizen and Community in the 1960 Anpo Protests." Ph.D. thesis, Department of History, Cornell University.

Sawayama Mikako. 1980. "Naze bosei ga towareru no ka" (Why is motherhood questioned?). *Kateika kyōiku* 54 (9): 51–63.

Saxonhouse, G. R. 1976. "Country Girls and Communication Among Competitors in the Japanese Cotton-Spinning industry." In H. Patrick, ed., *Japanese Industrialization and Its Social Consenquences*, 97–125. Berkeley, Los Angeles, and London: University of California Press.

Schorske, Carl E. 1981. *Fin-de-Siècle Vienna: Politics and Culture*. New York: Vintage Books.

Schwarcz, Vera. 1994. "Strangers No More: Personal Memory in the Interstices of Public Commemoration." In Rubie S. Watson, ed., *Memory, History, and Opposition: Under State Socialism*, 45–64. Santa Fe: School of American Research Press.

Scott, James C. 1976. *The Moral Economy of the Peasant: Rebellion and Subsistence in Southeast Asia*. New Haven: Yale University Press.

——. 1985. *Weapons of the Weak: Everyday Forms of Peasant Resistance*. New Haven: Yale University Press.

Scott, Joan. 1988. *Gender and the Politics of History*. New York: Columbia University Press.

Sedgwick, Eve Kosofsky. 1992. "Nationalisms and Sexualities in the Age of Wilde." In A. Parker, M. Russo, and P. Yaeger, eds., *Nationalisms and Sexualities*, 235–245. New York: Routledge.

Segawa, Kiyoko. 1950a. *Ama-ki* (The ethnography of women divers). Tokyo: Jipusha.

——. 1950b. *Hanjo* (Women sellers). Tokyo: Jipusha.

——. 1961. *Shikitari no naka no onna* (Women in traditions). Tokyo: Sansai-sha.

——. 1969. *Okinawa no kon'in* (The marriages in Okinawa). Tokyo: Iwasaki Bijutsu-sha.

——. 1970. *Mura no onna-tachi* (Women in the village). Tokyo: Miraisha.

——. 1972. *Wakamono to musume o meguru minzoku* (Folklore concerning young men and women). Tokyo: Miraisha.

Seton-Watson, Hugh. 1977. *Nations and States: An Enquiry into the Origins of Nations and the Politics of Nationalism*. Boulder: Westview Press.

Shinano Kyōiku-kai. 1898. "Tsūzoku joshi kyōiku-dan" (Discussions about secular education for women). *Shinano kyōiku* 141:10–16.

——. 1900. *Komori kyōiku-hō* (Methods for Educating *komori*). Tokyo: Kinkōdō.

Sievers, Sharon L. 1983. *Flowers in Salt: The Beginnings of Feminist Consciousness in Modern Japan*. Stanford: Stanford University Press.

Silverberg, Miriam. 1990. *Changing Song: The Marxist Manifestos of Nakano Shigeharu*. Princeton: Princeton University Press.

——. 1991. "The Modern Girl as Militant." In G. L. Bernstein, ed., *Recreating Japanese Women, 1600–1945*, 239–266. Berkeley, Los Angeles, and London: University of California Press.

Skocpol, Theda. 1985. "Bringing the State Back In: Strategies of Analysis in Current Research." In Peter B. Evans, Dietrich Rueschemeyer, and Theda Skocpol, eds., *Bringing the State Back In*, 3–37. Cambridge: Cambridge University Press.

Smethurst, Richard J. 1974. *A Social Basis for Prewar Japanese Militarism: The Army and the Rural Community.* Berkeley, Los Angeles, and London: University of California Press.

Smith, Anthony. 1971. *Theories of Nationalism.* London: Duckworth.

Smith, Dorothy E. 1987. *The Everyday World as Problematic: A Feminist Sociology.* Toronto: University of Toronto Press.

———. 1990. *Texts, Facts, and Femininity: Exploring the Relations of Ruling.* London: Routledge.

Smith, Robert J. 1983. "Making Village Women into 'Good Wives and Wise Mothers' in Prewar Japan." *Journal of Family History* 8 (1): 70–84.

Smith, Robert J., and Ella L. Wiswell. 1982. *The Women of Suye Mura.* Chicago: University of Chicago Press.

Smith, Thomas C. 1988. "Peasant Time and Factory Time in Japan." In *Native Sources of Japanese Industrialization, 1750–1920,* 199–235. Berkeley, Los Angeles, and London: University of California Press.

Stauder, Jack. 1974. "The 'Relevance' of Anthropology to Colonialism and Imperialism." *Race* 16 (1): 29–51.

Sugimoto, Etsu Inagaki. 1925. *A Daughter of the Samurai.* Garden City, N.J.: Doubleday.

Sugimoto Jin. 1975. "Yanagita-gaku ni okeru 'jōmin' gainen no isō" (Various aspects of the notion of "*jōmin*" in Yanagita's native ethnology). In Gotō Sōichirō, ed., *Yanagita Kunio no gakumon keisei,* 105–156. Tokyo: Hakugei-sha.

Suzuki Masayuki. 1977. "Taishō-ki nōmin seiji shisō no ichi-sokumen, I" (An aspect of peasants' political thought during the Taishō period, I). *Nihon-shi kenkyū* 173: 1–26.

Takahashi Yasutaka. 1976. "Nihon fashizumu to Manshū bunson imin no tenkai: Nagano-ken Yomikaki-mura o chūshin ni" (Japanese fascism and the development of migration to Manchuria to create branch villages: The case of the village of Yomikaki). In Manshū Imin Kenkyū-kai, ed., *Nihon teikoku shugi ka no Manshū imin,* 307–383. Tokyo: Ryūkei Shōsha.

Takai Toshio. 1980. *Watashi no Jokō aishi* (My "Jokō aishi"). Tokyo: Sōdo Bunka.

Takayama Sumiko. 1987. *Nono-san ni narun-dayo* (You will become a little buddha). Nagano: Ginga Shobō.

Takeuchi Yoshimi. 1983. *Kindai no chōkoku* (Overcoming the modern). Tokyo: Chikuma Shobō.

Tamanoi, Mariko A. 1988. "Farmers, Industries, and the State: The Culture of Contract Farming in Spain and Japan." *Comparative Studies in Society and History* 30 (3): 432–452.

Tambiah, Stanley. 1993. "Ethnonationalism: Politics and Culture" (in Japanese). *Shisō* 823:50–63.

Taussig, Michael. 1992a. "Maleficium: State Fetishism." In Michael Taussig, *The Nervous System,* 111–140. New York: Routledge.

———. 1992b. "Terror as Usual: Walter Benjamin's Theory of History as State of Siege." In *The Nervous System,* 11–35. New York: Routledge.

Thompson, E. P. 1967. "Time, Work-Discipline and Industrial Capitalism." *Past and Present* 38:56–97.

———. 1978. "Folklore, Anthropology, and Social History." *Indian Historical Review* 3 (2): 247–66.

Tokutomi Ichirō (Sohō). 1932. "Waga Haha to Nōgyo" (My mother and agriculture). *Nōson fujin* 1 (2): 2–3.

Tomio, Kentarō. 1986. *The Locus of Sexuality in Pre-modern Village Life.* Paper presented at the Midwest Conference on Asian Affairs, Champaign, Ill.

Tonkin, Elizabeth. 1992. *Narrating Our Pasts: The Social Construction of Oral History.* Cambridge: Cambridge University Press.

Tsujimura Teruo. 1966. *Sengo Shinshū josei-shi* (The postwar history of Nagano women). Nagano: Nagano-ken Rengō Fujin-kai.

Tsunoda, Ryūsaku, W. T. de Bary, and D. Keene. 1965. "Foundations of Our National Polity." In R. Tsunoda, W. T. de Bary, and D. Keene, eds., *Sources of Japanese Traditio*, 2: 278–288. New York: Columbia University Press.

Tsurumi, Patricia E. 1984a. "Colonial Education in Korea and Taiwan." In Ramon H. Myers and Mark R. Peattie, eds., *The Japanese Colonial Empire, 1895–1945,* 275–311. Princeton: Princeton University Press.

———. 1984b. "Female Textile Workers and the Failure of Early Trade Unionism in Japan." *History Workshop* 18:3–27.

———. 1985. "Feminism and Anarchism in Japan: Takamure Itsue, 1894–1965." *Bulletin of Concerned Asian Scholars* 17 (2): 2–19.

———. 1990. *Factory Girls: Women in the Thread Mills of Meiji Japan.* Princeton: Princeton University Press.

———. 1995. "Visions of Women and the New Society in Conflict: Yamakawa Kikue Versus Takamure Itsue." Paper presented at the conference on "Competing Modernities in Twentieth-Century Japan: Taishō Democracy," Maui, Hawai'i, November 1–5.

Ueno, Chizuko. 1987. "Genesis of the Urban Housewife." *Japan Quarterly* 34:130–142.

———. 1990. *Kafuchō-sei to shihon-sei: Marukusu shugi feminizumu no chihei* (Patriarchy and capitalism: The range of vision of Marxist feminism). Tokyo: Iwanami.

Umemoto, Katsumi, Satō Noboru, and Maruyama Masao. 1983. *Sengo Nihon no kakushin shisō* (Leftist thought in postwar Japan). Tokyo: Gendai no Riron-sha.

Uno, Kathleen S. 1987. "Day Care and Family Life in Industrializing Japan, 1868–1925." Ph.D. thesis, University of California, Berkeley.

———. 1991. "Women and Changes in the Household Division of Labor." In G. L. Bernstein, ed., *Recreating Japanese Women, 1600–1945,* 17–41. Berkeley, Los Angeles, and London: University of California Press.

Usuta-chō Fujin Shūdan Renraku Kyōgikai, ed. 1978. *Karatachi no hana* (Acacia flowers). Nagano: Usuta-chō Kōminkan.

Varner, Richard E. 1977. "The Organzied Peasant: The Wakamonogumi in the Edo Period." *Monumenta Nipponica* 32 (4): 459–483.

Vlastos, Stephen. 1986. *Peasant Protests and Uprisings in Tokugawa Japan*. Berkeley, Los Angeles, and London: University of California Press.

―――. 1994. "Agrarianism without Tradition: Radical Critique of Prewar Japanese Modernity." Paper presented at the Conference on the Invention of Tradition, Iowa City, Ia. (This paper will be published in the forthcoming book edited by S. Vlastos, *Mirror of Modernity: Invented Tradition of Modern Japan*. [University of California Press, 1998].)

Wakamori Tarō. 1975. *Yanagita Kunio to rekishigaku* (Yanagita Kunio and the discipline of history). Tokyo: Nihon Hōsō Shuppan Kyōkai.

Wakita, Haruko. 1993. "Women and the Creation of the Ie in Japan: An Overview from the Medieval Period to the Present." Trans. David P. Phillips. *US-Japan Women's Journal, English Supplement* 4:83–105.

Walkowitz, Judith R. 1980. *Prostitution and Victorian Society: Women, Class, and the State*. Cambridge: Cambridge University Press.

―――. 1983. "Male Vice and Female Virtue: Feminism and the Politics of Prostitution in Nineteenth-Century Britain." In A. Anitow, C. Stansell, and S. Thompson, eds., *Powers of Desire: Politics of Sexuality*, 419–438. New York: Monthly Review Press.

Walthall, Ann. 1991. "The Life Cycle of Farm Women in Tokugawa Japan." In G. L. Bernstein, ed., *Recreating Japanese Women, 1600–1945*, 42–70. Berkeley, Los Angeles, and London: University of California Press.

Waswo, Ann. 1988. "The Transformation of Rural Society, 1900–1950." In P. Duus, ed., *The Cambridge History of Japan*, vol. 6, *The Twentieth Century*, 541–603. Cambridge: Cambridge University Press.

Watanabe Tomio and Matsuzawa Shunsuke. 1979. *Komori-uta no kiso-teki kenkyū* (Basic studies of *komori*'s songs). Tokyo: Meiji Shoin.

Watson, Rubie S. 1994a. "Making Secret Histories: Memory and Mourning in Post-Mao China." In R. S. Watson, ed., *Memory, History, and Opposition: Under State Socialism*, 65–85. Santa Fe: School of American Research Press.

―――. 1994b. "Memory, History, and Opposition under State Socialism: An Introduction." In R. S. Watson, ed., *Memory, History, and Opposition: Under State Socialism*, 1–20. Santa Fe: School of American Research Press.

Weber, Eugen. 1976. *Peasants into Frenchmen: The Modernization of Rural France, 1870–1914*. Stanford: Stanford University Press.

Westerhoven, James. 1987. "Translator's Preface." In Dazai Osamu, *Return to Tsugaru*, xi–xxviii. Tokyo: Kōdansha International.

Wigen, Kären. 1995. *The Making of a Japanese Periphery, 1750–1920*. Berkeley: University of California Press.

Williams, Raymond. 1973. *The Country and the City*. New York: Oxford University Press.

Willis, Paul. 1977. *Learning to Labor: How Working Class Kids Get Working Class Jobs*. New York: Columbia University Press.

Wolf, Eric R. 1982. "Introduction." In E. R. Wolf, *Europe and the People without History*, 3–23. Berkeley, Los Angeles, and London: University of California Press.

Woolf, Virginia. 1938. *Three Guineas*. New York: Harcourt, Brace and Co.

Yamamoto, Akira. 1976. "Shakai seikatsu no henka to taishū bunka" (The transformation of social life and mass culture). In Asao Naohiro, et al., eds., *Iwanami kōza: Nihon rekishi*, vol. 19, *Kindai 6*, 301–336. Tokyo: Iwanami.

Yamamoto Shigemi. 1977. *Ah, Nomugi touge* (Ah, Nomugi path). Tokyo: Kadokawa.

Yamanouchi Mina. 1975. *Yamanouchi mina jiden* (The autobiography of Yamanouchi Mina). Tokyo: Shinjuku Shobō.

Yamazaki Nobukichi. 1906. "Fujin to yōsan" (Women and sericulture). *Den-en fujin*, May 1.

———. 1925. "Saika no shiori" (On the governance of the household). *Ie no hikari* 1: 16–19.

Yanagisako, Sylvia. 1979. "Family and Household: The Analysis of Domestic Groups." *Annual Review of Anthropology* 8:161–205.

Yanagita Kunio. 1934. *Minkan denshō-ron* (Theory on the oral traditions among *jōmin*). Tokyo: Kyōritsu-sha.

———. 1962a (orig. 1932). *Josei to minkan denshō* (Women and popular traditions). In *Teihon Yanagita Kunio Shū* (hereafter *Teihon*) 8:315–447. Toyko: Chikuma Shobō.

———. 1962b (orig. 1942). *Nihon no matsuri* (Festivals in Japan). In *Teihon* 10:153–314.

———. 1962c (orig. 1931). *Nihon nōmin-shi* (History of Japanese peasants). In *Teihon* 16: 161–236.

———. 1962d (Orig. 1929) *Toshi to nōson* (The city and the countryside). In *Teihon* 16: 237–391.

———. 1962e (orig. 1926). *Yukiguni no haru* (Spring in the snowy country). In *Teihon* 2: 1–136.

———. 1963a (orig. 1940). *Dai kazoku to shō kazoku* (Big families and small families). In *Teihon* 15:271–290.

———. 1963b (orig. 1931). *Meiji Taishō-shi sesō-hen* (Social conditions during the Meiji and Taishō periods). In *Teihon* 24:127–414.

———. 1963c (orig. 1941). *Minzoku-gaku no hanashi* (Story about native ethnology). In *Teihon* 24:493–503.

———. 1963d (orig. 1929, 1948). *Mukoiri-kō* (Thoughts on matrilocal marriage). In *Teihon* 4:152–98.

———. 1963e (orig. 1910). *Tōno monogatari* (The tales of Tōno). In *Teihon* 4:1–54.

———. 1963f (orig. 1917). *Yamabito-kō* (Thoughts about the mountain people). In *Teihon* 4:172–186.

———. 1963g (orig. 1925). *Yama no jinsei* (Life in the mountains). In *Teihon* 4:55–171.

———. 1964a (orig. 1904). "Chūnō yōsei-saku" (Policies to nurture middling farmers). In *Teihon* 31:409–423.

———. 1964b (orig. 1940). *Imo no chikara* (The power of women). In *Teihon* 9:1–219.

———. 1964c (orig. 1935). *Kyōdo seikatsu no kenkyū-hō* (Research methods on the everyday life in the countryside). In *Teihon* 25:261–328.

———. 1964d (orig. 1923). *Kyōdo-shi-ron* (Theory on the ethnography of the country). In *Teihon* 25:1–82.

———. 1964e (orig. 1934). *Minkan denshō-ron* (Theory on the oral tradition among *jōmin*). In *Teihon* 25:329–358.

———. 1964f (orig. 1939). *Momen izen no koto* (On matters before cotton affected our lives). In *Teihon* 14:1–218.

———. 1964g (orig. 1930). *Nihon no mukashi banashi* (Folk tales in Japan). In *Teihon* 26: 1–126.

———. 1964h (orig. 1928). *Ōnie-matsuri (Daijo-sai) to kokumin* (The festival of Onie and Japanese national subjects). In *Teihon* 31:373–375.

———. 1964i (orig. 1922). *Sairei to seken* (Festivals and society). In *Teihon* 10:397–427.

———. 1964j (orig. 1910). "Sangyō kumiai no dōtoku-teki bunshi" (Moral elements in the agricultural cooperatives). In *Teihon* 31:430–435.

———. 1964k (orig. 1928). *Seinen to gakumon* (Youth and learning). In *Teihon* 25:83–260.

———. 1964l (orig. 1941). *Shintō to minzoku-gaku* (Shintoism and native ethnology). In *Teihon* 10:315–396.

———. 1964m (orig. 1945). "Tokkō seishin o hagukumu mono" (Those who nurture the spirits of kamikaze). In *Teihon* 31:497.

———. 1967 (orig. 1935). *Kyōdo seikatsu no kenkyū* (Research on everyday life in the countryside). Tokyo: Chikuma Shobō.

———. 1970. *Josei to bunka* (Women and culture). In *Teihon* 30:211–214.

———. 1975. *The Legends of Tōno.* Trans. Ronald A. Morse. Tokyo: The Japan Foundation.

Yanagita Kunio and Miki Shigeru. 1944. *Yukiguni no minzoku* (Folklore in the snowy country). Tokyo: Yōtoku-sha.

Yanagita Kunio and Seki Keigo. 1948. *Nihon minzoku-gaku nyūmon* (Guide for Japanese native ethnology). 2 vols. Tokyo: Tōyōdo.

Yanagita Kunio Kenkyū-kai, ed. 1988. *Yanagita Kunio-den* (Biography of Yanagita Kunio). Tokyo: San'ichi Shobō.

Yasuda Tsuneo. 1979. *Nihon fashizumu to minshū undō: Nagano-ken nōson ni okeru rekishi-teki jittai o tōshite* (Rural fascism and people's movements: Seen through the historical conditions in the Nagano countryside). Tokyo: Renga Shobō.

Yokota Ei. 1988 (orig. 1976). *Tomioka nikki* (Tomioka diary). Nagano: Shinano Kyōiku-kai.

Yokota Hideo. 1914. *Nōson kyūsairon* (On rescuing the farm villages). Tokyo: Hakubunkan.

Yokoyama Gennosuke. 1949. *Nihon no kasō shakai* (Lower-class society in Japan). Tokyo: Iwanami.

Yokozeki Mitsue. 1990. *Shōwa: Onna o ikiru* (Showa: Living a woman's life). Nagano: Ginga Shobō.

Yoneyama, Lisa. 1995. "Memory Matters: Hiroshima's Korean Atom Bomb Memorial and the Politics of Ethnicity." *Public Culture* 7 (3): 499–527.

Yoshimi Yoshiaki. 1987. *Kusa no ne no fashizumu: Nihon minshū no sensō taiken* (Fascism at the grass roots: The wartime experiences of the Japanese masses). Tokyo: University of Tokyo Press.

Yoshimoto Takaaki. 1964. "Nihon no nashonarizumu" (Nationalism in Japan). In T. Yoshimoto, ed., *Gendai Nihon shisō taikei*, vol. 4, 7–54. Tokyo: Chikuma Shobō.

———. 1968. *Kyōdō gensō-ron* (Communal imaginary). Tokyo: Kawaide Shobō.

———. 1990. *Yanagita Kunio ron shūsei* (Compilation of essays on Yanagita Kunio). Tokyo: JCC.

Yoshino, Kōsaku. 1992. *Cultural Nationalism in Contemporary Japan: A Sociological Inquiry*. London: Routledge.

Young, Iris Morgan. 1990. *Throwing like a Girl and Other Essays in Feminist Philosophy and Social Theory*. Bloomington: Indiana University Press.

Young, James E. 1993. *The Texture of Memory: Holocaust Memorials and Meaning*. New Haven: Yale University Press.

Yuval-Davis, Nira, and Floya Anthias, eds. 1989. *Woman-Nation-State*. London: Macmillan.

Žižek, Slavoj. 1989. *The Sublime Object of Ideology*. London: Verso.

Index

abortion: prohibition of, 68; and rationalization, 188
Abrams, Philip, 41, 213 n. 9
Adachi, Seiko, 154, 232 n. 42
Adorno, Theodor W., 4, 175, 178, 238 n. 23
Africa: under colonialism, 41; nationalisms in, 225 n. 15
agrarianism, 21, 115, 119, 137, 152–153, 158, 167, 212 n. 24, 219 n. 19, 225 n. 14; definition of, 139; as an invented tradition, 152; traditional vs. popular, 139
agrarian myth, 224 n. 3
Agrarian Reform, 184–185
agribusiness, 192
agricultural cooperatives, 131, 192, 194–195, 200, 230 n. 17, 236 n. 11; as a multinational corporation, 194
Akamatsu, Keisuke, 59, 60, 61, 75, 77, 80, 216 n. 4, 222 n. 42; as a critic of Japanese native ethnology, 130–131, 228 n. 38.
Akamatsu, Ryōko, 96, 98, 99, 103, 106, 112, 221 n. 33, 234 n. 19
Akasaka, Norio, 124, 130, 226 n. 23
Allison, Anne, 29
Amamiya Silk Mill, 98, 112
American occupation, 12, 22, 43, 53, 180–185, 189, 235 n. 1. See also SCAP
anarchism, 50–51, 139. See also dangerous thought
Anderson, Benedict, 3–5, 10–12, 14, 19, 210 n. 12, 211 nn. 13, 14, 15, 22, 213 n. 6
Anthias, Floya, 14
antiprostitution movement, 221 n. 34
Aoki, Keiichirō, 141, 233 nn. 53, 57
Aoki, Takaju, 49, 66, 169, 174, 215 n. 29, 233 n. 53

Aoki Kidd, Yasue, 214 n. 20
Aomori (prefecture), 57–58, 216 n. 5, 234 n. 10
Arendt, Hannah, 49, 51
Ariès, Philip, 55
Arishima, Takeo, 141
Arndt, H. W., 11
Aruga, Kizaemon, 227 n. 26
Aryan race, 155. See also Nazi
Asad, Talal, 213 n. 11
Asada, Kyōji, 225 n. 12
Asian-brides-for-sale racket, 201–202, 204
Association for Enriching Japanese Nationals, 20
Association for the Promotion of Labor Unions, 98
autobiography, 32, 65, 213 n. 6
Avineri, Shlomo, 220 n. 27
Avon Cultural Center for Women, 38, 213 n. 8; diagram 39

Babior, Sharman, 201
Balibar, Etienne, 10
Basso, Ellen, 213 n. 6
Befu, Harumi, 211 n. 17
Benjamin, Walter, 4
Bernstein, Gail Lee, 47, 88, 214 n. 20, 234 n. 9
Bhabha, Homi, 10, 20, 210 n. 11, 212 n. 25
birth rate, 164, 212 n. 3
Bluestocking, 100
bon festival, 109, 223 n. 53
bosei hogo ronsō. See motherhood protection debates
Boyarin, Jonathan, 4
Braisted, William R., 214 n. 19
Branca, Patricia, 215 n. 1
Brandt, Anthony, 178, 235 n. 27
Breuilly, John, 210 n. 13
bride famine, 199, 200